D1129469

VICKSBURG

A People at War, 1860-1865

Part of the main battery aboard the USS *Richmond,* which dealt heavy blows at the city. Sketched by an officer aboard the *Richmond*. (From *Harper's Weekly*)

VICKSBURG

A People at War, 1860-1865

By

PETER F. WALKER

Chapel Hill

THE UNIVERSITY OF NORTH CAROLINA PRESS

Manufactured in the United States of America

For

Franklin T. Walker

and

Anna L. Walker

PREFACE

BEFORE the Civil War is understood as a complete historical experience it will be necessary to press beyond studies of military campaigns, finely spun constitutional theories, tenuous diplomatic negotiations, and significant individuals. This is not to question the validity of such studies, but merely to make the point that they are not enough. Putting an army into the field and maintaining it, for example, is nothing more than an expression of a peoples' will; so is a particular constitutional theory, if it is acted upon. But if a peoples' will can be determined, and the development of that will charted, it will be necessary to get right down among the people, if the historian is to do more than make generalizations, which may or may not be valid.

I have attempted to study the will and spirit of the people of Vicksburg. I have gotten as close to them as I am able. I advance no contention that the people of Vicksburg were typical Southerners of their time, but on the other hand I do not necessarily believe that they were atypical. Vicksburg was special simply because of its geographic location. The inhabitants of the city, except through chance, might well have lived elsewhere, and their actions might have been duplicated in another place. Before this statement can be proved or disproved more studies will have to be made on the state and local level. And, regardless of the bearing they may have on this study, they will enable Civil War historians to add dimension to their work which has heretofore been lacking.

Certain problems were encountered in this study which should be admitted: In some areas source material was lacking—the bare bones of the narrative attest to this. In other places I deliberately left unused some of the available material, for in my judgment its inclusion would have been repetitious. In dealing with manuscript sources the question of how they should be reproduced always arises. To avoid jogging the reader's attention I have omitted unnecessary interpolations in the quotations, and it should be understood that those errors of grammar, spelling, and mechanics which appear in the quotations exist in the original. Finally, I admit to the development of sympathies and biases—reactions which, I contend, are natural and ineluctable. It is hoped that they have not materially colored or distorted the work. If, however, it is marred by error of fact or interpretation, the responsibility rests solely with me.

If I have succeeded in combining demonstrable fact and sound interpretation in telling the story of Vicksburg, the credit, in large measure, accrues directly to these people:

Professors Herbert Weaver and Henry L. Swint of Vanderbilt University trudged every step of the way with me, from conception to completion, and were lavish with their time, patience, and understanding. To them, a great debt is due.

Miss Clara Mae Brown of the Joint University Libraries, Nashville, Tennessee, with an unflagging smile, looked up more things than should be asked of a reference librarian; Miss Charlotte Capers, Mr. Carl Ray, and the staff of the Mississippi State Department of Archives and History went far beyond the usual limits and made research a positive pleasure; Mrs. Eva W. Davis and the staff of the Old Courthouse Museum of Vicksburg opened many doors for me and allowed me unencumbered access to a precious set of newspapers; Professor John K. Bettersworth of Mississippi State University rifled his personal files for me, read the completed manuscript, and saved me from some previously undetected errors; Miss Sarah Gray, Assistant to the Curator of Manuscripts, Duke University Library, Mrs. Sara D. Jackson, Old Army Section, National Archives, and Mrs. Elsa B. Meier, Department of Archives and Manuscripts, Louisiana State University, extended to me an extraordinary courtesy and helpfulness which sets them apart in my mind.

And—the first shall be last—Judith Adams Walker, my wife, who possesses that most precious quality which is at once fragile and inextinguishable—faith.

PETER F. WALKER
Chapel Hill, N. C.

CONTENTS

ILLUSTRATIONS

The endpaper of the book shows the United States ironclad *Indianola* running the batteries at Vicksburg. (From *Harper's Weekly*)

INTRODUCTION

BRIGHT morning sunshine beat down upon the city. A few fleeting clouds did little to break the heavy heat. Heat waves shimmered off the sidewalks and the asphalt on the streets was soft underfoot. Crowds of people gathered under awnings and in the shadows of buildings while more hardy souls lined the sun-swept streets. Flags and bunting hung limply along the main streets and the faint popping of firecrackers sounded throughout the city.

On the surface the city appeared prepared for the annual Fourth of July festivities. The people were in a holiday mood; they had sent their men to war and the soldiers had crushed the European enemies and were now gathering for the final assault upon the Japanese. In the summer of 1945 a sense of victory hung over Vicksburg as it did over the entire country.

But this was no ordinary Fourth for Vicksburg; usual holiday moods were leavened with something distinct and separate, something that set the city and its people apart from the rest of the country as the moment of complete military triumph approached.

From up the main street came the sound of a military band, and the people turned to watch for the parade. Down the street the formations came—the band, the color guard carrying the flag of the United States, the marching troops; overhead a flight of aircraft roared above the city. The youngsters' eyes opened bright with excitement because many of them had never seen such a show. The eyes of some of the older people probably grew distant as the blare of the marching music faded from their consciousness and they remembered the stories of mothers and fathers and aunts and friends.

They were remembering a day almost a hundred years past, a day so etched into the historical experience of the city and its people that it linked them all together and made them as one. This distinctive thing had brought dignitaries and newspapermen from over the nation and had set them in the sweltering Southern city during the early days of July. This Fourth of July, 1945, was the first time the holiday had been observed in Vicksburg since Grant's victorious army marched into the city on the same day in 1863. Throughout the day and into the night the city celebrated. Vicksburg had finally accepted a decision made almost a hundred years before.[1]

The people of Vicksburg had bought dearly the right to choose the time they would observe this national holiday. They had been surrounded by the army and navy of this nation, isolated from friends and relief, and mauled as no community has been in the history of the American people. New York, Atlanta, Petersburg, and Boston have claimed the title "The Siege of," but these cities were never completely cut off, were never subjected to continuous and vehement attack as was Vicksburg. The city rises on its bluffs, possessor of a unique place in American history.

The story of a city and a people besieged has fascinated man since Homer told his stories. In the trapped city human life goes on; people go to their businesses, to market, they buy and sell, pray and love, are born and die amidst the clamor and the destruction. The written record leaves traces of unquestioning bravery, indomitable humor, and base selfishness that the screw of stress seldom presses out. It leaves the picture of a gentle bride from New Orleans cowering under the pounding artillery and musing, "Would it be wise like the scorpion to sting ourselves to death?"[2] It holds the dark image of a slave named Abraham blown by an exploding mine into the midst of the Forty-Fifth Illinois Regiment allowing that he had met his master going up while he was coming down and had traveled " 'Bout free miles, I guess."[3]

1. *Vicksburg Evening Post,* July 4, 5, 1945.

2. [Anonymous], "A Woman's Diary of the Siege of Vicksburg," ed. George W. Cable, *The Century Magazine,* XXX (September, 1885), 771. Hereinafter cited as "A Woman's Diary."

3. Osborn H. Oldroyd, *A Soldier's Story of the Siege of Vicksburg* (Springfield, Illinois, 1885), p. 67.

Although it is hard, it is a necessary imposition to rely solely upon the written record, for the great majority of the people remain unspeaking and dim in the background. Even so, the story of Vicksburg emerges in more than skeletal outline. The articulate inhabitants were observant; some knew that they were living a unique historical experience—and they wrote accordingly.

Theirs is the record of war-struck Vicksburg, the city which was the key to success or failure in the West and perhaps for the entire Confederacy. Confederate defeat at Gettysburg and Vicksburg occured on the same day. On this day the stamp of ultimate victory was set upon the Union. On the Fourth of July, 1863, Lee was moving back into Virginia, never again to take the initiative, never again to dominate the minds of the Union commanders. At the same time Lee's mangled corps turned southward, the Vicksburg river batteries were occupied by Federal troops and the Confederacy was cut in half. After successive failures Grant had achieved a brilliant victory. He had served his apprenticeship for Petersburg and was now ready to go east to impose his will upon the Army of Northern Virginia. He had imposed his will, and that of the Union, upon Vicksburg and its people.

This is the story of these people and their city, of how for over two years they stood against this will, and how, finally, they submitted to it. The climax of their record is the siege, but their story extends beyond this period alone. The siege, with its violence, carries an undeniable dramatic impact when set against the even tenor of the people first at peace and then far removed from actual war; but a thread of tragedy runs through the story of Vicksburg that transcends the importance of the violent weeks of bombardment. High tragedy was enacted on those hills overlooking the Mississippi (and let it be understood that it was tragedy and not irony that marked wartime Vicksburg). Here were a people, peaceful and reasonably content with the status quo, who in the tumultuous months of 1860 rejected the siren call of the Southern firebrands, who fought against secession and the implicit threats that secession carried, who went with their state out of the Union because there was really nothing else they could do, and who suffered more than any others when secession-brought armies poured into their state.

And a tragic condition of mind must be equated with the train of events. The tragedy is heightened because the people of Vicksburg, first eschewing secession, later chose to embrace the cause which would take them down into battered defeat. Distinct turning points stand out, directly related to specific events, that mark decisive changes in the Vicksburg mind. These points mark the shift of thought from peace and compromise to outright belligerency which, unlike that of Natchez was hard and determined, and not a brittle shell, easily punctured by a few shots from a squadron of gunboats. These turning points also mark the change of mind from burnished gallantry in the face of attack to acquiescence in surrender, and the reshaping of lives and attitudes in the shambles of defeat.

In sum, this is the story of a people reluctant to fling down the gauntlet of war, a people who played at war when the fighting was far away, who were greatly frightened when real war came to them, who sloughed off the most frightened ones and stood against attack with all the gallantry and sordidness of which human beings are capable; and finally it is the story of a people who found themselves defeated when the violence had passed.

Some persons stand out because they chose to write about what was happening to them, or because they were famous, or infamous, or because they merely caught the eyes of those who did write. The mass of inhabitants, white man, free Negro, and slave alike, stand mute; they are limned into the scene as best as their inarticulateness allows. There are no heroes—only the people who happened or chose to be in the city during its trial.

VICKSBURG

A People at War, 1860-1865

And he shall besiege thee in all
thy gates, until thy high and fenced
walls come down, wherein thou trustedst. . . .

—Deuteronomy 28:52

Chapter I

"A LARGE LOT OF SCRAPS"

THE soldier was sweat-streaked and tired, but most of all he was disgusted. He rolled a few choice curse words off his tongue and then said: "There [is] only one way to account for the hills of Vicksburg—after the Lord of Creation had made all the big mountains and ranges of hills, He had left on His hands a large lot of scraps; these were all dumped at Vicksburg in a waste heap." The major in charge of the detail did not bother to reprimand the soldier; he probably felt the same way. Both men were members of a party of army surveyors who were working their way along the crests of the tumbling hills. It was in July 1862, and it was hot work. Pine trees and scrub oaks, tangled and matted with underbrush and ropey vines, held them to a crawl-like pace. The summer sun caught the humidness rising from stagnant backwaters and sloughs and bathed the men with sweat as they toiled across the cut-up terrain. There was little time for rest as they leveled their transits and traced in the traverses; there was scarcely time for a quick bite of food and a hurried gulp of tepid canteen water. They went into the field early in the morning and stayed there until darkness stopped them. In the distance the sullen sound of cannon lent a sense of urgency to their work.[1]

The soldier who had to labor his way through this "waste heap" might well curse the scraps of hills, but these hills were the key to Vicksburg; and the city in turn was the key and the climax to a two-year struggle for control and possession of the Mississippi River.

1. Samuel H. Lockett, The Defense of Vicksburg—Notes and Sketches from an Engineering Point of View, Southern Historical Collection, University of North Carolina, p. 1.

The grand strategy of the United States in the Civil War was to divide the Confederacy and then slice up the pieces into succeedingly smaller bits. The Mississippi River, the great natural divider of the Confederacy, was the heart and core of this divide-and-strangle concept. Almost from the war's inception Federal forces were operating on the river in the form of gigantic pincers—moving centerward from both the north and the south—until finally they snapped together at Vicksburg.

They closed at Vicksburg because of the hills, the hills and bluffs which were the strongest point the Confederacy possessed along the river to withstand the might of the Union in the west. This rugged land and the city built upon it was, in 1862 and 1863, some of the most valuable real estate in North America. Vicksburg owed its supreme moment to the peculiar lay of the land, just as it owed its very existence to the land and the river.

The Mississippi River coils southward like a muddy snake to outline the western border of the state of Mississippi. About half way down the boundary a smaller river, the Yazoo, flows from the northeast and intersects the great muddy earth-bearing one at an acute angle. An inverted triangle is outlined, the confluence of the rivers forming the apex. The land lying between the two rivers is very flat and laced with innumerable streams, sloughs, and swamps. When the mighty river boils down in spring flood, the wash spreads over the triangle and deposits some of the richest soil in the world on the low land. At the river junction the land, in some ageless convulsion, heaved itself above the low country. Bluffs rise almost straight from the river, ripple back to the east, and gradually settle into rolling country. Across the river from the bluffs the land lies flat, almost at water level, as far as the eye can see. Vicksburg sits at the apex of this land-triangle watching over the river and the flat country which stretches out to the horizon.

Vicksburg has always been a river town, its pulse timed to the flow of the water which swirls at its feet. The city was founded and settled as the steamboat was developed; the city grew as the number of boats on western waters increased. From the river the city drew its life as skiffs, flatboats, and steamboats, laden with people and wares, tied up along its wharves.

Up the Mississippi from New Orleans came boats bearing china and clothes from France, knives and needles from England, gin machinery and nails from the North. These goods were unloaded at the docks and trundled up the hills to be displayed in stores or packed away in warehouses to await the orders of the planters and farmers. In return for the manufactured goods came bales of cotton, bushels of corn, and sides of bacon from the rich river lands, where the loamy topsoil lay twenty feet deep. The produce was carried by wagons and rafts and flat-bottomed boats that could work their way into the shallowest bayou landing and return to the city. The richest land in Mississippi was webbed by roads and waterways, and Vicksburg sat at the center of the web.

When Newitt Vick came to the Old Southwest some time before 1812, no city crowned the hills; there were only the vestigial remains of a Spanish fort. Soon after the turn of the century this Methodist parson, farmer, and father of thirteen

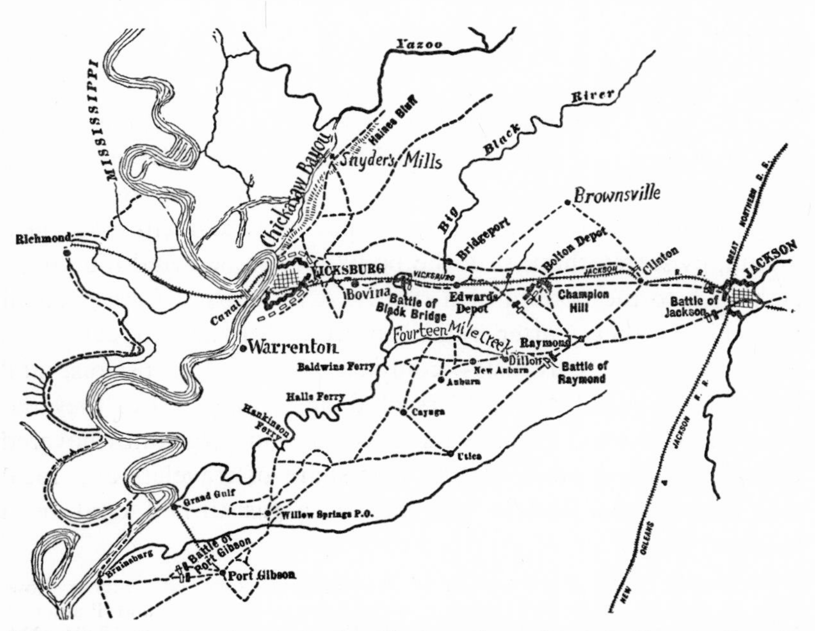

Vicksburg, showing the strategic railway and road net leading to the city. (Based upon a map in William Freeman Vilas, *The Vicksburg Campaign,* Wisconsin History Commission, 1908)

children, left settled Virginia society, moved to North Carolina, and then came to the bleakness of the Mississippi Territory. On a flatboat, he and his family floated down the Tennessee and Mississippi rivers and landed a few miles below the confluence of the Yazoo and the Mississippi. He moved inland about four miles to make his home and to lay out his fields. When other Virginians joined him and settled in the neighborhood, Vick pushed on toward the river to claim and to buy more land. In 1819 he died and left a portion of his estate to be divided into plots of land for the founding of a city.

Families from the east, from Kentucky, and from Tennessee moved into the vicinity until, in 1825, the preacher-patriarch's city became reality with the incorporation of the town of Vicksburg. Seven years later the Yazoo delta was opened to settlers; the dark, rich soil and the cotton crop it would yield brought the men who sought after it into the city. By 1835, the little town had prospered and become a bustling river port of some 2,500 persons. Cotton lust had swept the Old Southwest and held out great promises to the river town which served the great, loamy delta country.[2]

Life in a river town still on the frontier was turbulent, raw, and sometimes very brief. Territorial Mississippi's rivers and roads were infested with gangs of robbers and murderers. One of the worst outlaws was Little Harpe: he would kill and rob a victim, eviscerate him, stuff the body with stones, and hide it by sinking it to the bottom of a river. After Harpe, John Murrell with his partner Carter came up from Natchez to carry on. They posed as revivalists—complete with songs, psalms, and "the jerks"—to allay the fears of their victims before they did their bloody work. Gamblers, fleecers, and prostitutes hovered along the waterfront to catch their share of travelers and local men who succumbed to the lure of a fast-turned card or a flaunted smile.[3]

2. "Newitt Vick," *Encyclopedia of Mississippi History,* ed. Dunbar Rowland, II, 857-58; Willie D. Halsell, "A Vicksburg Speculator and Planter in the Yazoo Delta," *Journal of Mississippi History,* XI (October, 1949), 231.

3. Virginia P. Matthias, "Natchez-Under-The-Hill," *Journal of Mississippi History,* VII (October, 1945), 218.

Vigilance committees finally extirpated the most vicious river gangs—once by hanging five men and setting a sixth adrift in a skiff on the Mississippi with his hands tied behind his back.[4] Of the more settled elements in Vicksburg, newspaper editors especially had difficulty staying alive. The city was a political no man's land where pretentious, established Whigs clashed head-on with the brawling democracy. The newspapers spearheaded the political attack and editors were often called out to the city's streets or a river island to defend their editorials. Vicksburg, founded by a preacher's vision, was nurtured to the accompaniment of the "thunk" of bowie knives stuck solidly into human flesh and the mean little bark of derringers as well as Methodist hymns.

As the frontier washed past, life became more placid and society more stable, but a legacy of violence clung to the city. Yet in a short while the legacy would be claimed with a degree of violence undreamed of by the contentious frontiersmen.

A new courthouse, erected three years before the war, symbolized the transition from frontier town to ordered city. One of the highest hilltops was leveled for the building and its four-faced clock became a landmark of the city (later, the building's stuccoed façade and column-supported cupola would become a favorite registration point for gunboats and artillery). Below the courthouse more streets were cut into the hillsides, more gullies were bridged, and more land was leveled for new homes, stores, and churches. By 1860, the hills were tiered with buildings—long, low warehouses lay along the waterfront; three blocks up from the river the best stores and shops lined Washington Street; farther away from the river, Greek Revival homes, shielded by fences and hedges, stood aloof from the streets; less pretentious houses were stacked along the hillsides, and a visitor had to climb several flights of stairs to get to some of the front doors.

The architecture of the buildings, itself without a common pattern, followed in unconscious imitation the sprawling pattern

4. "Vicksburg," *Encyclopedia of Mississippi History,* II, 861. See also "Vicksburg Gamblers" in the Subject File of the Mississippi State Department of Archives and History, hereinafter cited as Miss. Arch.

The city at the beginning of the war, as a passenger on a riverboat from New Orleans might have seen it. (Courtesy of the Mississippi Department of Archives and History)

of the city. Rough, unpainted shacks held the human drift from the river and the families of immigrant Irish workers. Latin influence from New Orleans was manifested by broad verandas bordered with lacy iron grillwork. Duff Green, one of the leading grocery and commission merchants, built a house that rose four stories and was trimmed with ironwork. Ex-Governor Alexander McNutt lived in a little, neat, clapboard house that looked as if it should be set in New England rather than the South. Emma Balfour, a doctor's wife, lived in a two-story brick home whose simple lines reflected good taste. Atop one of the hills the Sisters of Mercy built a red brick convent which was square and undistinguished (shortly, the color of its weathering brick would be matched by the dull, brown bloodstains on its floors).[5]

The best view of the city was from the river. A passenger on a riverboat could see the city stretching out for almost a mile along the river, the streets rising up the hills from the waterfront, and the sky spiked by the spire of St. Paul's Church and the cupola of the courthouse.

As the war decade opened, the city's population numbered close to 4,500. These people, together with the agricultural community served by Vicksburg, supported almost one hundred shops, banks, stores, factories, and business houses of one sort

5. Bette E. Barber, Vicksburg: Home Town Gilbraltar, Miss. Arch., *passim*.

or another. Wholesale grocers, commission merchants, and cotton brokers held the largest business interests in the city. Druggists, gunsmiths, tailors, jewelers, insurance salesmen, publishers, bookbinders, carriagemakers, stove- and boilermakers, photographers, bakers, confectioners, nurserymen, liquor dealers, and dressmakers catered to the legitimate wants and wishes of the community. Professional men, too, found a good living in the city. There were enough teachers to staff both public and private schools, and the city supported a school system which kept an "average" of five hundred scholars busy at their books. Vicksburg's lawyers were probably the finest in the state, and the memory of the glittering eloquence of Seargent S. Prentiss left a luster that had not been matched in Natchez or Jackson.[6]

Vicksburg held out promises of opportunity across the nation and beyond the seas. Polyglot conversations could be heard in the streets and shops. Mme. Cognaisse fashioned Parisian-modeled gowns for the ladies. After a dress fitting a woman could stop by Saintsott's to be fitted with the latest-style shoe. From there she could go to Henry Scheulier's grocery store to select imported foods for her table. Then she might stop at Bazzinsky, Simmons and Company to choose material for her daughter's dresses, which could be sewn on a machine sold by L. B. Johnson. Clarke's Literary Depot was a popular place for the woman of leisure who wanted to read the latest novels or obtain a copy of Clarke's own *Household Almanac* for her kitchen. On her way home the woman might leave an order with Jacob Gisill for the next day's bread, then pause to look at the necklaces and bracelets displayed in the window at the jewelry store of Moody and Kuner.

A planter could come to town and spend several days mixing business with pleasure. He might check over his account with W. C. Raum, a commission merchant, then drive down to Bitterman, Wixforth and Company where a carriage was being made for him. From there he could go to place an order for plowshares at Paxton's foundry, then stop at A. N. Auguste's to

6. *A General Directory for the City of Vicksburg* (Vicksburg, 1860), pp. 50, 56. Hereinafter cited as *City Directory, 1860*.

replenish his wine cellar. John Baum would sell him some long, black Havanas which he could puff on while A. J. Carnahan fitted him with a suit. Over the span of a few days he could buy any of the six newspapers printed in the city. The *Daily Whig, Weekly Whig, Daily Sun, Weekly Sun, Daily Evening Citizen,* and *Weekly Evening Citizen* all supplied their readers with a diet of subjects ranging from national politics to patent medicine cures for maladies running from stomach ache and syphilis to young men's "dark and secret practices." The reader's choice was usually dictated by his political inclinations, for all of the papers were strongly partisan.

If a visitor was without an invitation to spend the night, he could find good accommodations and better food at the Washington Hotel, which reminded a titled English visitor of an old London tavern.[7] If the Washington did not suit his tastes, he could stay at either the Prentiss House, which was near the waterfront, or the Commercial Hotel higher up the hill. He might rest easier at night if he knew that four volunteer fire companies, the Washington, the Constitution, the Phoenix, and the Independent, raced one another to fires—and sometimes put them out.

If his visit carried him through the week end, and if he was so inclined, the visitor could worship in churches which covered the whole range of organized American religion. Baptist, Catholic, Episcopal, Methodist, and Presbyterian churches, and a Jewish synagogue were established in the city and they offered the citizen and the traveler ample fare for their souls.[8]

Satisfaction of the flesh as well as the soul could also be had in the city. Below Washington Street, where the hills dropped off sharply toward the river, "Vicksburg-Under-the-Hill" flourished and supplied items of pleasure and necessity that could not easily be obtained elsewhere. The scourings of the river worked in the houses and alleyways there, ready for anything if the price was right. In places such as Mollie Bunch's bordello a look, a word, or the flash of money could bring instant violence,

7. William H. Russell, *My Diary North and South* (Boston, 1863), p. 295.

8. The material presented in this paragraph and the preceding ones is based upon information obtained from *City Directory, 1860,* and the *Vicksburg Weekly Whig* and the *Vicksburg Daily Citizen* for 1860.

and a man's life could be snuffed out without causing a ripple of interest in the city or bringing more than scant official notice.[9]

But the city tolerated the sordid business heaped along the waterfront because it was an inevitable part of the river, and it was from the river that the city drew its life. The stores, the shops, the schools, the churches, and the dark houses on South Street were the surface of the city. The deepest meaning of the city—its very heart-throb—lay at the foot of the hills, where the river flowed.

As the people went about their business—as the newspapers were printed, as the plowshares were cast, as the clothes were tailored—the steamboats warped into the landings bearing newsprint, iron ingots, and yard goods. The wharves were the heart of the city, and the newspapers pridefully noted the forest of smokestacks gathered at the foot of their hills. They tallied the number of boats coming and going, and reserved special comment for particularly smart or fast vessels. In 1860, as he looked out of his office window down to the wharves, the editor of the *Whig* never dreamed that in three years the boats cruising past the waterfront would smash his newspaper plant to smouldering ruins.

Steamboats from New Orleans, Memphis, St. Louis, and Louisville arrived daily. Three times a week boats left Vicksburg for Memphis and New Orleans, and the Yazoo boat, which went deep into the delta to Greenwood, made its run four times a week. Every half hour a ferry crossed the river to De Soto City, Louisiana, the eastern terminal for the Vicksburg, Shreveport and Texas Railroad.[10]

The coming of the railroads gave Vicksburg lateral communications as well as the vertical lines provided by the rivers. The Southern Railroad of Mississippi spanned the state to connect Vicksburg with Meridian. Halfway across the line, at Jackson, the Mississippi Central Railroad and the New Orleans, Jackson and Great Northern Railroad provided rail links to the north and south. Two feeder lines, between Jackson and Vicksburg, connected Port Gibson and Raymond to the Southern

9. *Vicksburg Weekly Whig,* December 19, 1860.
10. *City Directory, 1860,* pp. 55-56.

Railroad. Across the river the Vicksburg, Shreveport and Texas Railroad pushed its way toward Texas.[11] The line was partially subsidized by taxes gathered in Vicksburg, taxes which the people had levied upon themselves in their enthusiasm to construct channels of commerce leading to their city.[12] As they built the railroad they did not know that they were also fashioning an iron noose about their necks.

During the war, as Confederate communication centers in the west fell, and as the Mississippi was swept clear of Southern traffic, the single line of iron running eastward from Vicksburg and the sorry little spur of track stuck out into Louisiana loomed larger and larger in military planning. After New Orleans and Memphis were lost, Vicksburg became the sole strong link holding the Confederacy together across the Mississippi River.

For two years Confederate supply lines, stretching from the Mexican border to Northern Virginia, passed through Vicksburg. English rifles, landed in Mexico and smuggled through Brownsville, were shipped with Texas beef and grain to the armies operating in the east. In Louisiana the supplies were joined by shipments of sugar and rice and were ferried across the river to Vicksburg depots. From there, loaded on rickety trains, they were sent to the east. So long as the city held, the supplies could come across to the eastern armies. The moment the city fell the trickle would be stopped and the Confederacy would be severed.

If, at the outbreak of war, a military man with a penetrating understanding of the importance of communications and terrain had studied a topographical map of the Mississippi valley, he would have jabbed a finger at the spot where Vicksburg was located, looked up, and said, "Here, a great battle will be fought."

11. Robert C. Black, *The Railroads of the Confederacy* (Chapel Hill, North Carolina, 1952), see fold-out map inside back cover. At the outbreak of war the Southern Railroad did not run quite to Meridian. In the spring of 1860 it was completed between Vicksburg and Newton, Mississippi.

12. City Council Minute Book, 1860-69, City Hall, Vicksburg, p. 125. Hereinafter cited as Council Minute Book.

Chapter II

"THE LOW RUMBLING THUNDER"

WASHINGTON Street was the city's main thoroughfare. It was smoothly graveled and lay parallel to the river. Jackson Street, at right angles to the river, ran up and down the hills. It was paved with widely spaced cobblestones so that horses and mules might set their hooves in the spaces to gain solid footing as they pulled their loads up the inclines; this gave carriages and wagons a hard bouncing, but it kept the animals from slipping and falling. Jackson Street got its name because, as it veered off to the north and left the city, it became the Jackson Road which connected Vicksburg with the state capital. The intersection at Washington and Jackson streets was the busiest place in the city. Throughout the day people crossed this corner as they went about their business. Within a given time such persons as C. W. Vick, Mahala Roach, Mrs. I. O. Smith, William Merritt, Max Kuner, and the Episcopal rector's maid Minnie might have passed by. They met and passed—a cross section of the population of Vicksburg.

The majority of the city's citizens were either native Mississippians or had come to the city laterally across the South from Alabama, Georgia, or the Carolinas. The remainder of the South had also contributed to the population and there was a sprinkling of New Englanders and Midwesterners, probably because Vicksburg was a handy place to step off (or be put off) a riverboat.

Some of the Vicks still lived in the city where they spent much of their time haggling over their patrimony. Seargent S. Prentiss, who came from Maine, got caught in the legal tangle of the Vick inheritance and left town a ruined man. When this was past, C. W. Vick, one of the heirs, found a measure of quiet tending the fruit trees and shrubs which he grew in his nursery on the edge of town.[1] The strength and the vision of the first generation was not transmitted to the offspring and the Vicks no longer sat with the men who directed the business of the city nor did their names appear on the important notices of the day.

Some people thought that Mahala Roach was a tragic figure. Mahala's mother was a bellwether of Vicksburg society and had not been pleased when Mahala married John Roach, an Irish immigrant. John Roach was a good husband and Mahala loved him, but he died young. Mahala, an attractive woman in her mid-thirties, was left with a marriageable daughter, a flock of young children, and the account books to study and puzzle with. Yet people could not guess that she preferred the company of her daughter's beaus, "Sturm und Drang" novels, and even the account books to the continuous round of her mother's tea parties and the blandishments of her own suitors.[2]

Just where Mrs. I. O. Smith fitted into the Vicksburg social structure is not certain. She might have been part of the mass that moved along the waterfront—as easily at home in Natchez or New Orleans as Vicksburg. She might have been the wife of a riverman or a laborer. This much is certain: she belonged to that part of the population which seldom put words on paper and which kept few account books. If she had a husband he was a tolerant man, because Mrs. Smith was ready to travel alone throughout the South and if she wanted company she knew "tow Laidiey" friends who were prepared to go with her.[3]

William Merritt had come from the leached soil of Virginia to find his fortune in Mississippi. He brought a gang of Negroes with him and set them to work clearing cotton land. Merritt and his slaves worked hard, and he prospered, but he could never cut himself away from his Virginia heritage. He regularly asked for advice and help from his father who remained in Virginia.[4]

1. Dallas C. Dickey, *Seargent S. Prentiss: Whig Orator of the Old South* (Baton Rouge, Louisiana, 1945), pp. 266-88; *City Directory, 1860,* p. 27.

2. Mahala P. H. Roach, Diary, Southern Historical Collection, University of North Carolina, *passim.*

3. Mrs. I. O. Smith to John J. Pettus, September 16, 1861, Governors' Correspondence, Series E, Vol. LIII, Miss. Arch.

4. William H. E. Merritt Papers, Duke University, biographical headnote.

Another portion of the population was neither native Mississippian nor American. This group of people had come to the city from Ireland, Scotland, England, France, Spain, Poland, Canada, Switzerland, Cuba, Russia, Finland, and the German and Italian states.

Max Kuner and his brothers left Bavaria in 1847. They made their way to a seaport and sailed—away from what or to what is unknown—for the New World. The brothers separated at New Orleans and Max took passage on a steamboat for Vicksburg. He landed there, found work as a watchmaker, and was given four months in which to learn the language. Max was a quick learner and a better businessman. By the outbreak of the war he was half-owner of a jewelry business which carried $56,000 in accounts, did not lose one per cent of the accounts because of bad debts, and had Jefferson Davis as a regular customer.[5]

There were more than a thousand Max Kuners in and about Vicksburg in 1861. This meant that almost one out of every three free persons who would go to war or stand the siege was not a native American, much less a Southerner. De la Hunts, Kellys, Genellas, Cohens, and Lowenhaupts were scattered throughout the town. Bridget Kelly took in washing; the Genellas sent their children in carriages to play with Mahala Roach's brood. The manner in which the immigrants cut across the Vicksburg social strata indicated that the town put as much value on ability and acquisitiveness as it did on the chance of birth.

Ability and acquisitiveness made no difference for one small group of free inhabitants. They were free, but that amounted to nothing so far as social or political status was concerned. The black man was black, free or slave, and that was all there was to it. He might have been a drayman or a fisherman or a preacher, or even as successful a businessman as William Johnson was in Natchez; but he left no mark on the city. The free Negro lived in a limbo shuffling between the prerogatives of a

5. [Max Kuner], "Vicksburg and After: Being the Experience of a Southern Merchant," ed. Edwin L. Sabin, *The Sewanee Review,* XV (October, 1907), 485. Kuner was identified as the merchant through the Warren County Census, 1860, Schedule I, p. 25, Miss. Arch.

free man and the status of a slave. Occasionally some note might be taken of him, but it was usually because he had brushed against the white man's law. In January 1861, a free Negro named Edgar was arrested by the police when they found "several suspicious documents, together with about $65 in money" in his possession. The mayor heard the case and told Edgar he must leave the state or be sold into slavery. Edgar decided to be sold, and the only comment this brought from J. W. Swords, the editor of the *Daily Citizen,* was, "Edgar is worth about $1800, which added to the State fund will help out considerably."[6]

The final segment of the population consisted of the slaves. Unlike the free Negroes, the slaves left their print upon the city. The landmark of the city, the courthouse, was built by slave labor. Many of the homes and buildings in the town were put up by their hands. The boilers of the steamboats which tied up at the wharves were stoked by slaves; the wagons which carried the bales and boxes off-loaded at the wharves were driven by slaves; the homes of the men who owned the boxes and bales were tended by slaves; the cotton upon which the city thrived was produced by slaves. It may be argued that the city existed because of the slaves. Whether this idea occurred to the Negro and what he thought of it is problematical because the strictly ordered system under which he lived and worked had no time or place for such speculation, nor did it have any desire to help the slave set it down on paper. Therefore as long as the system was capable of being enforced the slave remained mute. Only a fleeting glimpse of him remains, and that is usually through the eyes of a white person. Then as the system began to disintegrate the slave became more expressive. As before, he showed himself through the eyes and the pen of the white man, but his behavior had altered so much that the white man had to take notice of him and comment on him. But in 1861 the system was firm.

6. *Vicksburg Daily Citizen,* January 22, 24, 1861. See Charles S. Sydnor, "The Free Negro in Mississippi before the Civil War," *American Historical Review,* XXXII (July, 1927), 769-88, for a legalistic and statistical study of the free Negro. As Warren County (Vicksburg) was one of the four counties in which the free Negro was most numerous, this article is of some significance.

Occasionally a slave would run away, but the runaway notices carried in the newspapers were few, and the majority of the advertisements concerned slaves who had escaped from plantations rather than from owners who lived in the city. Sometimes when slaves ran away they made no attempt to put much distance between themselves and their owners, for they could effectively hide themselves within the city. One master posted notice that Martha, who worked as a "washer and ironer," was "lurking about town, and probably hiring herself to persons by the day."[7]

Instances such as this were the exception rather than the rule and, in January 1861, almost fifteen hundred Vicksburg slaves docilely followed their masters into the Confederacy. Most of the slaves probably knew nothing of the momentous happenings or what the implications held for them. One of them, Minnie, who was owned by Dr. William Lord, the Episcopal rector, did know; or at least she thought she did. The rector had been born in New York, but had lived most of his life in the slave states. He was prepared to remain in the South among the people with whom he had lived and served, but the question of Minnie's status bothered him. He could not justify keeping her as he shifted his allegiance from the country which would probably free her to a state whose avowed purpose was the maintenance and protection of slavery; therefore he offered Minnie her freedom. She rejected the offer and chose instead to remain with the family through war and siege, finally to be separated from the family when they moved on to unoccupied territory after the fall of the city. One of the children remembered Minnie as an "ardent defender of the cause" who was always called the "secesh darkey" by her colored friends.[8]

Minnie was in the minority, though she did reflect the attitude of some of the slaves. Subtle relationships existed between masters and slaves which breached the barriers of the class and caste system. These relationships would shift and change as peace gave way to war and war became siege. When siege

7. *Vicksburg Daily Citizen,* February 7, 1861. The same sort of advertisement appeared in *ibid.,* December 28, 1860.

8. Lida L. Reed, "A Woman's Experiences During the Siege of Vicksburg," *The Century Magazine,* LXI (April, 1901), 923.

ended in conquest the relationship between the Negro and the white man would be so twisted that it would be unrecognizable as akin to that which had existed three years previously. But this was all to come. In 1861 the slave did what he was bought to do, and he did it so well that his masters had scarce cause to remark on his presence.

These were the people of Vicksburg, the human sum of the city. Almost five thousand of them—[9] slave, free Negro, immigrant, and native American—lived in the hilled city unaware that it would bring them all to their lowest common denominator —that of human beings struggling to survive—and in doing so would give them a common name. The name would depend upon the particular writer and where that writer's sympathies lay. A Louisiana lady with literary inclinations called them "the keepers of the River."[10] The phrase occurred to her when she rather romantically recalled their behavior during the unsuccessful gunboat attacks during the summer of 1862. But in January 1861, the people of Vicksburg did not, any more than the inhabitants of New Orleans, Memphis, or St. Louis, consider themselves the keepers of the Mississippi, or any other river for that matter. The things they kept were homes, shops, horses, and slaves. This was their business. They did it well and they had become wealthy. There were not many romantic overtones to it, but there was a great deal of substance. They paved their streets for their carriages and wagons, guttered their sidewalks to carry off rain and refuse, lighted their streets with gas so they might travel at night more safely and securely, sent their children to the East to school, and traveled on vacation throughout the country.

9. The population figures are based upon the *United States Census Population of the United States in 1860* (Washington, 1864), p. 271, and the Warren County Census, 1860, Schedule I, pp. 1-82, and Schedule II, pp. 1-17, Miss. Arch. In 1860, 1,767 white males, 1,391 white females, 14 colored free males, 17 colored free females, 694 male slaves, and 708 female slaves lived in the city. The total population was 4,591. It would be reasonable to assume that this number increased somewhat by the outbreak of war. This population made Vicksburg the second largest city, after Natchez, in the state.

10. Sara A. Dorsey, *Recollections of Henry Watkins Allen, Brigadier General Confederate States Army, Ex-Governor of Louisiana* (New York, 1866), p. 122.

Their substance had a bourgeois quality to it. They were a new people and they smelled of the store and the shop and the rawness of new land rather than the secluded mustiness of the Battery and the Vieux Carrée. In their newness they had found wealth and the pleasures wealth could bring.

While schism and disunion were made in Charleston and compounded in Baltimore during the summer of 1860, some of the people of Vicksburg sought relief from the hot beat of the southern sun at Saint Anthony's Falls, Minnesota. There Emma Shannon, vivacious and articulate daughter of the editor of the *Vicksburg Whig,* amused herself with walks to the springs and buggy rides with a dashing man later rumored to be an absconder. Her father found pleasure in the summer society of both the Northerners and the Southerners at the resort.[11] But when he was home the editor was not too proud to print that his was a hard business, and he reminded his readers that they should be prompt with subscription payments.

The rubric which sets forth the Southerner's climb to wealth runs something like this: take a poor man with a little land; he will pick up a slave or two and work in the fields with them; with his increased income he will buy more land and produce more cotton; with his profits he will buy more land and more slaves until he is the master of a plantation and, *ipso facto,* is economically well off and socially acceptable and the peer of every gentleman. After he attains the desired economic and social status he will build a white-winged house and live in it like an English country gentleman.

There were white-winged houses in Vicksburg. Duff Green owned one which was as magnificent as any to be found along the river. But here the dialectic breaks down. Duff Green was a merchant. William Lum owned a house which was considered good enough for General Grant to live in when he stayed in Vicksburg. William Lum was a businessman. These men possessed little land and fewer slaves; in fact William Lum employed white women as servants in his home.[12]

11. Marmaduke Shannon to Lavinia Shannon, July 21, 1860, Phillip Crutcher Collection, Miss. Arch.

12. Charles J. Slack in a letter to the author, November 8, 1957; Warren County Census, 1860, Schedule I, Miss. Arch.

Vicksburg was a city of shopkeepers and the wealth of the people was measured by the goods stocked in the shops or stored in the warehouses rather than by acreages and slaves.[13] The pattern for the creation and acquisition of wealth was more like that of Max Kuner or Auguste Genella, who came from Switzerland to build one of the largest mercantile houses in the city, than the man who, with his own sweat and that of his slaves, hacked a plantation out of the delta wilderness.

The corollary to the status-through-land-and-slave dialectic is that everyone, small farmer, merchant, professional man, aspired to the plantation and the status it would give him. Yet the Vicksburg merchants and professional men were the social peers of the plantation owner. The planter was glad to come to town to visit and stay in their homes and also bring along his family so they might enjoy the social life of the city. The visiting was reciprocal; families from town were invited guests in the plantation homes and they were especially thankful for their plantation-owning friends when the gunboats started bombarding the city. No trace exists of a social barrier which is supposed to have rifted plantation owner and city dweller.

The Vicksburg economy was organized about the merchant and his business. This was only natural as the city was the warehouse for wide swaths of the Mississippi and Yazoo deltas, but the significance of the businessman's supremacy would not become apparent until his economic interests became imperilled by secession and the threat of war.

In addition to being a mercantile center the city also supported enough heavy and light industry to make the value of its

13. In 1860, the assessed valuation of property, both real and personal, in Vicksburg was $4,582,650. An analysis of this sum supports the textual statement. Merchandise was valued at $1,746,400, real estate at $1,538,400, slaves at $876,300, money loaned on interest at $183,450, horses at $28,200, and pleasure carriages at $9,900. Notice that the value of the merchandise was more than twice that of the slaves. As these figures represent evaluations for tax purposes, in all likelihood the real total far exceeded $4,582,650. This contention is supported by the fact that with a total value of $876,300 the average value of a slave would be little more than $700. This amount seems too low considering that town slaves were usually skilled or semi-skilled workers or trained household servants and they generally brought in more than $1,000 on the market. *City Directory, 1860,* p. 75.

manufactured products the second largest in the state.[14] Agricultural implements, books, shoes, jewelry, steam engines, carriages, clothing, firearms, and saddles were some of the articles produced in the shops and factories. The city could also claim a unique distinction in that it possessed the only gas works in the state. Clustered about the mercantile and industrial interests were the varied occupations which always exist in an urban area. Doctors, lawyers, bankers, dentists, newspapermen, teachers, barkeepers, railway workers, and servants were busy in the city. The newspapermen and the lawyers would play a prime role in molding and expressing the opinion of the people as the time approached when such an expression would bear heavily upon the course of events.

When the business, industrial, professional, and service interests are considered as an economic whole, the Vicksburg economy emerges as the most complex and variegated system which functioned in Mississippi. Natchez was a larger city, but it was tied to agriculture much more than its sister city up the river, and there was much less heavy industry located there. Holly Springs, which was the largest railroad town in the state, supported more heavy industry than Vicksburg, but its fortunes lay almost wholly with the railroads. This dispersal of economic activity linked Vicksburg to a wider group of interests than any other city or town in the state. Agriculture, industry, transportation and communications, as well as the various professions, raised the city to the place where it was not vitally dependent upon one of these interests alone. This tended to make the people less susceptible to the increasingly vehement arguments of the firebrand Southerners who preached secession as the panacea which would perpetuate slavery and make secure their peculiar economic and social system.

All of this was a matter of degree. Ultimately the economy of Vicksburg, as well as that of the state, rested upon slavery;

14. *Manufactures of the United States in 1860* (Washington, 1865), p. 292. The tabulations are by counties, but as Warren, Adams, and Marshall counties had only one major urban center it may be assumed that the great preponderence of industry was located in these cities, i.e., Vicksburg, Natchez, and Holly Springs. The total valuation of Warren County manufactures was $643,700.

but there were some citizens who believed that the city would be able to withstand the shock if the slave economy was dislocated, a belief the secession-bent planter or the man who aspired to land-slave status could never admit.[15]

Slavery became a very sensitive subject within the city as a vociferous minority agitated for the restoration of the African slave trade. The argument over the revival of the trade became so bitter that one of the leading citizens declared that "if African Negroes were imported into the South, he would move out of it." The "ultra," Davis-backed, Democratic paper seized this and printed a cartoon of the man, hair on end, eyes glassy with fear, lips drawn back in horror, as he contemplated the importation of slaves.[16]

This was mild compared to what was coming. As the abolitionists' shrill clamor increased, and as the undisguised threat to a basic element of Southern life and culture mounted, the state went into convulsion.

Anne Harris was a Vicksburg judge's daughter. The judge was a prosperous man and Anne had a fine home, house servants, and a carriage to keep her mind occupied with pleasant things. In the unsettled months of early 1861, war was a distant thing to her. Much later when she thought about it, she decided "the first mutterings of war were like the low, rumbling thunder that one hears on a quiet summer day, when there is hardly a cloud to be seen in the sky."[17] But Anne was just a child in 1861; she was not supposed to know that the thunder was long in coming and that the war clouds had been piling up for decades before she was born.

For over thirty years a discontent that bred disunion had worked its course in Mississippi. The state had bridled and tugged against Federal authority from the time of the nullification controversy. At the next great test Senator Henry S. Foote,

15. *Vicksburg Weekly Sun,* May 30, 1859, reproduced in Percy L. Rainwater, *Mississippi: Storm Center of Secession 1856-1861* (Baton Rouge, 1938), p. 80.

16. *Ibid.*

17. Anne Harris Broidrick, A Recollection of Thirty Years Ago, Southern Historical Collection, University of North Carolina, p. 10.

who labeled slavery "a selfish and semibarbarous policy," brought the state in line behind the Compromise of 1850. But soon the men who talked secession lured more and more Mississippians with their heady theme and Foote was beaten by fire-eating Albert Gallatin Brown when he ran for re-election in 1854. John J. McRae and John A. Quitman, ideological brothers of Brown, became governor and congressman in the same election. The presidential election of 1856 further widened the gulf which separated the Unionist and the secession-bent. James Buchanan's election, said Jefferson Davis, was merely a four-year truce which left the enemy standing "upon the field with flag flying, defiant and an army ready for attack."[18]

Three years later John Brown's raid blew new life into the sectional fears that Senator Foote had tried to allay in 1850. A month after the raid, John J. Pettus, called by one Mississippian "a disunion man of the most unmitigated order," was chosen to be governor of Mississippi. The train of events was building to the point at which men's reason would be subverted by passion, and those who clung to reason and to old loyalties would be shouted down in the race toward secession.

That point came with the election of 1860 when the Democrats split wide over the slavery issue. Stephen A. Douglas ran as the legitimate Democratic candidate. The South bolted the party and nominated John C. Breckinridge as the symbol of their discontent and secessionist tendencies. The Republicans, blatantly sectional and anti-slave, were dead in the South. A fourth party, the Constitutional-Unionists, selected John Bell to straddle party and sectional differences to try to hold the sagging nation together.

In Vicksburg, as throughout the state and the South, the election was the climax of a ten-year campaign of emotion-laden fears and hard, cold facts of political and economic dominance. The single issue stood out stark in its simplicity—secession. This time Jefferson Davis was determined that the enemy would not be left "upon the field with flag flying . . . ready for attack." He knew that Vicksburg, close by his plantation home, had strong Unionist leanings, and the night before the election he,

18. Rainwater, *Mississippi: Storm Center of Secession,* p. 40.

with Albert Gallatin Brown, L. Q. C. Lamar, and some lesser men, came to lead the "last Grand rally [of the] last great effort to save the right and honor of the South." In the dancing shadows cast by torches and gaslight, to a crowd whipped up by the Davis paper, they pleaded with the people to support Breckinridge as the only defender of Southern honor.[19]

At the same time Davis, Brown, and Lamar were holding forth, the Constitutional-Unionists met at the courthouse for their last effort before the people went to the polls. The courthouse hill was ablaze with the flare of rockets and roman candles as the Unionist speakers pointed their appeals to the young men of the city.[20] The conservatives felt secure with the older man, but the young men had found a liking for the hotspur chauvinism of the secessionists. The foppish glory of a military adventure stemming from secession caught their imagination and the Unionists tried to counter this emotional appeal with one of their own.

Marmaduke Shannon had aimed right at this point when he printed: "Young men! Will you see the Union of your fathers rent in twain? Will you see the Constitution torn in tatters by bands of secessional agitators and traitorous fanatics? No. NEVER, NEVER. Then buckle on your armor and go forth to do battle for the success of the Union candidates."[21] Shannon was a gentle man and these were strong words for him, but he would have dipped his pen in more vehement ink if he could have known that secession-brought war would kill five of his children and scatter others from Alabama to Texas.

The next day the people went to the polls. When the balloting was done the split Democrats gave eighty-three votes to Douglas and 580 to Breckinridge. The Old Whig-Conservative-Unionist men had a solid majority—816 of them voted for Bell.[22] Vicksburg agreed with Marmaduke Shannon and rejected Jefferson Davis' storming for Southern rights and secession if necessary.

19. *Vicksburg Weekly Sun,* November 5, 1860, reproduced in *ibid.,* p. 158.
20. *Vicksburg Weekly Whig,* November 7, 1860.
21. *Vicksburg Daily Whig,* October 10, 1860.
22. Returns for Presidential Electors, 1860, Series F, Vol. LXXXV, Miss. Arch.

Though set upon a slave culture, the people of Vicksburg were strongly Unionist. They had weighed the issues for years and when the matter came to a head they unequivocally set themselves against disunion. Marmaduke Shannon took note of the election returns and registered the mind of the people when he wrote: "The Union party [is] a Permanent organization. . . . It is founded upon a rock and the gates of hell shall not prevail against it."[23] The rock of which he spoke rested within the framework of an orderly settlement of differences. It would turn to sand under the onslaught of inflamed passions called States' Rights.

When all of the abstruse involutions of States' Rights doctrines were set aside, the base upon which secession rested was slavery, and slavery was the foundation of the state's culture. Neither the wealthy Vicksburg-Natchez merchant-planter nor the small slaveholder nor the yeoman farmer would care to have that foundation changed. For the wealthy man it was his stake in the present; for the man on the make it was his stake in the future. But secession was another matter. Secession probably meant war with all of war's attendant risks of loss. The wealthy man of the river counties and cities stood to lose if war came. He was well established and could afford to wait and bargain and hope that his culture would be left intact. The man on the make had less to lose and more to gain with war. If he could free his section for once and for all from Northern meddling he would know that his future was secure, that someday he too might amass land and slaves and social status. He was not afraid to gamble on war. The man of property was. When all of the prolix arguments were stripped away and the nub of the matter was exposed, the prospect of war was the thing which separated secessionist from conservative.[24]

Vicksburg voted conservative. Economic ties with the North—especially the river connection with the Midwest—fear

23. *Vicksburg Weekly Whig,* November 7, 1860.

24. This interpretation is set forth at greater length and in greater detail in John K. Bettersworth, *Confederate Mississippi* (Baton Rouge, Louisiana, 1943), p. 5. It has a decided economic emphasis and neglects other motivations such as a genuine love and regard for the Union, fear of war which did not stem from fear of property loss, and sincere political differences.

of war stemming from property and personal hazard, genuine love for the Union, and strong partisan political feelings which made the conservatives distrust the demagogic, secession-inclined Democrats, were the forces which worked to hold the city apart from most of the state. The vote characterized the population—they were a people established, entrenched, and content with the status quo.

When the national election results were announced the state quivered with wrath and apprehension. The Black Republicans had won, and Abraham Lincoln, a minority president, was bound for the White House. The announcement that Lincoln was to be the next president shivered even some of the staunchest Unionists, and the pressure of the secessionists mounted on all sides.

Crisis was a word on everyone's lips. The shops, the streets, the homes were filled with the word. It even crept into the sanctuary of the churches. Emma Shannon excused herself from the Methodist Church on the Sunday following the election and went home to find peace and to send a note to her fiance: "Sunday school was so dismal this morning, that I needed to come home . . . . Mr. Marshall preaches, or *speaks,* rather, for I suspect he is eager for an opportunity of airing his peculiar political views in the present crisis. But I don't care anything for the present crisis. . . ." She closed her letter by saying that country and crisis could go hang, that all she cared for was her sick lover.[25] Political upheaval might be forced into abeyance by a young woman in love, but other persons in the city searched deep into their conflicting and torn loyalties to try to find a solution to their dilemma.

A week after the election the conservatives made their decision: "The die is cast . . . Abraham Lincoln is Presdent of the United States . . . What is [our] duty in this crisis in our national affairs . . . . Shall [we] follow the rash and mad advice which the Governor of this State . . . urge? We do not mean to rebel against the Government because an obnoxious man has been made President! We do not mean to raise the standard of

25. Emma Shannon to William O. Crutcher, November 11, 1860, Crutcher Collection.

resistance . . . . Let others do what they will, for us, we will stand by the *Union, the Constitution, and the laws.*"[26]

This was the will of the people. They had taken measure of the election and they, like the rest of the South, loathed the thought of Lincoln being in the White House. They readily admitted that a crisis existed. Their loyalty to the Union bent and was re-scrutinized, but then it snapped back firm. Republicans, with all of their sectional and abolitionist trappings, were distasteful but not unpalatable. In mid-November, Vicksburg was strong for the Union, but the inexorable current toward secession had set in across the state.

There were men who tried to halt the flood, or at least hold it back. Late in the month a state-wide Union mass meeting was held in Vicksburg during which the speakers counseled patience and the settlement of difficulties within the constitutional framework. They found the people of Vicksburg a receptive audience, but as far as the state was concerned they cried in the wind.[27]

At the same time the Union men were gathering in Vicksburg, the state legislature called for an election of delegates to a secession convention. The election was to be held December 20, six weeks after Lincoln's victory. This time lag gave the secessionists ample time to intensify their clamorings of the dire fate that awaited the South at the hands of the Republicans.

In Warren County, Thomas A. Marshall and Walker Brooke were nominated by the conservatives, now called "co-operationists." W. H. Johnson and William H. McCardle (of *ex parte* McCardle fame in Supreme Court reports) ran as avowed secessionists. All of the candidates were citizens of Vicksburg, and they spent several weeks campaigning in the city and out in the county.

When the ballots were counted the condition of mind of November 6 was re-affirmed. Vicksburg remained Unionist. The co-operationist candidates gathered 561 votes, only 173 voters selected the secessionists. The editor of the secessionist *Citizen* cried fraud, but the returns stood and Vicksburg

26. *Vicksburg Weekly Whig,* November 14, 1860.
27. *Vicksburg Daily Whig,* November 30, 1860.

sent Unionist delegates to the convention.[28] Soon after the election Marshall wrote to Joseph Holt, a native of Vicksburg and Postmaster General: "I am a member of the convention . . . and will certainly do all I can to bring about a satisfactory settlement of our difficulties *in the Union. . . .*"[29]

Marshall and Brooke would sit with the minority. Most of the counties nominated secessionists and they had vowed to take the state out of the Union as quickly as they could. Vicksburg was one of a few islands of resistance which dotted the state. The cruel jaws of dilemma clamped closer on her people. J. M. Swords, the editor of the *Citizen,* was now sure of the outcome; he could joke about his city's impossible situation. He wrote that Vicksburg "distinguished herself by voting in favor of co-operation, which is a modest term for submission. As the State is certain to secede in less than two weeks, it is a matter of great curiosity to some, to know what is to become of [Vicksburg]. Will she secede too, or will she hang on to Lincoln's Union?"[30]

Swords could make his joke, but it was a hard question for most of the people in the city. Untimately there was but one answer. When the state seceded it would do so as an entity—everyone would go with it or risk the brand of traitor. That much was plain. The use of force against the state was, as it turned out, more repugnant to the people than was the use of force against the Union. And there was a practical aspect to the situation. The state, as weak as it was, could easily crush

28. *Vicksburg Daily Citizen,* December 21, 1860. The breakdown of the voting was as follows: Marshall received 283 votes in the city and 177 votes in the county; Brooke received 278 votes in the city and 167 votes in the county; McCardle received 158 votes in the city and 4 votes in the county; Johnson received 15 votes in the city and 71 votes in the county. This gave the Unionist (co-operationist) candidates a total of 805 votes to 248 votes for the secessionists. The Unionists lacked only nine votes of matching their total in the November election. The secessionists fell short by 332 votes. This great disparity in the totals might be explained by a feeling of apathy or complacency on the part of the secessionists in Warren County. They knew that they would be beaten in the county election, but were confident that the state would return a secessionist majority to the convention, so they did not bother to vote.

29. Thomas A. Marshall to Joseph Holt, December 29, 1860, Joseph Holt Papers, Library of Congress.

30. *Vicksburg Daily Citizen,* December 22, 1860.

any internal armed opposition to it. If this thought occurred to the Unionists they quickly dismissed it, for they were men who stood for the law and for the peaceful settlement of difficulties within the law. They saw no peaceful settlement at the end of the course the state was now set upon, yet they knew that they would have to be part of the decision when it was made. They were caught. The press of events and numbers had become too great for some of them to stand against.

In the closing weeks of December the Unionist opposition, which up to this point had been a more or less solid front, began to break up as the people tried to accommodate their loyalties with the inflexible situation. They followed two separate and distinct patterns. Succumbing to the intense pressure were "some of the strongest and most prominent men who were in favor of co-operation." They gave up the struggle, acquiesced in secession, and became "among the most rampant Southern Rights men."[31] Whatever their reasons for submission (and they varied with the individual) they were finished as an articulate faction. The other group remained staunch. They would fight secession until the final vote in the convention, and then they planned to go underground to try to wrest political control of the state from the secessionists. Brooke and Marshall were members of this group.

The state convention met in Jackson at the turn of the new year. The city was gay and bright with a holiday spirit of impending revolution, and Marshall and Brooke, with the minority of co-operationists, arrived grim-faced in the revelling capital. They knew that they were set upon an unpopular course, but they were determined to stick it to the end.

One of the first bits of business in the convention showed the handwriting on the wall. A secessionist delegate moved that copies of the firebrand *Daily Mississippian* be furnished the members during the session. Marshall countered with an amendment that the *Vicksburg Whig* should also be given to the delegates. He was voted down.[32]

31. *Ibid.*

32. *Journal of the State Convention and Ordinances and Resolutions* (Jackson, Mississippi, 1861), p. 11.

The main business was soon at hand when L. Q. C. Lamar moved that a committee be appointed to draft an ordinance of secession. The minority proposed to amend this to read, "An Ordinance providing for the final adjustment of all difficulties between free and slave states . . . by securing further Constitutional guarantees within the present Union." They were outvoted.[33] Walker Brooke fought the rearguard action when he submitted an amendment that the Ordinance should not become effective until the people could vote for it in a general election. Most of the river county delegates and a few of the hill county men supported Brooke. They were not enough.[34]

Thomas Woods was the youngest delegate in the convention; he mostly sat, listened, and watched. He knew that outside the capitol's walls the city was ablaze with excitement, but he was impressed by the brooding spirit of gravity and seriousness which hung over the convention itself. The speeches which he listened to were plain and unpurpled with rhetorical flourishes. This was heavy business and Woods did not find much thrill in it. When he later thought about it, he could recall only one "dramatic and thrilling" moment. That was when the Ordinance was put to the final ballot.[35]

In the vaulted north chamber of the capitol Walker Brooke rose to cast his last vote. Then he spoke: "I was elected by a large majority, as what is known as a co-operationist. . . . I have . . . endeavored to carry out the views of my constituents. . . . I have acted in good faith . . . I have failed." His head bowed and his voice faltered. After a moment he continued. A vote now against the Ordinance would be a "vote for this Convention to do nothing" and this would "make ourselves obnoxious to the scorn and ridicule of the world. . . . I therefore feel it my duty, painful as it may be, to . . . assume the responsibility of casting at least one of the votes of Warren County for the passage of the Ordinance."[36]

33. *Ibid.,* p. 9.

34. *Ibid.,* p. 10.

35. Thomas H. Woods, "Sketch of the Mississippi Secession Convention of 1861—Its Membership and Work," *Publications of the Mississippi Historical Society,* VI (1902), 95.

36. *Proceedings of the Mississippi State Convention Held January 7th to 26th, A.D. 1861. Including the Ordinances, as finally Adopted, Important Speeches, and a List of Members* (Jackson, Mississippi, 1861), p. 14. Thomas

Thomas Woods sat on the edge of his chair in rapt attention; he thought this was high drama. Vicksburg Unionism was bowing before the weight of numbers and a sense of honor. Neophyte and seasoned secessionists eased back in relief, then they broke into the only applause of the session.[37]

The business was done. Cannon and fireworks exploded throughout the city, bells pealed out over the crowds. Mississippi was out of the Union.

There were no cannon or fireworks in Vicksburg. The city sat unrejoicing on its hills while the river lapped quietly at the bluffs. The swift march of events and the crushing weight of numbers had committed the city to secession, but though they were committed the people did not have to celebrate their defeat.

Now they had to do two things: they had to devise a rationale which would enable them to work with the rest of the state in the new adventure and they had to look to the future and lay plans for righting what they believed to be a dread political mistake. But at the moment they were bereft of the power of great expression. The swift action of the convention and Walker Brooke's collapse left them dizzied. Even articulate Marmaduke Shannon was at a loss for words. The best he could manage when the news was announced was a laconic "We trust that the prosperity of the new Republic may even exceed the expectations of the most sanguine secessionist."[38]

The key to the whole question now lay in the people's concept of their dual loyalties to the state and to the Federal Union. Though they professed love and loyalty for the Union, they lived in a time when the states were not considered mere appendages of the central government, but, conversely, were regarded as the creators of the central government. The government at Washington was far away and it did not greatly manifest its power. The state was close at hand, readily identifiable, and bound to the people in countless homey and everyday ways. When the last wrench occurred, when the ultimate choice was de-

---

Marshall remained faithful to his instructions. He was one of the fifteen delegates who voted against the Ordinance.

37. Woods, "Sketch of the Mississippi Secession Convention," *Publications of the Mississippi Historical Society,* VI, 95.

38. *Vicksburg Weekly Whig,* January 16, 1861.

Surrender of Vicksburg. View of the city from the ri

manded, the state, and not the Union, held the loyalty of the people.

As spokesman for the conservatives, Marmaduke Shannon took over a week to work these thoughts and feelings into print. Finally he thought he had captured the mind of the city. He began with a rhetorical question: "What of the law abiding, conservative, patriotic men who fought so gallantly in the late election against acknowledged odds under the banner inscribed with the glorious motto, *'the Constitution, the Union and the enforcement of the laws?'* " Then he supplied the answer:

> We do not think there can be any doubt as to the duty of patriots at this crisis—*it is to follow the destiny of the State and abide its fate, be it for weal or be it for woe.* We are . . . Mississipian[s]. Our State has spoken. It has taken its stand . . . . It has declared its

owing part of the river batteries. (From *Harper's Weekly*)

independence . . . . We did not approve it. But it is not for any citizen of the State, to set . . . himself against the ACT of the State . . . . It is enough for us to know that Mississippi, *our* State, *our* government has taken its position. We, too, take our position by its side. We stand ready to defend her rights and to share her fate.[39]

This summed up and settled the question of loyalties. But here the conservatives made an important distinction. They reserved their loyalty for the state, not for a particular faction—the secessionists. The will of the state was secession; they would abide by that will. But if the will of the state could be changed they would then accept the new expression. This theory opened up a new avenue through which they could at once

39. *Ibid.,* January 23, 1861.

remain loyal to the state and reassert their allegiance to the Federal Union.

Outwardly the conservatives closed ranks with the secessionists, but they did so merely to give an external appearance of state unity and to keep away the taint of disloyalty. Horace Fulkerson, who lived in Vicksburg, knew that Brooke and some of the other conservatives had voted for the Ordinance in order that they might keep favor in public eyes. They wanted to have an opportunity to wage a state-wide campaign in the coming fall elections to repeal the Ordinance of Secession and get the state back into the Union.[40]

This involuted logic did not satisfy a small number of men in Vicksburg. Their loyalties were straightforward and could not be led along such a devious route of accommodation. They were for the Union and that was all there was to it. Alexander Arthur, a banker, wrote Joseph Holt: "We have just learned from Jackson that our Convention has just passed the Secession Ordnance . . . . [Secession cannot] be justified upon any plea of necessity of law, or of morals . . . . *Peaceable* secession is nothing more . . . than Revolution." These were not empty words; he would remain true to them through the war.[41]

It made no difference if a man was an overt Unionist or an accommodationist who waited for the autumn elections. Fall would be too late. When autumn came Bull Run had become history and the state was firmly set in the Confederacy; the fire-eaters who had boasted that they would drink every drop of blood shed in battle had long since fallen silent; and up at Cairo, Illinois, a stubby man who had failed in the army and in business, and who some said was too fond of the bottle, made his first move down the Mississippi River. The tragedy of the situation was that the people who did not want war, and who waited for fall, lived on the Mississippi.

40. Horace S. Fulkerson, *A Civilian's Recollection of the War Between the States,* ed. Percy L. Rainwater (Baton Rouge, Louisiana, 1939), pp. 5-9.

41. Alexander H. Arthur to Joseph Holt, January 10, 1861, Joseph Holt Papers.

CHAPTER III

"EVERY AVAILABLE MEANS"

THE *Silver Wave* was a riverboat, and the men of Vicksburg who watched the river knew her familiar outline. She had been in and out of the city many times, bearing passengers and freight loaded at Cincinnati and New Orleans and everywhere in between. The familiar *Silver Wave* was the thing that shattered Unionism in Vicksburg. The subtle reasoning in Marmaduke Shannon's theories and the Union leaders' quiet plotting were lost on the people after they heard her name.

The people had stolidly accepted the secession of their state. They had done their best to forestall secession, but when it became an accomplished fact they abided by the decision. They were passive in their acceptance, and they knew that men were talking of peaceful secession and were working for compromise. Then overnight the mood of the city changed from stolidness to fighting fervor—a martial spirit swept the people.

Mutterings of force and reprisal had begun to drift down the river. Shipments of goods were held up in Cincinnati, and it was rumored that Northern Unionists planned to send steamers loaded with volunteers to attack seceded towns along the river. The *Silver Wave* was supposed to be one of the boats.

On the morning of January 12, the city's alarm bells rang. The *Silver Wave* was reported to be on her way to Vicksburg. The "Vicksburg Battalion" rushed out to Fort Hill, a high bluff north of the city, and hauled up four artillery pieces to halt the steamer. The afternoon train brought volunteers from the little hamlets of Bovina and Edwards Station. Under the beat of a cold winter rain they hurried out to Fort Hill and helped emplace the cannon. For three days they waited by their dripping guns, watching the river. On the third day the battalion was dismissed, and its members straggled back into the city soaked and bedraggled. The *Silver Wave* had not come (and when she did arrive she bore her usual cargo of passengers and freight), but Vicksburg had gotten its first taste of war.[1]

Across the divided nation men still talked of peaceful secession and compromise. In Vicksburg the people talked of war. The state convention and legislature were asked to move from Jackson to Vicksburg because there were better accommodations in Vicksburg and because the city was "now the seat of war."[2]

On January 6, the people unresponsively heard the news that they were out of the Union. On the fifteenth they proudly proclaimed that they were at the center of armed conflict, and they had cannon frowning over the river to lend substance to their statement. What could explain the transilience of minds that within a week's time leaped from passiveness to pugnacity?

The simple answer was the *Silver Wave*. But the boat was merely a symbol; the real reasons lay deeper and were more complex. Marmaduke Shannon had put his finger on it when he said "we are Mississippians." The people of Vicksburg were Mississippians first and citizens of the United States second. In innumerable ways they were bound to a culture which they identified as Mississippian or Southern and not American. The more abstract concept of political allegiance to a Federal Union could not possibly hope to compete for loyalty against something as close and as compelling as a pattern of life created by fathers and grandfathers and passed down from father to son. Even as they fought against secession the Unionists acknowledged this. They had sought to accommodate their way of life to the radical ideals of the Republicans so that the Union might be preserved. They had not dreamed of sacrificing the former to retain the latter.

Compromise and peaceful solutions were one thing, but a naked threat to the culture for which their state stood was an

1. *Vicksburg Daily Citizen,* January 14, 15, 1861. The January 31 edition of the *Citizen* carried this about the *Silver Wave:* "Even the *Silver Wave* herself, after unloading her guns in Pittsburg, and taking other freight aboard was kindly received at our landing the other day, and no manifestations were made to interrupt her in her peaceful commercial voyage."

2. *Ibid.,* January 14, 1861.

entirely different matter. The *Silver Wave* was that naked threat. She was the carrier (so they thought) of armed men bent on attack and destruction. The *Silver Wave* was the catalyst that hurried a people into precipitate but determined action. She did not threaten slavery or States' Rights or any of the other shibboleths of the secessionists per se. She threatened homes, business, and life itself; and the threat was not rhetorical or abstract; it was gun-metaled and grim. Vicksburg's response to her threat was equally grim.

In this response the city resembled the upper South more than the state to which it belonged. Three months later Virginia, Tennessee, and North Carolina would react in the same manner to Lincoln's call for troops. In Vicksburg, as in the upper South, the majority of the people hung back from violence until they were faced with overt coercion. The fear of force was the thing which drove the conservatives into the secessionists' arms.

The city began to prepare for war. On January 16, the city council met to consider the first large expenditure for war. A citizen had offered to give five thousand dollars for the purchase of munitions if the city would build an arsenal to house and protect the supplies. The council voted to match this sum provided the county would do likewise, yet they did not let their enthusiasm become boundless, and a note of caution crept into their deliberations. They wanted the arsenal, but they did not want it inside the city. It was decided to build it "outside the city limits, and within a mile thereof." This action was reported to the state convention.[3] A week later Thomas Marshall, who was one of the fifteen who had voted against secession, offered a resolution in the convention that the city's proposal should be favorably reported to the state military board, which was supposed to co-ordinate the defensive preparations being made in the state. The convention refused to do this, and the rejection left the council perplexed and dismayed.[4]

Though they were rebuffed by the state, the council went ahead with its local preparations. They could not wait for the cumbersome, ill-prepared state machinery to move. The men in

3. Council Minute Book, p. 57. 4. *Ibid.*, p. 62.

Jackson could dally and play politics, but Vicksburg sat on the river and lay exposed to attack.

Six volunteer companies were raised in the city. The Volunteer Southrons, the Sharpshooters, the Warren County Guards, the Warren Dragoons, the Hill City Cadets, and an artillery company started to fill their ranks with men who responded to the threat of force by creating force of their own. There was talk of forming a company of Zouaves. The dash and glitter of their uniforms appealed to some of the men, but the idea was soon dropped. The name Zouave and the brightly colored jackets, blousing trousers, and gaiters were foreign. The people were raising units for the defense of their homes; they wanted nothing foreign in them (this attitude would soon become drastically modified).[5]

All of this was local business, there was no doubt of that. Later, when the state finally got some semblance of organization patched together, the city and the state would work together, but in the earliest stages of conflict the city moved alone.

These early manifestations of war fervor cannot be attributed solely to the pressure of the secessionist minority or to the hot-bloodedness of the young men, though the situation lent itself to these things. The action of the city council must be taken as an expression of the will of the majority of the people, for the council held office at the majority's pleasure. The council eagerly seized the opportunity to build the arsenal and in the same meeting they voted to find "suitable Rooms" for the volunteers to use, and requested the board of police to defray one-half of the cost.[6] As they did these things the council reflected the changing attitude of the city.

H. C. Clark, printer and book dealer, also caught the shifting of the mind, and in it he saw an opportunity to increase his profits. With his novels, almanacs, newspapers, and journals, he now carried a stock of Gilham's *Military Manual,* Hardee's *Cavalry Tactics,* and McComb's *Tactics.*[7]

Though talk and rumor of war lay over the city, the patterns of life were not greatly altered. The men in the volunteer com-

5. *Ibid.* 6. *Ibid.,* p. 57.
7. *Vicksburg Daily Citizen,* February 11, 1861.

panies took a few hours out of the week to drill, but the rest of the time they stayed at their businesses and homes. Paxton's foundry continued to cast plowshares, the Sisters of Mercy to teach, Northern steamers to tie up at the wharves, and the city council devoted as much time to balancing accounts and chastising property owners for not keeping gutters and sidewalks in proper repair as it did in making defensive preparations.[8] The first alarm had passed and the people settled back into familiar routines of living. It took Jefferson Davis to remind them of the new order of things. He was now president-elect of the Confederate Provisional Government, and he planned to pass through Vicksburg on his way to his inauguration at Montgomery, the temporary capital.

On the morning of February 11, the city council held a special meeting to prepare for Davis' arrival in the city. Three months before they had repudiated Davis and all that he stood for. Now they bubbled over with welcoming praise: "Resolved: That the Mayor and City Council of the City extend to that distinguished Soldier Statesman and Patriot the Hospitality of this City, and that they will unite with the Military and Citizens in greeting him with such cordial welcome on his arrival here as his emenent position and services demand."[9]

The council did not have much time to prepare, for Davis arrived early that afternoon. He stepped off the *Natchez* before the crowd that lined the wharves. The volunteer companies were out in full dress, and their cannon and musket shots roared over the cheers of the people. Davis spoke briefly, then boarded the eastbound train for Montgomery. He was dressed in homespun, which some people thought was in "good taste" and an example worthy of being imitated.[10] Expenditures for his reception included gunpowder and music. It was an omen that twice as much was paid for powder as was spent for music.[11]

Davis went on his way and the city followed his actions and the deliberations of the Provisional Government in the newspapers. A week after the inauguration the *Whig* was still carrying details of the Montgomery ceremony, but Marmaduke

8. Council Minute Book, p. 66. 9. *Ibid.*, p. 68.
10. *Vicksburg Daily Citizen*, February 12, 1861.
11. Council Minute Book, p. 82.

Shannon had already turned his attention back to his own city. It was probably with a little glee that he juxtaposed the story of Davis' inaugural with a glimpse into a Vicksburg bedroom. One column of his paper carried the story of Davis' triumph; in the next column this was printed:

> A few nights since, a resident of this city, moved by the green-eyed monster, determined to detect an imaginary rival in the affections of his wife. It appears that the room occupied by himself and wife was in the rear of the house, the front room, which also opened into his, being occupied by another family. On the evening in question, locking his own door, and triumphantly putting the key in his pocket, he waits till the "sma' wee hours," and proceeds to hunt up the police. Finding them, he states his suspicions, and stations them in front of the house, while he arranges that he shall rush through the front room and detect his unfaithful spouse before her lover can have time to escape. No sooner said than done, but as he dashes through the front room, the male occupant taking him for a robber, springs out of bed, knocks him down and after beating him severely, hands him over to the police already present, with instructions to take him to jail. In a few moments, however, he explains his position, and proceeds to his own rooms, where he finds his wife quietly reposing alone, it having never occurred to the jealous husband that by locking the door to prevent his rival from escaping, he also prevented his entrance.[12]

The prosaic mixed with the prominent; one as newsworthy as the other, and an indication of the mind's inability to sustain itself at a high pitch of intensity. The course of history was being shaped in Montgomery. In Vicksburg a jealous husband's shabby foolishness caught the people's eye. Shannon made a joke of it. Perhaps he felt the need of comic relief from the ominous march of events. Or perhaps he understood his readers, and knew they relished the earthy as well as the momentous.

A war spirit can be subtle as well as explosive and can lie seemingly dormant under a calm exterior until something triggers its violent expression. It manifests itself in countless ways. The *Silver Wave* brought out grimness; Davis' reception brought out gaiety. The next explosion mixed violence with frivolity and carried puritanical overtones.

12. *Vicksburg Weekly Whig,* February 27, 1861.

It all started when the girls from Mollie Bunch's gave a ball. A prostitutes' ball was not uncommon; it had been done before, and if the city authorities did not sanction it, at least they ignored it. But this time the girls went too far, for they did not confine themselves to South Street; they sent invitations to the ministers and to "the most respectable families" in the city.

On the evening of the ball, fire alarms rang. The alarm was false; and instead of the firemen, outraged citizens trundled the engines down to South Street. They drenched Mollie's house and destroyed the furniture, then went on to the corner of Mulberry and Crawford streets where the ball was in progress. They turned the hoses on the dancers, washed the food from the banquet tables, and were still not satisfied. On they went to Pat Gorman's tavern. Gorman shot one of the men, but his bar was demolished and his liquor and lager flowed with the water in the gutter.

The sentiment of "the most respectable families" was, "As much as we deprecate mobs . . . we have no words of censure for the movement on Thursday night." In a masterpiece of understatement Marmaduke Shannon called the mob action "A quiet but determined way of correcting an evil."[13]

Mollie Bunch and Pat Gorman petitioned the city council for "the payment of monies . . . for losses of property and valuables . . . destroyed and stolen from them by a mob." The council rejected the petition and revoked Gorman's liquor license. They did nothing to Mollie.[14]

Arrests and jailings increased during the spring. Thirty-five people were in the workhouse in February. The number increased to forty-seven in March, jumped to seventy-three in April, and seventy-four in May.[15] It seemed as though the city was purging itself in anticipation of war. The purity of romantic heroes and heroines was idealized in the city, and a strong strain of the Covenanter lay in its heritage. War would be a sacred cause and God would be on the side of the pure and the righteous. Evil must be extirpated. And perhaps a puritanical war-

13. *Vicksburg Daily Citizen,* February 22, 1861; *Vicksburg Weekly Whig,* February 23, 1861.
14. Council Minute Book, pp. 72, 81-82.
15. *Ibid.,* pp. 72, 85, 93, 99.

catharsis, as well as honest outrage, boiled up on the night of Mollie Bunch's ball.

A steamboat, the President of the Confederacy, and a bordello's madam caused spectacular outbursts by the people, but they did not measure the true extent of the drift of the minds of the people. The minds moved slowly, and attitudes were still crystallizing. J. M. Swords felt this and it prompted him, almost two months after the *Silver Wave* scare, to write: "The Vicksburg *Citizen* is the ONLY TRUE Southern paper published in this city or county."[16]

A week later he lamented the fact that not until March 7 did a volunteer company recruit enough members to make the unit eligible for mustering into state service. The other companies were still trying to enlist men, and Swords urged "Merchants and Manufacturers" to support the recruiting and to help equip the units.[17] He thought that the men of influence in the city had not thrown themselves behind the preparedness movement. He must have spurred the recruiting, for on March 12 the Sharpshooters reached their quota, and on the following Saturday they and the Artillery Company were mustered into service.[18]

Though they were the first to be mustered into state service, the Sharpshooters and the Artillery Company stayed camped by the city. The first unit to leave to seek adventure and to sustain honor was the Hill City Cadets. They awoke in early morning blackness on March 27, fumbled about for their equipment, and got themselves aligned in ranks. The sun was barely up, but the town was wide awake. The Cadets marched to the railroad depot, escorted by the other companies and followed by cheering civilians. The Cadets broke ranks at the station, gathered in hampers of food, extra clothing, and embraced families and friends. They climbed abroad the cars, and at six o'clock sharp the train pulled out of the station. As the last cheers died away J. M. Swords looked about him. He saw tears, but thought the families were brave. The train was gone now, and the people moved slowly back to their homes and breakfasts. The Cadets

16. *Vicksburg Daily Citizen,* March 6, 1861.
17. *Ibid.,* March 13, 1861. 18. *Ibid.,* March 18, 1861.

were on their way to Pensacola to join in the game of cat and mouse being played at Fort Pickens.[19] For a while the city would turn out to send their soldiers on their way, but finally the rumbling, loaded trains would become so familiar that they scarcely caused comment.

A few days after the Cadets left, Mayor Crump took stock of the situation. He had seen the armed troops leave the city and before that had heard of the guns which had reached out for the *Star of the West,* but he was still not disturbed. In fact, the Mayor was quite optimistic. On April 1, he told the people: "The last few months have developed a mighty political revolution which as yet bloodless, promises to so continue and to result in placing the Confederate States among the Independent nations of the earth with every prestige of peace, prosperity and happiness."[20]

He thought he had some basis for this optimism since his financial committee had reported that there were fewer delinquent debtors and fewer worthless banknotes in the city than ever before. This was considered to be especially reassuring because "financial matters have been in a disturbed condition."[21] Trade was brisk, Northern steamboats still tied up at the city's wharves, luxury items were plentiful, and one family thought nothing of running up a bill of $123.04 for yard goods, mostly silk.[22]

The ardent secessionists were not so sanguine as the Mayor. They had got secession, but they wanted more. They wanted a complete hold on the minds of the people so they could never be returned to thoughts of union with the North. The fire-eaters were not reassured as they saw that only three volunteer companies had been brought up to full strength, and they suspected that the men of substance were still dragging their feet in the preparations for war. They needed to whip up a chauvinistic, hyper-Southernism in Vicksburg. On the first of April their plans had matured to the extent that they could be made public.

19. *Ibid.,* March 27, 1861.
20. Council Minute Book, p. 84.
21. *Ibid.,* p. 75.
22. Receipted bill dated April 14, 1861, Phillip Crutcher Collection, Miss. Arch.

The rabidly partisan *Sun* was resuscitated.[23] As before it "espouse[d] the true Southern cause." At the same time the *Sun* resumed publication a prospectus for another paper appeared in the city. This newcomer would be named the "Confederate States" and the publisher promised that his paper would be "just the kind of a paper the city of Vicksburg and the Southern Confederacy, and all the rest of Mankind are in need of."[24] Combined with the *Citizen,* the fire-eaters would have three papers to howl down the *Whig,* which was still, despite Shannon's protestations to the contrary, regarded with a jaundiced eye.

This move was backed up by an inundation of Confederate propaganda devices. Several shops in the city now stocked "Jefferson Davis" letter paper, envelopes, visiting cards, framed photographs, note paper, rosettes, and badges. Alexander Stephens, Vice-President of the Confederacy, either because he was a Whig or because he was of second-magnitude importance, was allowed letter and note paper.[25]

The fire-eaters could have spared themselves the trouble. In twelve days the Charleston batteries would force the issue far beyond the point which newspapers and insignated note paper could carry it. A little more than a week of peace remained for the city. Inside that time, within a four day span, the pendulum of human passion would swing in full arc.

On the evening of April 8, two of the city's girls became novitiates in the Sisters of Mercy. This was the first time the ceremony had been performed in Vicksburg, and Protestants as well as Catholics made up an "immense audience" at St. Paul's. They watched as the Bishop of Natchez, assisted by three of the Vicksburg priests and eight little girls dressed as angels, con-

23. The *Sun* failed the previous year when its columns became too violent even for Vicksburg.

24. *Vicksburg Daily Citizen,* April 1, 1861. There is no record which indicates that the "Confederate States" got beyond the prospectus stage. The *Sun* resumed its fitful life, then died later in the year.

25. *Ibid.,* April 6, 1861. There is little indication that Confederate stationery was popular in Vicksburg. Practically every note and letter handled by the author was written on plain bond paper or on shoddy notebook paper. Most of the documents written before late 1862 were written on good, heavy paper. After that time, as the blockade began to take effect, the paper was of a poorer quality. Very few documents carrying a Confederate device were seen by the author.

ducted the ceremony. Protestant and Catholic alike "were deeply impressed with the solemnity and appropriateness" of the service. They filed out of the church and left Sisters Agnes and Philomena to ponder their vows of mercy, charity, and usefulness, which, they would soon discover, held in war as well as peace.[26]

Very early in the morning on April 12, the Charleston batteries opened fire on Fort Sumter. On the same morning a cannon at the railroad depot in Vicksburg blew off James Gilvan's arm. The cannon were firing salutes as the Artillery Company climbed aboard the outbound train, and the premature explosion of a piece gave the civilians and the soldiers a minute glimpse of the battlefield. The crowds were at the depot again, but this time instead of cheers J. M. Swords heard "shrieks of distress" as final goodbyes were said.[27] These troops were going to war and the people who stood beside the cars knew it.

There was little rejoicing or celebration when the news of the firing upon Sumter reached the city.[28] The inevitable had occurred, but attitudes shifted by secession and the *Silver Wave* still did not coalesce into monolithic solidity. The young men seemed ready for war, but the men of property and influence remained reluctant. On the day war broke out J. M. Swords was prompted to say, "We would suggest that our business men should encourage [the young men] to go with their corps when ordered," and not remind them of inconveniences or threaten to fill their jobs with other men.[29]

There were other indications of hesitancy. The Artillery Company left their cannon in the city when they moved out. The guns sat there, unused, unmanned. At first there was some talk of forming a new company, but then interest faded. A week after the artillerymen had gone, a week after the outbreak of war, the *Citizen* stopped appealing to the "ardor" of the citizens to recruit a new company. The paper took a new approach, probably one that was closer to the desires of the men who might

26. *Ibid.*, April 9, 1861. 27. *Ibid.*, April 12, 1861.
28. The *Citizen* reported no celebrations at the outbreak of war.
29. *Vicksburg Daily Citizen*, April 12, 1861.

make up the unit. It was now suggested that the company be raised "for home service alone, in case of necessity."[30]

The city council took an even more practical view of the matter. They appropriated five thousand dollars for "placing the Guns in battery, which are now lying in the City in a useless state, and of purchasing the ammunition required for their use in case of an emergency and also of forming and training a company of artillerists."[31]

In other ways the council tried to put the city on a war footing. They passed a resolution stating that "every available means of defense should immediately be put in a condition to be as effective as possible [because] Vicksburg in a military point of view occupies an important position upon the Mississippi River whose upper banks are now occupied by declared enemies." That took care of the rhetoric. The council then appropriated the five thousand dollars, appointed a committee to discuss defensive preparations with the governor, appropriated a subsidy of two hundred dollars for each military company going into service, and thankfully accepted the gift of 4,700 rounds of ammunition for the city defenses.[32]

The sound of gunfire was not carried by the telegraph or in the newspaper dispatches. The men charged with the safety of Vicksburg could see that their city sat at a strategic spot, but they talked in terms of "emergency" and "in case of necessity." They saw only the faintest glimmerings of the implications of the Sumter bombardment, and in their city there was the curious but natural blending of the ways of war and peace.

30. *Ibid.,* April 18, 1861.
31. Council Minute Book, p. 91.
32. *Ibid.*

Chapter IV

"WAR IS NEAR US INDEED"

MR. MacMeehan, the proprietor of the Washington Hotel, stood in the center of his dining room. Perspiration stood out on his forehead, and he alternately wiped his wet face and swatted at flies. A look of satisfaction crossed his face as he watched the packed dining tables. He took another swipe at a fly, then bawled out in a loud voice, "Now, then, here is a splendid goose! Ladies and gentlemen, don't neglect the goose and apple-sauce!" His eye caught another loaded platter, "Here's a piece of beef that I can recommend! Upon my honor you will never regret taking a slice of the beef." Then on to another dish, "Oyster-pie! Oyster-pie! Never was better oyster-pie seen in Vicksburg." He mopped his brow and called out again, "Ladies and gentlemen, just look at that turkey! Who's for turkey?"

He paused for breath and the clatter of voices and silverware filled the room. Officers dressed in braided grey uniforms and planters wearing summer linen worked at their filled plates. At other tables soldiers in privates' uniforms sat and talked with finely dressed women. At one end of the room a long table was laden with the joints and dishes that MacMeehan begged his guests to taste. Negro waiters, men and women, stood by the loaded table carving the roasts and sending the filled dishes to the diners. The steamings from the roasts, oysters, and turkeys mixed in the June heat and lay redolently over the noon-day diners.[1]

William Russell sat at one of the crowded tables. He had just come to America from England and he felt at home in the crowded dining room. MacMeehan's loud pleas reminded him

1. Russell, *Diary*, p. 295.

of London tavern owners as they called out invitations to passers-by on the streets. But one thing was decidedly not English. As Russell watched the uniformed men and listened to the conversations he caught an undertone of a people at war. When he put down the day's events in his diary he also noted: "war fever is rife in Vicksburg."[2]

Russell wrote this two months after the editor of the *Citizen* had begged the men of property in the city to support enlistments in the army. The minds of the people had shifted again.

The guns at Fort Sumter had not forged a common spirit at Vicksburg. No instant sense of outrage coalesced the will of the people into a single purpose. The news of Sumter had left the city passive and still divided, just as the news of secession had done.

The outrage came three days later when Lincoln issued a proclamation calling for troops to suppress "combinations . . . too powerful to be suppressed by the ordinary course of judicial proceedings." Here again was naked force, though magnified a thousand fold, and the people reacted as they had done when the *Silver Wave* had threatened them.

For four months the people had lived in a never-never land, alternating an occasional show of belligerency with the hope that Horace Greeley's policy of "let the South go in peace" (or some other peaceful solution) would come to pass. Lincoln's call for troops on April 15 crushed this naïve hope. And as it crushed it also created. A new sense of common purpose sealed over countless schisms and antagonisms. The Artillery Company, which languished a few days before, was filled up. New volunteer units were raised. Troops from Louisiana and western Mississippi started pouring through the city.

Marmaduke Shannon took the measure of the people's outrage—the same Shannon who four months previously had said that secession was rebellion and that the Union would stand against the gates of hell. Nine days after Lincoln's call for troops he printed: "THE SPIRIT OF OUR PEOPLE . . . . The history of nations does not present an example of unanimity among any people comparable to the extraordinary spectacle

2. *Ibid.*, pp. 295-96.

now presented in the Confederate States. We can speak confidently of Mississippi. In the fervor of patriotic feeling, all devisions about mere details have been completely merged . . . . This spirit pervades all sects—all classes—all ages."[3]

"Spirit" and "classes" and "ages" are abstract terms, but they now took on form and substance. On April 12, J. M. Swords chided the businessmen of the city for their lack of enthusiasm in war preparations. Twelve days later he had nothing but praise for them as seventy-one of the city's "oldest and most prominent" men—merchants, physicians, lawyers, and judges—formed themselves into a company named the Old Guard.[4] As a fighting unit they were not worth much, but as a symbol they were worth several regiments. They had been the hard core of conservatism and Unionism; now they were banded together and armed against the very things they once espoused.

The Old Guard came from one end of the Vicksburg class structure. Another new military unit came from the opposite end (all of which lends truth to Shannon's rhetorical generalizations). In January plans to form a Zouave company had been dropped because the term smacked of something foreign and less than reliable. In April this feeling went by the boards. If there had ever been doubt as to the loyalty of the city's foreign-born it was now laid to rest. The foreigners were actively recruited and some of them were officers in the volunteer units. A language barrier kept others out of the units—they did not know enough English to comprehend the simplest military commands. This problem was attacked by the tentative organization of the "Foreign Legion," which was designed to gather up all of those men who because of language difficulties were excluded from the other units. The most significant thing about the Foreign Legion was that the non-English speaking men proposed it themselves. They did not want to be left out of the fight.[5]

3. *Vicksburg Weekly Whig,* April 24, 1861.

4. *Vicksburg Daily Citizen,* April 24, 1861.

5. *Ibid.,* April 29, 1861. There is no indication that the unit was formed. It surely would not have solved the problem of language barriers because its members would still have been polyglot.

When William Russell got to Vicksburg in early June he found no indications of class distinctions in the war spirit. He made this entry in his diary: "Irish and German laborers, to the extent of several hundreds, have gone off to war."[6] One group of Irishmen formed a unit named the Jeff Davis Guards.[7] The majority of the foreign-born had identified themselves so closely with Vicksburg's life and culture that they were as eager to have it preserved as were the native Mississippians.

William Newman and Henry Lee also identified themselves and their interests with those of the city and the Confederacy. They were unable to join a military unit, yet they did manage to indicate their feelings. When the first Confederate war loan was offered in Vicksburg, Newman and Lee made it a point to be among the earliest subscribers. They each bought $250 worth of bonds. Other people in the city subscribed more, but there was a greater difference. William Newman and Henry Lee were free Negroes.[8]

All of these actions took place within the space of two weeks —the last two weeks of April. Yet they were merely reactions to a single event. The pivotal point of the tangled ganglia of hopes and fears, voiced and unvoiced, was April 15, when Lincoln called for troops. From that moment on everything the people did was a reaction to external forces. Only one opportunity to display initiative was left to them, and when it did come the people would confirm rather than change everything that had passed before.

This is not to say that war fever was a blaze which consumed every doubt, every qualification, and every contrary motivation. Marmaduke Shannon might extol the "example of unanimity," but the city still held unbending Unionists, cowards, and men who put personal gain before honor and duty. In the first fit of war these men could be overlooked, though in the long run they would

6. Russell, *Diary,* p. 296.

7. *Brokenburn: The Journal of Kate Stone, 1861-1868,* ed. John Q. Anderson (Baton Rouge, Louisiana, 1955), p. 16.

8. *Vicksburg Daily Citizen,* April 24, 1861. It is also interesting to note that the amount they subscribed—$250—was no small sum at that time. Evidently the free Negro in Vicksburg had the opportunity, perhaps greater than some of the whites, to accumulate wealth.

crop up from time to time and rip at Shannon's bright promise of unanimity.

Nevertheless, at the end of April, Vicksburg was war-minded. J. M. Swords, as well as Shannon, believed "the spirit of patriotism now so prevalent in our community" permeated practically every house in the city.[9] As the people talked of war they thought of only one result—victory. "There is but one opinion upon this subject . . . . We can and will whip the Black Republican . . . hordes . . . if they ever attempt to subjugate the South." This was Swords's statement, but it fairly well was the opinion of the city. There could be no other outcome. They were the outraged, they were on the defensive, they fought not to impose their will on someone else but for "those birth rights bequeathed to us by our fathers . . . and . . . inherited from the God of Jacob and our God."[10] Theirs was the pure cause, theirs was the just cause, theirs was the God-sanctioned cause, theirs was the inevitable victory.

War with its justifications, its course, and its outcome was minutely spelled out by the propagandists; but they did not stop to mention or to count the cost. Two men named Catching and Porter did, and they thought they saw some honest profit in it. They owned a dry goods store and, on May 1, they announced with pride that "our stock of Mourning Goods was never so complete." Offered for sale were: black organdie, black silk grenadine, black mosambique, black silk mitts, black kid gloves, and black lace veils.[11]

Catching and Porter were Cassandras. They would have done better if they had stocked their shelves with Confederate grey and material for women's party dresses. In the late spring nights the city was bright with lights, and the sound of familiar songs and recently composed music lay over the hills. On May 29, Dr. Morris Emanuel, druggist and president of the Southern Railroad, gave a dinner for over two hundred people. The 105 officers and men of the Volunteer Southrons were the honor guests, for they were leaving for camp the next day. Music and laughter lasted late into the night and grandmothers as well as

9. *Ibid.*, April 29, 1861. 10. *Ibid.*, May 1, 1861.
11. *Vicksburg Weekly Whig*, May 1, 1861.

young belles danced with the troops. The following morning over two thousand people were at the railroad depot to bid the Southrons farewell. The troops were doubly honored; not only were they going to war, they were also the first persons to make the trip from Vicksburg to Meridian without changing cars. The troops loaded aboard the cars and as the train pulled out of the station both the soldiers and the civilians were singing the "Marseillaise." They also knew other songs of revolution. The night before they had danced to "Adieu to the Star-Spangled Banner Forever," "The Banner of the South," "Our First President's Quickstep," and the "Grand Secession March of the Eight Stars."[12]

The railroad depot was used for several purposes. Soldiers and supplies were gathered there before starting their movement to the east; less war-like activities went on there as well. One June afternoon Mayor Crump and some other men took William Russell to the depot to discuss politics and current events. Russell thought a railway station was an odd place to hold such a meeting and he was pleasantly surprised when he saw the arrangements which had been made for the occasion.

One of the rooms was set up with large china bowls filled with blocks of ice. Decanters of wines and liquors flanked the ice bowls, and boxes of cigars were placed around the room to aid the discussions. The men talked until late in the afternoon, mainly about Chief Justice Taney's protest against Lincoln's suspension of habeas corpus. The clink of ice against glass and the blue haze of good cigar smoke reminded one very little of a railroad station.[13] The memories of goodbye wailings and of troops singing the "Marseillaise" faded with the afternoon.

The reminders of conflict were countless and not confined to troop movements and lavish parties of farewell. The post office stopped delivering letters bearing United States stamps unless Confederate postage was also paid. Kate Stone, who lived across the river at thousand-acre "Brokenburn," read

12. Elizabeth Eggleston, unaddressed, undated letter, Roach-Eggleston Papers, Southern Historical Collection, University of North Carolina; *Vicksburg Daily Citizen,* May 30, 1861. The "Eight Stars" in the last title refer to the eight seceded states as of April 18, 1861.

13. Russell, *Diary,* p. 296.

Harper's Weekly and *Monthly,* the *New York Tribune,* and even the *Journal of Commerce.* Northern journalism, especially Greeley's *Tribune,* made her angry, but she read the papers and magazines anyway and plaintively asked, "What shall we do when our mails are stopped and we are no longer in touch with the world?"[14] *The Southern Field and Fireside* was supposed to be the answer to Kate's query. If Kate saw a copy of the magazine she would have thought it a poor substitute for *Harper's,* but it found its way into more and more Vicksburg homes where some people bought it simply as a matter of patriotic duty.[15]

The Warren Artillery, now up to strength after a languishing beginning, also got involved in a matter of patriotic duty—or perhaps honor, if the two may be separated. A rumor was circulated in the city that the Artillery was simply a home guard unit, that it would serve at Fort Hill and no other place. The artillerymen took this to be a slur on their patriotism and they printed a resolution stating that there was no truth to the rumor and that they sought "active service at the seat of war."[16]

The martial spirit also caught the women and they were not content to cheer the troops as they left for war (and then weep after they had gone) or prepare their men for the field by lining heavy blankets and sewing pockets in the blankets to hold soap, combs, brushes, and other sundries. This was not enough.

This war was a struggle to preserve a particular culture, a culture in which woman was idealized to the extent that she had become a pedestaled goddess. If the war was lost and the culture destroyed, woman would no longer occupy her idealized place in society. Not only could war destroy her men and her home, but it could also destroy her as woman—at least as the woman that had been created by a slave society liberally laced with the romanticism of Scott and others.[17] Perhaps the women were intuitive enough to recognize this threat; at any rate they plunged into war work.

14. Stone, *Brokenburn,* p. 14; *Vicksburg Daily Citizen,* May 30, 1861.
15. *Vicksburg Daily Citizen,* May 30, 1861.
16. *Ibid.,* May 16, 1861.
17. With respect to the continued veneration of the Southern woman see such works as Lucian L. Knight, *Stone Mountain* (Atlanta, 1923), pp. 60-61.

They banded into sewing societies and made clothing, not for soldier relatives alone, but for all the volunteers. The women who needed no income worked without recompense; seamstresses working with them were paid for their efforts. Women got out on busy Washington Street and solicited money and supplies from passers-by. They organized the Ladies Military Association to solicit donations from planters who lived out in the country. Some of them volunteered to follow the army as nurses.[18] Mary Jane Stevenson also wanted to go with one of the units bound for Fort Pickens, but she merely wanted to be with her husband and she thought that the state should furnish the funds for her to make the trip.[19]

Activities such as these are the kind women are always involved with in wartime, but they are not extraordinary. There was nothing in them in this instance that foretold total war or indicated that the women had recognized and had responded to the most basic threat that the war held for them—the extinction of the cultural base which supported the idealization of Southern womanhood. That recognition and response came in late May when Captain John Travis came up from Natchez. Travis had a singular profession, but the ladies in Vicksburg were assured that he was "a gentleman of very pleasing and refined qualifications"; and besides that he had been a success with the ladies of Natchez. Travis came to Vicksburg to teach the ladies "the art and science of pistol and rifle shooting."[20] Something deep-seated and elemental had been stirred when it became socially acceptable for women to meet in a shooting gallery to learn to load and to aim pistols and rifles.

In the first rush of outrage and patriotism many schisms were closed over; then as the weeks passed by they widened again, and as they were laid open the vindictive and intolerant spirit of a people at war was exposed. The Southern states moved toward civil war because they had found the wishes of the majority intolerable. As the beset minority they broke away

18. Mrs. I. O. Smith to J. J. Pettus, September 1, 1861, Governors' Correspondence, Series E, Vol. LIII, Miss. Arch.; *Vicksburg Daily Citizen,* May 8, 15, 1861.

19. Mary Jane Stevenson to J. J. Pettus, May 19, 1861, Governors' Correspondence, Series E, Vol. LII, Miss. Arch.

20. *Vicksburg Daily Citizen,* May 27, 1861.

from the Federal Union so they might preserve those things they held to be dearer than the Union. Yet as they established their own government, and in doing so became a majority, they became intolerant of the minority. It was a simple case of "If you are not for us you are against us."

On May 1, even as he spoke of binding patriotism, J. M. Swords hinted at the rising spirit of fear and intolerance. He said, "If there are any persons in our midst who refuse to join us in our cause, they should at once be invited to leave the city as speedily as possible and relieve us of their presence and the duty of keeping a vigilant watch on them."[21]

By May 11, Swords was so concerned with the possibility that Unionists might still be in the city that he proposed to mark every good and loyal citizen. They would wear badges bearing the motto "Southern Rights—For This We Fight," and all strangers coming into Vicksburg would be given badges, too—after they had taken an oath of allegiance to the Confederacy.[22] If any Unionists escaped this measure Swords was sure that the county grand jury, composed of the "best and most devoted citizens," would investigate all cases of disloyalty and indict as traitors all people who spoke against the Confederacy. Some of the citizens, the city's "best citizens," were not content to let the grand jury handle matters and formed a vigilance committee which operated at night making "thorough examinations for spies, emissaries, and Unionist Sympathizers."[23]

This was mostly talk, but it was ugly talk. The Southerner could scornfully point to Lincoln's suspension of habeas corpus and howl despotism, but the veneer of constitutionalism—the bulwark of secessionist theory—lay just as thin in the South and would be just as easily contravened. The extra-legal vigilance committee met and threatened. Alexander Arthur bit his lip and kept quiet as he watched the committee members. He thought they were a tawdry bunch: "overzealous patriots who did not want to go to the wars, but [who wanted] to show their zeal and bring *out others*." Arthur remained silent—he was a Union man—and stored up three years of bitterness. But he

21. *Ibid.*, May 1, 1861.
22. *Ibid.*, May 11, 1861.
23. *Ibid.*, May 14, 1861.

would not be frightened; he stayed in the city and kept his thoughts to himself.[24]

Property rights as well as personal liberties began to feel the weight of war's intolerances. Late in the summer the directors of the Vicksburg Gas Company voted to confiscate the dividends of all stockholders living outside the Confederacy and to invest the expropriated money in Confederate bonds.[25]

Despite the talk of repressive measures and the sequestration of Northern property there were lingering indications of a lack of enthusiasm for the Confederate cause. Some of the leading businessmen still refused to help equip the volunteer units or donate to the women's fund-raising committee. J. M. Swords complained that they had "made immense fortunes in business . . . and . . . are deeply and vitally interested in the maintainance of Southern institutions and Southern rights," but they were "unwilling to make any drafts upon their overburdened coffers." One ardent Confederate proposed to give the recalcitrant businessmen a final opportunity to donate; then if they failed to do so he suggested that a 10 per cent "contribution" be levied upon their estates. If everything else failed they were to be hounded out of the city.[26]

A civilian's war can be more vicious and ruthless than that of the line soldier who comes to know and respect his enemy and share the fear, the wet, and the boredom with him. The civilian rarely knows the enemy as a man or learns the common bonds which can make all soldiers brothers, but instead regards him as something which must be extirpated by whatever means are at hand. In time the people of Vicksburg would come to learn the enemy well, and to respect him; but at first they could not, and investigations in the night, taunts, threats, and coercion were those means of extirpation. They went hand in hand with

24. Alexander H. Arthur to Joseph Holt, February 2, 1865, Joseph Holt Papers, Library of Congress.

25. This action, was taken under the authority of an act of the Confederate Congress of August 30, 1861, entitled "An Act for the sequestration of the Estates, property and effects of alien enemies. . . ." Isaac E. West to John McArthur, December 20, 1863, Records of the Bureau of Refugees, Freedmen, and Abandoned Lands, National Archives, Record Group 105. Hereinafter records in the National Archives are indicated by the symbol NA, followed by the record group (RG) number.

26. *Vicksburg Daily Citizen,* May 10, 1861.

dancing in the night, saluting cannon, and cheering. It was not a gallant nor an honorable side of war, but it was an inevitable one because the civilians could not do otherwise. For the most part the mean and the vicious acts were the result of individual or small group action; there was no over-all concerted drive against the slacker and the Unionist, and the city officials made no record of traitor-hunting thoughts or actions. In fact, imprisonments took a decided drop at this time. Only one-third as many people were jailed during the summer as were in the spring.[27]

The burst of intolerance following the outbreak of hostilities might have been an emotional catharsis similar to that which occurred on the night of Mollie Bunch's ball. In time it spent itself, but it did serve notice that the powerful admixture of pride, outrage, patriotism, and honor was not so strong that it could bind a people tightly together and quiet petty jealousies, evils, and differences of opinion.

This was a fitful period as the city accustomed itself to war, yet at the same time tried to hold on to the ways of peace. It was a time of anomaly and paradox. A citizen with a knowledge of the South's industrial capacity (or incapacity) urged the people to begin to practice economy, especially by saving scraps of paper and cotton goods to use in the manufacture of paper. Another person counseled the rationing of eggs in order that more chickens might be produced. Yet as these persons asked for economy the merchants of the city advertised a plethora of goods and begged the people to consume them. There was no war shortage, for the stores held foods ranging from fish to firkins of Congress Water shipped from Saratoga. Spices, coffee, and tea, which soon would become nonexistent, were plentiful. One merchant offered for sale pepper, cloves, allspice, ginger, nutmeg, and mace; Rio, Java, White and Brown Mocha coffee; and Im-

27. Council Minute Book, pp. 99, 104. The number of imprisonments fluctuated sharply during this period and this fluctuation may be of some significance when related to the sequence of events. There were forty-seven imprisonments in March, seventy-three in April, seventy-four in May, twenty-four in June, thirty in July, and twenty-six in August. From August 1861 until the siege the number did not rise above thirty-two, and that was in December when Christmas spirits became too boisterous.

perial, Gunpowder, and Young Hyson tea.[28] Though the guns had opened there was no bite of war in Vicksburg.

The Warren Female Academy showed no indication that war would touch it. Plans were laid for the coming autumn's session in which the students would acquaint themselves with Ancient and Modern Geography, English Grammar, Rhetoric, Belles Lettres, Botany, Astronomy, Geology, Pure Mathematics, Music, and Ancient and Modern Languages.[29]

The churches, like everything else, reflected the mingling of war and peace. Just before they left the city the Jeff Davis Guards attended a special mass during which their company flag was consecrated and blessed. The following Sunday, Father LeRay celebrated the mass with his civilian communicants.[30]

The first rush to war subsided, the volunteer companies left the city, and the quiet weeks stretched into summer. War was dispatches printed in the newspapers. War was letters from the soldiers printed for public consumption or read privately in the homes. War was Emma Shannon's marriage to William Crutcher before he left with the King Cotton Guards. War was staying in the hot city and not escaping to cool lakes in Minnesota. Only the distant echoes from the guns at Bull Run came to Vicksburg and the city waited in the summer sun far from the sounds of war.

Kate Stone became bored at Brokenburn and her mother let her cross the river to visit in Vicksburg. Kate spent three weeks in town during the latter part of the summer, but she found little to do there. The hurried excitement of April and May was past, and there were few officers to outfit or to dance with. She went from home to home and found pleasant moments in gardens and on rides, but most of the men were gone and those who remained wanted to talk of war news. The girls and women were little better; practically every one of them had joined a sewing society and they sat and sewed and talked of war. When Kate returned to Brokenburn at the last of August she wrote in her journal that she had had a "quiet" stay in Vicksburg, and she found

28. *Vicksburg Daily Citizen,* May 11, 24, 1861.
29. *Ibid.,* May 3, 1861.
30. *Ibid.,* May 25, 1861.

much more to write about at home than she did while she was in the city.[31]

Fall was a time of complacency. There was little else of war in the city but the cannon being cast in Reading's and Paxton's foundries and the clank of trains carrying Louisiana and Texas soldiers and supplies toward the east.

In the quietness, and without a clear and pressing threat to close it over, man's petty nature was at work. The autumn elections which some of the Unionists had looked forward to were coming, but there would not be the vigorous campaigning that they had hoped for early in the year; Bull Run had decided that. Though the state was sealed in the Confederacy and Unionist sentiment had been effectively silenced, there was no political unanimity in Vicksburg. Party politics still operated, and some men put personal and political advantage before everything else. The loyalty of the conservatives—the editorials of the *Whig* and the formation of the Old Guard notwithstanding—remained suspect, and the Davis-linked "ultras" still sought to crush the power of the men who were the acknowledged leaders of the city.

T. S. Martin, who edited the *Sun,* had been unable to put his paper on a paying basis since it had been resuscitated in the April heat of secession and war. When he learned that the people of Vicksburg would not buy it, Martin asked Governor Pettus to let him have the state printing contracts so he might bolster his paper's finances. If he did not get the contracts the *Sun* would collapse, Vicksburg would be without an "ultra" newspaper, and this, Martin wrote the governor, "would create as much Exultation among our enemies as the news of the fall of man caused in Hell."[32]

With the outbreak of war Marmaduke Shannon had adopted a non-partisan editorial policy for the *Whig,* but Martin still thought of the Old Whig conservatives as "enemies" and appealed to Pettus for aid on the grounds "that the *Sun* ever since it was established has done as much for the party as any other paper."[33] Shannon might say that war brought unanimity to Vicksburg,

31. Stone, *Brokenburn,* p. 47.

32. T. S. Martin to J. J. Pettus, October 7, 1861, Governors' Correspondence, Series E, Vol. LIV, Miss. Arch.

33. *Ibid.*

but time after time the people would prove the falseness of his optimism.

During this time the city council cast its accounts and found that the city was not as prosperous as it had been the previous year. The river flowed on, but the boats from Cincinnati, Louisville, and St. Louis no longer came south on its current. The first symptoms of economic paralysis began to creep in.[34]

When the boats stopped, the heart beat of Vicksburg slowed. Steamers from Baton Rouge, New Orleans, and Memphis still came to the city, but they brought few manufactured goods and the clatter of the wagons on the wharves had a hollow ring. Men were laid off from their jobs; not even the absence of the soldiers created a job market. Reading's and Paxton's foundries worked full time, but theirs were among the few businesses which did not feel the slack.

People began to go hungry. Men without work and privates in the army with scant pay could not feed their families. The city council did what it could—they appropriated money for food and fuel, though it was just a pittance, for they lived in an age when the unfortunate had to depend upon the charity of other people and of God, not of the government.[35]

Some of the people, recognizing the plight, organized a charity named the Benevolent Society which operated a "Free Market" to care for the jobless and the hungry. Emma Crutcher joined the Benevolent Society and she took particular interest in filling the baskets for the families of two men who were in her husband's company on the Virginia peninsula. As winter came the Free Market supplied almost one hundred families with meal, potatoes, sugar, salt, molasses, peas, turnips, cabbage, soap, and fresh beef. William Crutcher wrote his son that the Free

34. Council Minute Book, p. 120. The assessed valuation of property decreased one-third of a million dollars from the previous year. Practically the entire sum was lost in merchandise. The value of slaves also decreased. Though the number of slaves increased by 140, their average value dropped $68 per slave. On the other hand, the value of real estate increased $110,000 and money loaned on interest was almost doubled. Cf. *City Directory, 1860,* p. 75.

35. Council Minute Book, p. 127. The council also created the position of "Dog Killer." The dog killer was supposed to dispose of the stray and hungry dogs which had begun to infest the city.

Market was a great boon, for "no one can get work now, and there would be great suffering if it were not for the [charity]."[36]

Those who had jobs had food. Lavinia Shannon had lived in Vicksburg for twenty-seven years and had never known food to be so plentiful. Eggs were priced at fifteen cents a dozen, chickens were twenty cents each, venison was ten cents a pound, and pork the same. As Christmas drew near, Emma Crutcher reported to her captain in Virginia that "provisions are . . . abundant" and asked, "Now doesn't it look like God was providing for our wants, and taking special care of us?"[37]

A more cynical person might have answered that instead of God, Reading and Paxton were providing for the wants and needs of the people. As the holiday season opened the foundries' furnaces glowed long into the night and it became quite proper for the ladies to visit the factories and watch the cannon being cast. The women paid close attention to the details of the work and were pleased that they could talk knowingly of the "sixty brass cannon and 30,000 bombshells" being cast in their city. Emma Crutcher told her husband that she was "very much interested" in the casting, and the afternoon she visited the foundry she saw several other groups of women there watching the cannon being made. When she became tired of inspecting the war work she returned home where she "rattled away nonsense to Brother Clinton, discussed metaphysics with Brother Harrington—Benevolent Society with Sister Howe, and knitting with Sister Harrington."[38]

Christmas came warm and spring-like. Flowers of every season bloomed in the city—morning-glories, hyacinths, jasmine, violets, chrysanthemums, roses, and holly were bright in the sunlight. The Hill City Cadets were home on furlough before re-enlisting and their uniforms gave the city a splash of color that had been lacking for several months.

Emma Crutcher thought the Cadets looked strong and healthy, but she did not care for their "impudent stare." She wrote her husband: "I should not be surprised if they were a most

36. William Crutcher to William O. Crutcher, January 19, 1862, Phillip Crutcher Collection, Miss. Arch.

37. Emma Crutcher to William O. Crutcher, December 25, 1861, *ibid.*

38. *Ibid.*, December 16, 1861.

depraved set, for they are just old enough to feel all the temptations that allure men, and at the same time, are without the strength which is an accompaniment of manhood." The city, however, was glad to have the Cadets back, even if for a short while, and on Christmas day families gathered together, exchanged gifts, and sat down to Christmas dinners.

Emma gave her servants eight dollars, but made no other gifts. The day dragged by slowly for her: "I cannot say that there has been much merriment about this [Christmas], but it has passed, somehow, as all days do." Her family circle was thinned and when they sat down to dinner Emma thought: "What a contrast between the condition of this family this year and last, and how many members it has lost." She became so upset that she was excused from the table and she had no heart for the visitors who came to play the piano, sing, have tea, and hold a long prayer meeting. All she wanted was her captain whom she imagined was chilled and hungry in Virginia. While the guests sang she sat in the warm afternoon and dreamed of peaceful Christmas-times: "Poor baby, to be pining after the *sugar plums* of life, when the substantial *bread and meat,* in the shape of religion, love of family, and plenty of work to do, lie around in such profusion. But I want the *sugar plums,* and I should die without them."[39]

Later in the day the wind shifted and came whipping in bitter and cold from the north. It streamed into Vicksburg and the blooming flowers withered in its path.[40]

On the same day, hundreds of miles to the north on the Tennessee line, a Mississippi regiment was in camp where Christmas was celebrated by "all hands and the cook getting drunk."[41] The enemy was being held at the Tennessee boundary, but in Mississippi plans were underway to strengthen the Vicksburg defenses (though it had taken the state authorities eight months to get around to even thinking about the necessity of defending Vicksburg).

39. *Ibid.,* December 25, 1861. 40. *Ibid.*

41. "Civil War Diary of Captain James Litton Cooper, September 30, 1861, to January, 1865," ed. William T. Alderson, *Tennessee Historical Quarterly,* XV (June, 1956), 145.

Edward Fontaine, Ordnance Officer for the Mississippi Army, planned to be in Vicksburg during Christmas to lay out fortifications. He had asked Governor Thomas O. Moore of Louisiana to co-operate in the building of defenses along the river. The governor referred the request to General Mansfield Lovell, Commanding General of Department Number One, who replied: "We [have] no officer of Engineers and no guns to spare, and I [think] it too late to commence a . . . work. If they [Mississippi] wish to build it, however, let them do it . . . but I can give them no competent officer, no guns, and no powder."[42] In the spring General Lovell would reverse his decision and send to Vicksburg the men and equipment he salvaged from the New Orleans debacle. In the meanwhile the people of Vicksburg were undisturbed by military preparations in their city.

The second war year commenced. As the new year opened the armies were still along the lines of the previous summer, but suddenly the balance would be tipped and the sound of cannon would reverberate off the hills of Vicksburg. That would come; when the new year began Vicksburg was quiet.

Fewer boats came to the wharves, jobs became scarcer, and Emma Crutcher plunged into her work with the Free Market—it helped to pass the long hours and kept her from being so lonely.[43] She bought a little dog to give her companionship but found the animal a poor substitute for her husband. On New Year's Day she wrote him that she would keep the dog until he returned and then give it away, because, she said, "I think that after you get back, I can dispense with any other companionship for my evenings. Don't you think we can contrive to get through the time without any outside help?"[44]

Sometimes the loneliness would become unbearable and she would sit in her room for long hours and write: "To know that my love, my life, my other self, the dear object round which my

42. *War of the Rebellion: A Compilation of the Official Records of the Union and Confederate Armies* (Washington, 1880-1901), Ser. I, Vol. VI, 783. Hereinafter cited as *Official Records Army.*

43. Emma Crutcher to William O. Crutcher, January 19, 1862, Crutcher Collection.

44. *Ibid.*, January 1, 1862.

heartstrings are so knitted that I can never disentangle them . . . is exposed to the cold blasts of winter blowing colder from the sea . . . is too dismal for a comment." Then, like the Spartan women of whom she had probably read, she would tell her husband: "If you get into a battle and are left with *no* choice between surrender and death, *surrender*. Not till the last moment, not until resistance becomes suicide, for I had rather see you dead before me than dishonored, but save your life for me if it can be done short of dishonor."[45] War held little glamour for this bride of twenty-two, but winter was not all bleakness and loneliness.

One of her friends had been engaged for two years to a man who lived in Baltimore. He could not get through the armies' lines to come to Vicksburg and the Federal naval blockade had shut off commercial shipping to the southern ports. But he was a determined man—one day in January he arrived in the city to claim his bride and the people cheered his exploit. He had disguised himself as an oysterman and had slipped by the patrolling men of war.[46]

The blockade provided the people with another topic of conversation. The *Trent* Affair—stemming from the forceable removal of two Confederate diplomats from an English packet boat—was discussed in the city, and some people speculated on the possibility of England taking punitive measures against the United States. If this came to pass they believed the war might soon be over, "for these difficulties with England must seriously embarrass our enemies." They were not sure that England's "interference" would be best however—they were confident of the Confederacy's ability to win the war alone and they wanted the United States "all to ourselves."[47]

Suddenly optimism and complacency were jarred by a series of military disasters. On January 19, the right wing of the Army of Tennessee was shattered at Mill Springs. Three weeks later at Forts Henry and Donelson, Grant's army and Foote's gunboats battered the center of the Tennessee line into submission. The great screen which had shielded the tier of Gulf

45. *Ibid.*, January 4, 1862.
46. *Ibid.*, January 26, 1862.
47. *Ibid.*, January 10, 1862.

states was now a disorganized and defeated mass and for the first time the people of Vicksburg felt the shock of catastrophe.

On the second Sunday in February the city "had its usual round of Sunday School and Church," but beneath the outward forms of activity there was an air of expectancy and unrest which had been absent for many months. Emma Crutcher returned from church to write her husband: "The town is fermenting again . . . and everyone is going to war right off."[48] This pleased Emma, for a month before she had asked J. W. Edwards to join the King Cotton Guards, but he had begged off.[49] Three new companies were being raised and Emma found the reawakened tensions rather exhilarating: "Some of the old ladies think they are going to eat us up right away, but I defy the Yankees to scare me."[50] She might protest her fearlessness, but even as she did so the many-pronged attack along the Mississippi, which would culminate at Vicksburg, gathered weight and momentum.

As the Union armies began to press down from the north and as the Union ships tightened the blockade on the Gulf ports, the people began to feel the pinch of war shortages.

Scarcity changed Mahala Roach's daily routine. Until mid-February she had used the time after dinner to sew, read, and work with her account books. Now she stopped trying to do much work after dark. In flickering firelight she made this entry in her diary: "After dinner I . . . subsided into utter idleness; because my eyes are weak, and we have not candles enough to burn, light wood is not good enough to sew or read by, therefore I make use of the time after tea only to *chat,* or doze."[51] A few days later she began to experiment and found that cottonseed oil would burn in her lamps. It was not as satisfactory as candles or oil, but it was better than firelight and she was happy to be able to read again at night.[52]

48. *Ibid.,* February 9, 1862.

49. J. W. Edwards to William O. Crutcher, January 12, 1862, Crutcher Collection.

50. Emma Crutcher to William O. Crutcher, February 9, 1862, *ibid.*

51. Mahala P. H. Roach, Diary, Southern Historical Collection, University of North Carolina, p. 50.

52. *Ibid.,* p. 56.

Soap became scarce and the experimenters turned to native ingredients to try to manufacture a substitute. A "splendid soap" was made with china-balls—the fruit of the chinaberry tree. The berries were soaked and dissolved in a lye solution to yield "a fine soap."[53]

Women's fashions also suffered. Homespun now clothed the prosperous and the poor alike as women worked at long unused spinning wheels and looms. Homespun became a badge of sacrifice and loyalty and the women in Judge Harris' family were proud to wear it. They solved the problem of new hats by fashioning them from plaited oatgrass and palmetto. If they were going to church or to a party and wanted a trim for a hat, they went out in the garden, cut a flower, and stuck it on.[54]

The winter days began to lengthen, but so did the casualty lists. The people knew that Albert Sidney Johnston was trying to re-organize his army along the northern border of Mississippi, but it seemed to be a slow job and there was little to encourage them. An air of melancholy and foreboding seeped into Vicksburg. Emma Crutcher stopped writing cheery news to her husband and she let her sagging spirits come out in her letters. On March 6, she wrote: "It is impossible to enter the details of little events that fill up my life . . . . I wanted to make my letters interesting but there is no use in trying now—they will just have to answer the purpose of letting you know that everybody is well." Then she added: "I saw Mr. Martin this evening. His company go into camp tomorrow. Somehow I have gotten the idea into my head that he will not return."[55] Less than a month before Emma had defied the Yankees to frighten her; now she looked at her friends and saw death.

Foreboding and uneasiness were not confined to a single, lonely woman. On March 13, the city council passed an ordinance prohibiting the storage of cotton within Vicksburg. No more cotton could be brought into the city and the cotton already

53. [Anonymous], "War Diary of a Union Woman in the South," ed. George W. Cable, *The Century Magazine,* XXXVIII (October, 1889), 938. Hereinafter cited as "War Diary."

54. Anne Harris Broidrick, A Recollection of Thirty Years Ago, Southern Historical Collection, University of North Carolina, p. 13.

55. Emma Crutcher to William O. Crutcher, March 6, 1862, Crutcher Collection.

there was to be moved outside the city so "the Same may be Safely burned, should it be necessary to do so, to prevent it from falling into the hands of our Enemies." In the same meeting the council tried to spur enlistments by authorizing the payment of two hundred dollars to each infantry company, two hundred and fifty dollars to each artillery company, and three hundred dollars to each cavalry company raised in the city.[56]

Mayor Lindsay watched the deteriorating situation. On March 24, he told the council: "The unfortunate condition of our country, the voice of the people, and the protection to our soldiers passing through our city, call for the closing of all houses where liquors are retailed, at an early hour . . . and that no more licenses be granted to such houses whilst the present state of affairs exists." He also recommended economy in city expenditures "keeping in view the decrease in our revenue, and the imperative necessity from time to time of assisting our Military Companies, and the Families of Volunteers. . . ."[57]

The mayor was especially concerned with the maintenance of law and order in the city. Martial law had been declared in Memphis and New Orleans and he expected "a large floating Population of Thieves, Gamblers, Swindlers, and Suspicious Persons" to leave those cities and flood Vicksburg. The city police would not be adequate to cope with this situation; therefore the mayor recommended that the military companies, which had previously assisted the police, continue and increase their activity and that citizens who were not already members of a volunteer unit be requested to form themselves into squads further to augment the police forces.[58]

The men who governed the city were worried, but they could (and would) still direct the affairs of the city, though the time was fast approaching when this would not be so.

Individual citizens continued to do what they could to help the war effort. Emma Crutcher gave her pony to the army. This was quite a sacrifice because the animal was her one remaining pet and she had ridden it out in the countryside during her courtship days with her husband. She told her husband,

56. Council Minute Book, p. 157. 57. *Ibid.*, p. 160.
58. *Ibid.*

when she let the pony go: "Instead of writing a model, patriotic note about laying the sacrifice on the altar of my country etc. such as you see in the newspapers, accompanying a pair of *salt-spoons,* I wrote the shortest and simplest note possible, merely saying that I wished to give my pony to the Confederacy . . . ." But she gained little comfort by making the sacrifice and said: "If it were not for religion (and it sometimes escapes me for a moment) life's problems would remain forever unsolved."[59]

Other women organized the Ladies Hospital Association. Money was sent from throughout the state to the Association and the women used it to care for the sick soldiers in the city's hospitals.[60] Mahala Roach took her turn nursing the soldiers, though little did she dream that it was just a trifle compared with what was to come. On the last day of March she returned home and made this entry in her diary: "Went early to the Hospital—nursed the sick all day, got home after 7—had many pleasant moments—and am too tired to do anything tonight."[61]

The city council also took notice of the men in the hospitals and of the fact that some of them would not recover. The council set aside special lots in the cemetery for the burial of the dead soldiers in order that they might be assured of a "decent and Christian interment."[62] The lots would soon be filled to overflowing.

On Mississippi's northeast boundary Albert Sidney Johnston had pulled together the remains of his Tennessee army. He organized his forces in a weird battle formation and, on the morning of April 6, he sent them crashing into unsuspecting Grant at Shiloh. When the day was over Johnston was dead, Beauregard had called off the attack, and Grant had managed to salvage his army and a victory from the tangled battle. Two hundred miles to the southwest the people of Vicksburg awaited news of the outcome.

April 11 was cold and wintry. Rain beat down on the city and lightning bolts cut the sky. Messengers from Shiloh,

59. Emma Crutcher to William O. Crutcher, March 14, 1862, Crutcher Collection.

60. Morris Emanuel to Elizabeth Eggleston, April 9, 1862, Eggleston-Roach Papers, Department of Archives and Manuscripts, Louisiana State University.

61. Roach, Diary, p. 86.

62. Council Minute Book, p. 166.

more eloquent than any dispatch, lay at the railway depot, their bandages and blankets sopped with water. The men and women of Vicksburg were at the station, but this time there were no cheers for the troops, and throughout the day and into the night the people worked to move the wounded to homes and hospitals. Mahala Roach spent the day with the wounded and she was worn out when she returned to her home that night; but before she went to bed she made a short entry in her diary: "It was a sad sight, and makes us realize that the war is near us indeed."[63]

63. Roach, Diary, p. 92.

CHAPTER V

"MISSISSIPPIANS DON'T KNOW HOW TO SURRENDER"

GOOD Friday. The churches were open and the ministers were conducting Holy Week services. Suddenly the whole town was in an uproar; the courthouse bell rang in alarm and the congregations were hurriedly dismissed. When Mahala Roach left her church she heard the bare outline of what had happened: one of the Carroll Dragoons had shot a woman and then had resisted arrest. He was not taken into custody until the militiamen were called to overpower him.[1]

Later in the day the city council met in response to the request of "many citizens." The people themselves wanted martial law declared in Vicksburg—an almost unprecedented occurrence. The incident involving the dragoon seemed proof enough that the civil police were incapable of maintaining the peace and the city council admitted that they could no longer govern the city. The council empowered the mayor to appoint a provost marshal and to establish martial law because "the establishment of martial law in New Orleans, Jackson, and Memphis, and other points of easy communication with Vicksburg, has driven many of the idle, the visious and the profligate of those Places to [seek] refuge in this City, and . . . the City authorities, although adequate to the quiet government of the City under ordinary Circumstances, are powerless to govern, and control this influx of vice, and lawlessness."[2] The breakdown of the local government

1. Mahala P. H. Roach, Diary, Southern Historical Collection, University of North Carolina, p. 97.

2. Council Minute Book, pp. 166-67. Though the people wanted their local officials to declare martial law, they had ambivalent feelings on the matter. General Van Dorn instituted martial law in July 1862, much to the

had commenced and the rot of war had begun to sap the city. Yet on the surface there were few indications of the nearness of actual conflict.

Tending the wounded from Shiloh was still the closest touch the people had with war. The wounded, the few militiamen who garrisoned the small river batteries, and the casualty lists printed in the newspapers reminded the people they were at war, but these things were slight and remote from conflict. Martial law gave a military fillip to the atmosphere, but other than that the city was placid; and war, real war, was far away.

Farragut patrolled and blockaded the Gulf Coast to cut off imports and to make cotton pile up in the warehouses, but there was nothing immediate about that. Halleck was stalled in front of Corinth with an army sitting in his way, and "Old Brains" was so slow that it would have taken him five years to move to Vicksburg if he had gotten in motion. The Northern fleet on the Mississippi was far above Memphis, and the Confederate rams gathered at Fort Pillow blocked its movement southward. If distance was measured by the sinuous path of the river, which was the course the gunboats would have to follow to get to Vicksburg, war was over four hundred miles away, and the only sound of guns heard in the city was the booming of the cannon as the gunners computed and checked their ranges.

Then it all changed very quickly. War, which up to this time was something that happened to people in Tennessee and Virginia, came flooding into the lower Mississippi valley. The pincer movement was on again. It had been sidetracked in Tennessee while Grant cleaned out Forts Henry and Donelson and pushed Albert Sidney Johnston down the Tennessee River to Shiloh. That was finished now, and the might of the Union was hurled up and down the river toward Vicksburg.

On April 24, Farragut stopped patrolling and smashed by Forts Jackson and St. Philip, the guardians of the approaches

---

people's displeasure. The reason they bridled against Van Dorn's edict is not clear. It might have stemmed from the fact that Van Dorn over-stepped his authority—only the president could declare martial law—and too, Van Dorn had the military force really to enforce the law, while Mayor Lindsay had only a few volunteer companies, which would make for a much less stringent enforcement.

to New Orleans. The next day he steamed up to the wharves of the city to land Federal troops which occupied the city. The news was telegraphed up the river to shake the towns and cities from their lull of safety. When the message clicked out in Vicksburg it stunned the people. Forts Jackson and St. Philip were the strongest fortifications on the river; there was nothing left between New Orleans and Vicksburg to hold back the gunboats, and New Orleans was less than five days steaming away. The boats, with gunports yawning black in their hulls, would soon be up the river to anchor off the city.

Five days grace, then Union gunboats. The shock spread through the city like ripples made by a stone cast into a mill pond. The sounds of the business day were muted and the people "walked the streets aimlessly, as one does when troubled, with bowed heads and saddened mien. It was like the slaying of the first born child of Eygpt. Sorrow was in every house."[3]

The time had come when the life of the people could not be separated from the military operations. Though they were civilians and noncombatants, they were now subject to the same conditions as were their soldiers: the guns of the enemy threatened them. Like their soldiers, they were both brave and fearful, had fits of dejection and apathy, had moments of supreme detachment in the midst of crisis; and in the end they made their way in the face of circumstances as well as they were able. But they were without one of the greatest comforts of the soldier. They had no leader. They were not bound to follow orders with the knowledge or the hope that someone of greater ability knew what was going to happen and what was best for them. But though they were not subject to orders, they were no longer free in the broad sense of the word. All they could do was to react to the military situation as it ebbed and flowed around them.

The news of the fall of New Orleans came early on Saturday morning, April 26. The shock, with its debilitating aftermath, was severe but brief, and as soon as the thought of being under Federal guns registered in their minds the people began a frantic scurrying.

3. Anne Harris Broidrick, A Recollection of Thirty Years Ago, Southern Historical Collection, University of North Carolina, p. 12.

Sundays along the Mississippi were drowsy days. In late April the sun was warm, the woods along the river showed green, and people went to church and visited one another. There was no time to enjoy the spring now. The gunboats had not come yet; but the five days' grace was drawing to a close, and there was no telling when the boats might arrive. There was no drowse in Vicksburg—no time for worship and leisurely visiting. People stayed away from church and were in the streets hurrying to homes, shops, warehouses and the railroad station. Gangs of workers were in the factories dismantling machinery, packing it, and carting it off to the depot. Cotton was hauled out of warehouses and carried to fields outside the city ready for burning. Merchants stayed in their stores closing account books and packing their goods. The clatter of hooves filled the streets as drivers whipped their horses up the hills and out of the city. That night Mahala Roach made this entry in her diary: "This has been a singular Sunday, no Sabbath stillness has pervaded its air, but bustle and confusion have reigned everywhere!" The clatter and confusion went on into the night, and the next day the wagons still streamed out of the city.[4]

Until this time war had been a distant thing, touched with a kind of glory. War had been the Volunteer Southrons singing the "Marseillaise" as they climbed aboard the railroad cars, eager for battle; war had been Emma Crutcher's love letters to her captain in Virginia; war had even been the terribly dirty, bloody wounded from Shiloh, but it had never been close. It was close now, and it was different. War was fear, and the people of Vicksburg were afraid. War was the urge to close up shop, pack up, and get out of town. Even some who stood aloof from the confusion and took the time to record the day's events were making preparations to leave the city. As they left they began a movement which was to be an integral part of the story of their city under attack.

Never before did a civilian population caught in the midst of military operations have the opportunity or the equipment to move as did the Southerners in the Civil War. The improved

4. Roach, Diary, pp. 103-5; and Charles B. Allen, Plantation Book, Miss. Arch., p. 67.

A Confederate transport bringing cattle to Vicksburg. (From *Harper's Pictorial History of the Civil War*)

roads, waterways, and railroads of the mid-nineteenth century gave the people a mobility they had never before possessed. With roads clogged and cut up by soldiers, with rivers scoured and dominated by Federal boats, and with railroads falling into decrepit disrepair and requisitioned for military use, the Southerner was still able to move fast and far, though often at the peril of his person and his property.

Under the threat of attack the people's first inclination was to leave the city. Though the possession of the river hung in doubt, Southern shipping still moved between Memphis and Baton Rouge and up the secondary streams into Mississippi, Arkansas, and Louisiana. Large troop movements were just beginning, and the railroads and the roads were open to the civilians. They could move in any direction, north and south along the river, or deeper inland to the east and west. But it was not that easy. Factors other than ready access to transportation had to be taken into consideration. It was an expensive proposition to close a place of business and a home, pack household belongings, load a family into a carriage or a railway car, and relocate them in the country or in another town. Not many people were able to do this. Instead they worked out compromises which gave them the most safety with the least expense and which took the form of "visiting." In this manner the movement followed a loose pattern and was partially confined to a particular socio-economic class and geographic locale.

The threat the people most wanted to escape was gunboat bombardment—land operations were not a factor yet—and they knew that the range of the boats' guns was limited. This meant that they could move only a few miles into the country and find safety. Another limiting factor entered at this point. Warren County was a rich agricultural county, and most of the land was held in plantation-sized farms. This would further tend to limit the type or class of person who could find refuge in the county. The planters' homes were open to their friends and social equals, but the laborer-artisan families got short shrift. Living close by the city also meant that businesses and shops would not have to be closed. The owner might commute if he chose, or he might even stay in his town house once he had moved his family and knew that they were out of gunfire range.

Charles Allen, who lived on the Big Black River, owned a plantation with the jaw-breaking name "Nanachehaw." Four days after the fall of New Orleans one of his friends from Vicksburg, S. B. Day, came out to inquire if he and Mrs. Day might visit Nanachehaw. Mr. Day bluntly told Allen that his wife was "scared about the gunboats" and wanted to leave the city. Allen replied that the couple would be welcome and they were soon at the plantation, away from the gunboat threat.[5]

Mahala Roach remained calm during the frenetic week end and her routine did not differ from that of the previous days; but in the back of her mind she, too, was making preparations to leave the city. By May 7, she had her children and their belongings packed and they traveled out to "Woodfield," which was also on the Big Black. Mahala did not relish the prospect of leaving her house deserted in the city and as soon as she got the children settled she returned to Vicksburg to spend two lonely nights in the house. By May 12, she was satisfied that there was little chance of harm coming to her property and she left again for Woodfield. During the next three months she would be in and out of the city.[6]

5. Allen, Plantation Book, p. 68. 6. Roach, Diary, pp. 113-14.

The Days and Mahala Roach moved toward the east, the direction most of the refugees took. They probably moved into this section because it was more densely populated—the little hamlets of Bovina, Edwards Station, Bolton Station, Clinton, and Raymond were there—and it was easier to find a place to stay. The Southern Railroad also ran to the east; this made movement back to Vicksburg easier and quicker than travel by road and by water, which were the only routes open to those who moved north, south, and west, but plenty of people moved in these directions.[7] Across the river at Brokenburn, Kate Stone watched the refugees pass by. On the first day of May she was told: "The Yankees were hourly expected in Vicksburg. Numbers of people were leaving the city."[8]

One of the families who moved in a northwesterly direction had a different motive from that of most of the refugees. Though they left town about the same time as the others, they were not fleeing the gunboats. On the last day of April, in a little village by a lake in Arkansas, a young bride sat down and made this entry in her diary: "The last two weeks have glided quietly away without incident except the arrival of new neighbors—Dr. Y., his wife, two children and servants. That a professional man prospering in Vicksburg should come now to settle in this retired place looks queer."[9]

The unexpected arrival of these new neighbors provided the young woman's family and friends with a new conversational topic, and they tried to guess the reason which impelled a prosperous, established man to pick up and move so far to such a secluded place. One of the men weighed all of the evidence and said, " 'that man has come here to hide from the conscript officers. He has brought no end of provisions, and is here for the

7. At this time the Vicksburg, Shreveport and Texas Railroad, which ran westward from Vicksburg, was completed only to Monroe, Louisiana, and the first eighteen miles of it were under water from the overflowed river. *Official Records of the Union and Confederate Navies in the War of the Rebellion* (Washington, 1904), Ser. I, Vol. XVIII, 465. Hereinafter cited as *Official Records Navy*.

8. Stone, *Brokenburn,* p. 103.

9. "War Diary," *The Century Magazine,* XXXVIII, 937.

war. He has chosen well, for this country is so cleaned of men that it won't pay to send the conscript officers here.' "[10]

The others did not know it but there was double irony in the situation because the motivation which was attributed to the doctor was the same for the bride and her husband. They had fled New Orleans because the husband, though a Southerner, had no love for the Confederacy and believed "the result will inevitably be against us."[11] He did not want to fight for the Confederacy, yet he would not fight against his people. The only solution was to go into hiding. The irony was compounded when the spring floods drove the couple out of their water-bound hideaway and forced them into Vicksburg, where the husband would not fight for his people but where both of them would suffer with them.

At the same time the exodus was taking place, a cross-current of incoming refugees set in. During the first week in May a paradoxical situation developed; some people were desperately trying to flee the city while others were eager to come in. Most of the ones who were arriving were from New Orleans and the vicinity already occupied by Union forces—they were glad to exchange life in an occupied territory for the meagre comfort they could find in Vicksburg, which was only threatened with attack and capture.[12]

Hurried flight was merely one aspect of the people in alarm, but it was typical of the conditions of the time. Fear opened a Pandora's box of sudden changes and evils. Property which could not be moved was changing hands as owners liquidated real-estate holdings in anticipation of damage and loss through bombardment and occupation.[13] The old bugaboo of a Jewish conspiracy—a lingering reminder of Know-Nothing days—crept out in the tension and strain. Benjamin L. C. Wailes wrote Jefferson Davis: "The shopkeeper Jews in Vicksburg are buying up real estate—one bought the Washington

10. *Ibid.* 11. *Ibid.*, 936.

12. Allen, Plantation Book, p. 69.

13. The number of recorded real-estate transfers for April and May was almost four times the number recorded in February and March. Warren County Deed Book CC, Courthouse, Vicksburg, entries for February-May, 1862.

Hotel and other property has fallen into their hands."[14] The taint of disloyalty was implied in this accusation.[15]

Flight and bigotry were indications of the temper of the people in a time of uncertainty and fear. Those who could, or wanted to, fled. Some of those who stayed caught up old shibboleths and flung them about, heedless of the truth. All of them sought to salvage and hang on to something of their old way of life in a situation that threatened to strip them bare of their common culture. In sum, they acted no better nor worse than anyone else in a similar position. They groped about in an amorphous situation as individuals, without leadership or direction. As individuals they tried to find a place of safety for themselves in the face of the unknown, and as individuals they made a muddle of it. The situation was not altogether their fault; they were without organized direction. At a time such as this order and disciplined movement could be restored only by force of leadership, by an authority who possessed that force and who was willing to use it. Such power rested with only two sources—the civil authorities and the military officers—and neither was capable of applying it.

The city government was completely unable to cope with the situation or to offer any rallying point around which the people could gather, catch their breaths, and make a common guided effort to stabilize themselves. Problems such as civilian defense (to apply a twentieth-century term to the situation), the housing and feeding of refugees, and the preparation for the occupation of the city by Confederate soldiers were all sloughed off. Only one meeting of the city council was held during these critical weeks. There was no leadership from this quarter. The men who governed the city failed to provide any direction for the frightened people, and they did not even try to go through the motions of leadership. Government collapsed into an ignominious interregnum.[16]

14. Benjamin L. C. Wailes to Jefferson Davis, May 6, 1862, Jefferson Davis Papers, Duke University.

15. There is little indication that this accusation was based upon fact. William Lum owned the Washington Hotel, and the names of the property purchasers in the Warren County Deed Book, although inadequate evidence, do not indicate that many Jews bought property during this period.

16. The news of New Orleans' fall came on April 26; the council did not

The other potential source of leadership and force was the military authorities. There was a void here also for the simple reason that there were no officers in Vicksburg with the rank or the power to act. Perhaps it was just as well that military force was not applied because when it was used two months later such a howl arose that Jefferson Davis had to disavow the action.

The frightened city moved in a leadership vacuum—perhaps it was better that way. The lack of leadership threw the people back on their own resources and, though for a while they wallowed in the morass of their own confusion, they slowly began to take the temper which would be required of them to stand attack and siege. This temper—this spirit—could not be created by military edict or by civic regulation; it could not be pressed upon the people; it had to come from within themselves. At some time during the first weeks of May the people began to take the temper. The panic of the weekend of April 27 was spent with the first mad rush to the country. This cleared out most of the thewless ones. Those who were left might be afraid, but they would not be stampeded.

As one day lengthened into the next and Farragut's gunboats still did not appear, the people began to take heart and their backbones began to stiffen. There was a new atmosphere in the city when Charles Allen came in on business on May 3. As he made his rounds to the wholesale grocers and the commissions merchants—and that the business houses were still open was a good sign in itself—he watched and listened to the people. What impressed him most was not the flight from the city, but the fact that large cannon were being emplaced along the riverfront. He sensed something wholly different from fright in the city. When he returned home he wrote in his journal that the people of Vicksburg were "determined to show fight."[17]

Allen did not know it, but on the day before, General Mansfield Lovell, the man who had said in December that he could

meet until May 5, ten days after the first burst of panic and flight. The minutes of the meeting of May 5 indicate a routine business session. Nothing is recorded concerning the fall of New Orleans or the threat to Vicksburg. Then, no further meetings were held until June 16, and at both meetings a bare quorum (four out of seven councilmen) was present. Council Minute Book, pp. 166-69.

17. Allen, Plantation Book, p. 69.

not defend Vicksburg, had reported to Beauregard that he had ordered troops to the city and also had heavy artillery on the way.[18] Most of the troops were artillerymen and had served the guns at Forts Jackson and St. Philip and the batteries of the Chalmette; they knew the gunboats and they wanted another chance at them. These veterans began to arrive in the city on May 1.[19]

At the same time these Louisiana troops were pouring into the city, more soldiers were coming from the east as reinforcements were ordered from the camp at Enterprise, Mississippi. The night before the trains started for Vicksburg, the officers appropriated a school building, decorated it, set up dining tables, and installed a band for a final ball and banquet.

Little William Hart, whose father commanded a company of the Eighth Louisiana Heavy Artillery, was allowed to stay up to watch his parents dance and dine with the other couples. This was an exciting time for a four-year-old boy far from home; as the hours passed he remained wide awake watching the uniformed officers dancing and laughing with their hoop-skirted ladies. Occasionally he would look through the windows of the school and see the faces of the enlisted men who stood outside peering in at the brilliant display. His young mind was not keen enough to catch the undertones of brittleness in the laughter or the current of tension which underlay the party, for the gaiety of the evening was set against the thought of the morning, when the men would leave to tend the guns of Vicksburg. The officers of the Eighth Louisiana had served the guns at the New Orleans forts; they knew what was in store for them, but all little William knew when they sat down to eat was that "everybody was gay and happy because the sound of war had not yet reached that place." The next day they were on the trains bound for Vicksburg.[20]

The arrival of the troops marked a psychological turning point for the civilians. Here, finally, was someone doing some-

18. *Official Records Army,* Ser. I, Vol. X, pt. 2, 481.

19. S. H. Lockett, "The Defense of Vicksburg," *Battles and Leaders of the Civil War,* eds. Robert U. Johnson and Clarence C. Buel (New York, 1884), III, 482. Hereinafter cited as *Battles and Leaders.*

20. William O. Hart, "A Boy's Recollection of the War," *Publications of the Mississippi Historical Society,* XII (1912), 149-50.

thing positive. The placement of the guns spoke eloquently and decisively of what was to be done. Though there were still people who would leave the city, those who remained caught something of the resoluteness of the black cannon and the cheerfulness of the soldiers.

General Martin Luther Smith, who was placed in immediate command of the defense, arrived on May 12, the same day that Natchez was occupied by Federal forces. The weak show of force and the apathy of the people at New Orleans and the flaccid collapse at Natchez made him doubtful as to what he would find at Vicksburg.[21] He was immeasurably heartened as the people—both men and women of all ages—sought him out to tell him that they had made their decisions about themselves and their city. They wanted Vicksburg defended and held. General Smith saw no wavering among the people at this time; he thought they were ready to stand the gaff. Their response was so cheering that "the defense became an affair of more than public interest" to him.[22]

The metamorphosis of the mind was completing itself. Two weeks previously the people had stumbled over themselves in their fear. Now they were sticking behind the military forces. This two-week span is the period in which the people were most brave, braver than when the gunboats finally came and braver than when Grant locked them in under seige. At this time they faced the unknown—the unknown that is always more frightening than the reality, and which requires stronger stuff to stand against it. War had never really touched them and they could only guess and fear what it would do to them.

The gunboats were the carriers of war and of the unknown. They had scourged the western waters; Forts Henry and Donelson, Island Number 10, and New Orleans had been felled by them. The unanswered question which preyed on the minds of

21. Brigadier General C. G. Dahlgren, who commanded at Natchez, reported that he could raise only fourteen men who were willing to defend the city, and that "the conscripts positively refus[ed] to do duty." *Official Records Army,* Ser. I, Vol. XV, 737. Though the author raises the point of a difference in the condition of mind between the citizens of Natchez and Vicksburg, he does not, though admittedly he makes an invidious comparison, attempt to explain the reason (or reasons) for the difference.

22. *Ibid.,* p. 7.

the inhabitants of Vicksburg was "What will the fleet do when it gets to our city?" After the gunboat bombardment started, and later when Grant encircled the city, the gnawing dread of the unknown vanished. The people learned what to expect; and as they learned they found that they could stand against it. Actual attack was a physical thing, and the courage required to stand up under it became more of a physical exercise than a solely mental process. From this standpoint the period between the fall of New Orleans and the onset of actual attack was the most critical time, at least for the civilians, of the entire, extended Vicksburg campaign. The whole business pivoted on these few weeks in which, though there was no military clash, it was decided that there would be a campaign instead of a quick capitulation.

Seen in retrospect, the civilians were an inevitable part of the military operations, but at the onset the military leaders hoped that they could be kept separate, and General Smith directed that the artillery batteries should be sited out of the town limits, sometimes at the expense of not using better locations inside the city, in the hope that the fight would "be confined to the armed points, and the city itself, which could have no bearing on the ultimate issue, be made to suffer as little [as possible]."[23] Later he would ruefully report that "events did not justify our expectations."[24]

Once defensive preparations were set in motion, and the more elaborate they became, the more they impinged upon the civilians. There was no clear-cut or consistent reaction on the part of the people to the inexorable encroachment upon the city and their lives. The frailty and inconsistency of their nature were highlighted by the manner in which they would seek out General Smith to tell him with "great unanimity" that their city ought to be defended "at all hazards," yet at the same time disregard pleas for Negroes and tools to work up the defensive positions.

Before the fall of New Orleans the slaveholders were requested to send one thousand Negroes to the engineer in charge of building the defensive works. They were not sent. Even

23. *Ibid.*, p. 12.

24. *Ibid.*

the fall of New Orleans and the immediate naked threat to their city did not make the owners comply with the request. Finally the engineer in charge, who had the authority to impress the slaves and equipment, was forced to use it.[25]

When Charles Allen heard that horses as well as Negroes were being impressed he sent a messenger off in the night to catch and turn around a wagon and team he had sent to Vicksburg.[26] Though he lived only a few miles out of town, and though his fate was closely linked to the military decision which would be made there, he would have no part of aiding in the defense. Even when the gunboats lay out in the river, and after his guests had left his home because they were more afraid of the possible landing of troops at Nanachehaw than the gunboats, he remained adamant. Two weeks after he sent out in the night for his wagon he was still unmoved by the requests for help. "I have paid," he wrote in his journal, "no attention to any of their requisitions, thinking more than half are by scoundrels to get planter's teams to haul private property . . . one gentleman found his team hauling out a family and their truck and wanted to know if they were Gov't. stores?"[27] And this was written after the gunboat flotilla commander had threatened to blow the city to rubble.

This sort of reaction was not limited to the early weeks in May as the civilians were feeling the demands of the military for the first time. Some of them would never adjust themselves to the realization that they were an integral, though perhaps unwilling, part of a military struggle and they kept criticizing—sometimes justifiably, sometimes captiously—right to the end of the siege. But this was merely one aspect of the people as the time of attack came nearer. In other respects they appear in a more favorable light.

During the period of stabilization the city militia was reorganized. Up to this time it had been a haphazard sort of

25. *Ibid.*, p. 813.
26. Allen, Plantation Book, p. 70.
27. *Ibid.*, p. 74. In Allen's behalf it must be stated that the requisition for slaves was for one night only. Allen could see little reason in walking a gang of slaves on a twenty-five mile round trip for one night's work. Also there was "no overseer to work them when they got there."

organization and most of the men who would have ordinarily been a part of it had already gone on duty with either state or Confederate units. On May 15, an order went out which included all men of military age who were left in the city—between eighteen and fifty years old—and mustered them into the militia. They were required to meet in front of the courthouse the following Saturday morning "when their organization will be completed." They were further required to bring their own guns and have them in good order. The brigadier general directing their organization was Charles E. Smedes, who was better known as a grocer.[28]

At first reading this seemed to be a routine announcement, but there was more to it than met the eye. First, the militia was a local organization and it functioned under the direction of local authorities; therefore, at last, some initiative was being exercised by the local officials. The sweeping inclusion of every male of serviceable age indicated the temper of the city—everyone will turn out and there will be no shilly-shallying about it. The sorry display at Natchez—where only fourteen men could be dragooned to defend their city—was not to be tolerated in Vicksburg. This was fine. Then, in contra-distinction to the bold tone of the order, a pathetic note underlined its wording. Here were men called out to protect their own homes. It had taken twenty-two days from the first alarm to get them out just for organization, they had to find their arms by themselves, and they were commanded by a grocer.

As a military unit the militia was a weak reed, but that was not the point. The point was this: the militia was a symbol of the great seethe and reaction which had occurred in the minds of the people since the time of secession. A year and a half previously they had fought against secession in every way they could. They had voted for a Unionist candidate for president; when that failed they had sent anti-secession delegates to the secession convention. All of this had been to no avail, and the guns and blood of battle had pushed them into the arms of the secessionists. The casualty lists which trickled back from Virginia and Tennessee had sealed the embrace. In this they

28. *Vicksburg Daily Whig,* May 15, 1862.

were no different from the people of Natchez, who though Unionist, also had sent their men to war and had learned that they had been killed and maimed. But something had happened in Vicksburg that was not repeated in Natchez. Both cities had been loyal in 1860; yet when the moment came to make the ultimate decision, Natchez, which pitted fourteen men against five gunboats, chose complaisant submission while her sister city, equally Unionist in 1860, volunteered defiance. The militia was the city's articulated defiance. The change in the mood of the people was the real significance of the militia gathered in front of the courthouse on a Saturday morning in May. The final, irrevocable setting aside of old loyalties was the true meaning of the old men and young boys who, dressed in whatever they chose to wear and armed with whatever they could scrape up, went through military motions under the command of a grocer general.

This defiance was neither brash nor rash, but considered and calculated. At the same time the *Whig* carried the notice to muster the militia the paper was engaged in a debate with the Jackson *Mississippian* concerning the fate of the city. The editor of the *Mississippian,* forty miles from the gunboat threat, had exhorted the citizens of Vicksburg to show their earnestness in the struggle and to "make a example of heroism and devotion to the cause" even if it meant putting the torch to the city to prevent its capture. Across the river at Brokenburn, Kate Stone, whose mother was burning $20,000-worth of cotton, was also in an incendiary mood. On May 9, she wrote in her journal that "it seems hopeless to make a stand at Vicksburg. We only hope they may burn the city. . . . How much better to burn our cities than let them fall into the enemy's hands."[29] Kate's private thoughts and the *Mississippian's* public urging were contradicted by the people who would feel the fire.

Marmaduke Shannon, the Old Whig-Unionist, spoke for the majority of the citizens when he replied to the editor of the *Mississippian*:

We observe that our patriotic contemporary of the *Mississippian* urges the denizens of this 'burg' to consign the city to flames before

29. Stone, *Brokenburn,* p. 101.

surrendering. We trust that our authorities and citizens will have a little more discretion than to commit such a rash and impolitic act. Vicksburg is no Moscow, and its destruction would be of no injury whatever to the enemy, but would be a severe blow to the many families here whose husbands, sons and brothers are now in the army . . . . Vicksburg has shown and will 'show her earnestness in this struggle,' but her people will not destroy the city . . . . We will 'make a example of heroism and devotion to the cause,' but it will not be by destroying the city. If the enemy shell it there will not be a murmur, but we will not apply the torch ourselves.[30]

This was written by the editor who had told his readers eighteen months before that resistance was rebellion. Now he was doing his best to rally the people to "the cause." War was a Procrustean bed and few people escaped the stretchings and shrinkings that the passions and pressures of conflict forced upon them; but though the citizens' minds were changing and hardening into resistance they would not adopt the tinny heroism that outsiders tried to foist on them. Shannon's answer to the editor of the *Mississippian* was an exercise in quiet courage, and the only florid phrases in it were quotations from the *Mississippian* which would never see the gunboats and only momentarily feel the weight of Grant's army.[31]

A condition of mind is shown in many ways. An editorial is a more eloquent statement of that condition, but homey, everyday things sometimes come closer to the true state of affairs. The editorial printed on the front page of the *Whig* was one man's opinion, though it was synthesized from a fair segment of the people's ideas. The advertisements carried in the inside of that paper were the statements of many people of the city. They offered French clocks, velvets, Scotch plaids, laces, French china, stoves, silverware, and pins for sale. In mid-May the city's

30. *Vicksburg Daily Whig,* May 15, 1862.

31. Shannon was not blind in his allegiance to the Confederacy. In the same issue of his paper he struck out at the government: "The Government has lost the popular confidence and heart, never to regain them. . . . By gross neglect and incompetency, we have met with such severe disasters that the public confidence has been shaken in our leaders. . . . For one long year . . . has war . . . raged on Southern territory . . . not a southern musket has been fired beyond Southern limits. . . . We are playing the part of the frogs in the pond, pelted with rocks by cruel boys, and only . . . find safety in dodging as best we can the dangerous missiles."

stores were open and luxury items as well as many staples could be bought in them. On the same page with the advertisements there were announcements of candidacies for probate judge and county sheriff in a coming election.[32]

These notices—the advertisements for pins and plaids and the election announcements—were really better indicators of the temper of the people than Shannon's editorial. There was something stolid in these advertisements that lent additional substance to the higher pitched editorial. Shannon had acted as their spokesman in the rejection of old loyalties, and the merchants and office-seekers confirmed their confidence in the new loyalties, even in the face of attack, by refusing to be stirred from the everyday course of their lives and activities.

The refusal to be stirred went further than strivings for business and political gains. Among those people who remained in the city, social activities went on much as before. Kate Stone was again in town during this period visiting a friend whose home she thought was "delightful." While there she visited several other friends whom she had known at the Nashville Female Academy and they "attended a meeting to get up a fair."[33]

Yet beneath the surface of resoluteness and gaiety a different current ran counter to the outward mood of the city. Speculation and profiteering are ugly words and the practice is even uglier, but it was inevitable that the sordid business would creep out in the city. Without regulations of any sort on merchandise and foodstuffs the public lay at the mercy of the merchants, and they had to depend upon the fairness and patriotism of the sellers to pass on their goods at reasonable prices. The temptation to increase profits through hoarding and price raising was too great for some of the merchants to resist, and the worst part of the whole business was that the price pinch went on necessities rather than luxury items. Stoves and silverware went begging, but salt became very dear.[34]

32. *Vicksburg Daily Whig,* May 15, 1862.

33. Stone, *Brokenburn,* p. 104.

34. The lack of salt in Vicksburg, as throughout the state, became so acute that in the summer of 1862, Governor Pettus sent agents through the South to scour the country for it. Ella Lonn, *Salt as a Factor in the Confederacy* (New York, 1933), pp. 292-96.

Charles Allen returned to Nanachehaw on May 10, after buying supplies in Vicksburg. He was still choleric when he opened his journal to write: "V'burg is now full of men and those there are [the] oldest merchants in the produce line, who are playing the game of 'Number One;' I am done with them." Then he became more specific: "Could not get a sack of salt—offered $100—Duff Green and Company and Rigsby have it, but won't sell—will quit Green and Crump if Duff Green is in the concern; believe he and Benj. Thomas are partners in speculation on necessaries of life."[35]

Allen could not see that he was a victim of war's poetic justice. Three days earlier he had refused to let his horses be used in defensive preparations; now the shoe was on the other foot and he did not like the way it pinched. But this was of no comfort to the people who aided with the defenses and still could not get the precious salt.

Charles Allen was just one of the many who discovered that some of the merchants were hoarding and profiteering. By May 15, the practices had become so flagrant that the *Whig* printed: "Someone has said: 'All men think all men mortal except themselves.' How true is this in reference to extortion! All men think all men extortioners but themselves! . . . They forget that in the Holy Book . . . extortioners are classed with murderers, adulterers, and liars, and not with common sinners. Think of this, ye church members, who are selling articles at one hundred times their value, and are thus preying upon the life blood of the people, and seriously jeopardizing the liberties of the country."[36]

This was a mere indication of what was to come when the city was surrounded by the enemy and there was no way to get foodstuffs through the lines. The concept of mobilization and control of civilian resources as well as military resources—or the concept of total war—was far in the future; and the hypersensitive attitude which the Southerner held toward the encroachments of a powerful government on his precious liberty—the attitude which goes a long way in explaining secession and the

35. Allen, Plantation Book, p. 71.
36. *Vicksburg Daily Whig*, May 15, 1862.

subsequent collapse of the Confederacy—would have scarcely allowed city officials to impose and enforce any sort of regulations on the buying and selling of food. When a sense of honor and humanitarianism failed the merchants, and it surely did, the people who were hungry had to depend upon the charity of their fellow citizens and that of the generous people in Mississippi and Louisiana.

On the same day Charles Allen vented his spleen on the profiteering merchants another link in the chain of river defenses broke and the gunboats steamed closer to Vicksburg. On May 10, Fort Pillow, guarding the approaches to Memphis, fell and the Confederate rams gathered there were brushed aside. General Jeff Thompson, who commanded the fort, watched the fleet as it was being wrecked. When it was done he turned from the river, said, "They are gone, and I am going," and mounted his horse and rode off.[37]

From the south Farragut's gunboats were moving nearer to Vicksburg. After holding his fleet back for over a week following the fall of New Orleans, he moved northward. On May 3, he ordered "three or four of the gunboats" to proceed to Vicksburg under the command of S. Phillips Lee.[38] A week later he urged Lee to move quickly because he had just talked with a man from Vicksburg who said that there were only six guns emplaced at the city, but that more batteries were being built. He also told Lee to try to get a gunboat up the Yazoo River to destroy the ironclad ram which was being built there. The destruction of the ram was "a thing of the first importance."[39] Lee dawdled on the way. He got to Natchez on May 12, but then it took him six days to move his boats on to Vicksburg.

On Sunday, May 18, three weeks to the day from the scrambling rush to leave the city, the gunboats steamed into view. Here finally was war. But it was not the kind of war the newspapers reported or the wounded from Shiloh told about.

37. Henry Walke, "The Western Flotilla at Fort Donelson, Island Number Ten, Fort Pillow and Memphis," *Battles and Leaders,* I, 452.

38. *Official Records Navy,* Ser. I, Vol. XVIII, 465. When Lee finally started for Vicksburg he had in his flotilla the *Oneida, Kennebec, Winona, Sciota,* and *Itasca,* and two transports loaded with troops. *Ibid.,* pp. 533, 705.

39. *Ibid.,* p. 478.

It was merely several dark, squat shapes lying silently out in the swollen river.

Noon. The sun stood straight over the river and there was no activity. Then, twenty minutes past the hour, the *Oneida* put a gig over the side; a white flag fluttered above it. The gig moved in toward the city, a faint movement in the silent scene. A single shot—the first shot fired at Vicksburg toward the enemy—split the stillness. Its echo bounced off the bluffs and the projectile raised a ruffle in the river. The gig stopped and a steamer moved out from the wharves to see what message it carried.[40] The dispatch was exchanged and an agreement was made that the gig would return at three o'clock for an answer. The message was addressed to "The Authorities at Vicksburg."

U.S.S. Oneida
Near Vicksburg, May 18, 1862

The undersigned, with orders from Flag-Officer Farragut and Major-General Butler, respectively, demand the surrender of Vicksburg and its defenses to the lawful authority of the United States, under which private property and personal rights will be respected.

Respectfully Yours,
S. Phillips Lee,
Commanding Advance Naval Division.

The same ultimatum had gotten quick results with the officials at Natchez. The Natchez mayor had replied that his city had "no alternative but to yield to an irresistible force, or uselessly . . . imperil innocent blood."[41] Lee was probably thinking of the mayor's reply while he awaited an answer from Vicksburg. Three o'clock came; the gig set off for the answer, but there was none. Finally, at five o'clock the steamer left the wharves and met the gig.[42] She carried three messages—and it was well that Lee had addressed his ultimatum to "The Authorities":

Headquarters' Vicksburg,
May 18, 1862.

Sir: As your communication of this date is addressed to "The Authorities of Vicksburg," and that you may have a full reply to

40. *Ibid.*, pp. 782-83.
41. *Ibid.*, p. 491.
42. *Ibid.*, p. 783.

said communication, I have to state that Mississippians don't know, and refuse to learn, how to surrender to an enemy. If Commodore Farragut or Brigadier-General Butler can teach them, let them come and try.

As to the defense of Vicksburg, I respectfully refer you to Brigadier-General Smith, commanding forces at and near Vicksburg, whose reply is herewith enclosed.

Respectfully,
Jas. L. Autry,
Military Governor and Colonel,
Commanding Post.

General Smith had this to say:

Headquarters Defenses of Vicksburg,
May 18, 1862.

Sir: Your communication of this date addressed to "The Authorities of Vicksburg," demanding the surrender of the city and its defenses, has been received.

Regarding the surrender of the defense, I have to reply that having been ordered to hold these defenses, it is my intention to do so as long as in my power.

Respectfully,
M. L. Smith
Brigadier-General, Commanding

General Smith and Colonel Autry replied for the military and for the Confederate government. A third message came from the mayor; he spoke for the people of Vicksburg:

Mayor's Office
Vicksburg, Miss.,
May 18, 1862.

Your communication of this date addressed to "The authorities at Vicksburg" has been delivered to me.

In reply, I will state to you that as far as the municipal authorities are concerned we have erected no defenses, and none are within the corporative limits of the city; but, sir, in further reply, I will state that neither the municipal authorities nor the citizens will ever consent to a surrender of the city.

Respectfully yours,
L. Lindsay,
Mayor of the City.[43]

43. This series of documents may be found in *ibid.,* pp. 492-93.

If Lee was not satisfied with the replies, at least he was sure that all of the "authorities" had seen his ultimatum. He studied their notes, decided that nothing more could be done at the present, and ordered the *Oneida* to drop below the city. The remainder of the flotilla followed him and just about twilight their anchor chains rattled through the hawse-pipes.

The next day was quiet. During the morning the officer of the deck on the *Oneida* saw a large fire above Vicksburg, which was probably someone's cotton crop going up in smoke. That afternoon he saw three little river steamers go scuttling into the city's wharves. That was all and the gunboats remained silent on the river.

The following day, Tuesday, began quietly, but ended with gunfire. In the late afternoon the gunners on the *Oneida* saw some troops on the bluffs and blasted away at them.[44] Captain Lee tried to force the issue. On Wednesday, May 21, he notified Mayor Lindsay that he would commence an attack on the town. He gave Lindsay twenty-four hours to remove the women and children "as it will be impossible to attack the defenses without injuring or destroying the town, a proceeding which all of the authorities of Vicksburg seem determined to require." He closed his message with the hope that "the same spirit" which prevailed at New Orleans would be manifested at Vicksburg, thus sparing the city from damage.[45]

The message got to Lindsay late in the afternoon. He replied that it was too late in the day to make the public announcement, and that he would compute the twenty-four hour period as commencing at 8:00 A.M. on the twenty-second.

The next day Lee answered that this was unacceptable. It was his "option to fire or not . . . at the earliest moment." On the afternoon of May 22, the guns opened in earnest.[46]

44. *Ibid.,* p. 783.
45. *Official Records Army,* Ser. I, Vol. XV, p. 13.
46. *Ibid.,* pp. 13-14.

Chapter VI

"WE CAN FEEL THE SHOCK VERY SENSIBLY"

An eleven-inch naval cannon was a murderous weapon. Swollen at the breech, long and grey-black, it tapered toward the muzzle where its almost foot-wide bore gaped dark and empty. A heavy iron and oak carriage, lacings of chains, ropes, and pulleys, and a number of men were required to pull the gun into battery, serve its projectile, then haul it back after it was fired. Its projectile weighed 166 pounds and had a range of several miles; it could smash through brick walls and dig great gouges out of the ground. The gun's shock action, the capability of causing fear, was almost as great as its destructive power. It was the personification of war—with the waiting, the fear, the moment of clamor and impersonal destruction, then the waiting again.

Vicksburg shuddered under the naval gunfire. The shelling was not heavy or concentrated, but it was enough to start a new exodus from the city. Many of the people who had refused to be frightened by rumor and who had remained in their homes when the first wave of refugees left the city now departed. They had waited to see what would happen; now they knew, and a second movement of civilians commenced.

The shelling decided Max Kuner. A friend offered him the use of an abandoned plantation house about ten miles out in the country, which he was glad to accept "because all available shelter for miles around was being rapidly taken up." Finding a place to stay was one problem; moving there was another, for all of the serviceable horses and mules had been requisitioned for use by the artillery and the cavalry. Finally Kuner found an old, broken-down horse, which cost him ten dollars, and the tired beast pulled the family out of the city.

When the Kuners arrived at their new home they found the "walls in tatters" and pigs in the basement. Four other families joined them and Kuner had to support them all. He even took in an old Negro and a decrepit mule, but he did not mind for they were all safe.[1]

Doctor William Lord, the Episcopal rector, moved his family. He would remain in the city to keep his church open and serve as a chaplain, but he wanted his wife and children to be out of gunfire range. He buried his silverware in the churchyard, packed books and clothing into a wagon and a carriage, and sent the family to a plantation on the Big Black. Mrs. Lord remained on the plantation a few days to get the children settled, then returned to Vicksburg. She was worried about her husband and wanted to be with him, even if it meant facing the shelling.[2]

Rowland Chambers could stand on his front porch, see a cottony puff of smoke and hear a dull report from the river, then hear the snapping rush of air as a shell passed overhead. He was an itinerant dentist and jack-of-all-trades who had been in Vicksburg for only a few days. He had brought his family and servants with him and had just opened his practice when the shelling started. The cannon fire did not bother him, but as it frightened his wife and daughter he sent them to the country with two servants.[3]

Emma Crutcher left Vicksburg with a light heart, for her husband had returned from Virginia. Captain Crutcher had been invalided out of the army and Vicksburg was manifestly no place in which to convalesce. The couple moved to Clinton, found a place to themselves, and Emma began to nurse her husband back to health. After a while he was strong enough to be up, and they attended church services held in the Clinton Hotel because all of the churches were filled with sick and wounded soldiers. Much of their conversation centered about

1. [Kuner], "Vicksburg and After," *The Sewanee Review,* XV, 486.

2. William W. Lord, "A Child at the Siege of Vicksburg," *Harper's Monthly Magazine,* CXVIII (December, 1908), 44.

3. Rowland Chambers, Diary, May 28, 1862, Department of Archives and Manuscripts, Louisiana State University.

the attack on Vicksburg, and Emma, with a touch of pride, wrote her mother: ". . . the country people seem to think it strange that Father has not moved his printing office—knowing, as they do, that everything else has been taken out of Vicksburg."[4]

General Smith inspected the city during this period. He observed that many homes were closed, that the city was "sparsely populated and somewhat prepared for . . . attack," that other people were preparing to leave, but also that there were still "many who had determined to remain and take the chance of escaping unharmed."[5]

Vicksburg was now a garrison and was rapidly becoming a fortress. The raw slash of earthworks cut across the springtime green; roads were rutted by wagons and caissons; stores were closed and some of the merchants who remained had begun to demand cash for all purchases.[6] Major Winchester Hall looked about him and decided: "Vicksburg looked as if the simoon of war already had swept over it, the lowlands were flooded, the city deserted by all who could leave, [and] business houses that were not closed were barren of goods . . . ."[7]

But life did not cease, values merely changed, and they took some strange twists. War might be gunboats on the river and the possibility of death, but it was also merely doing without some things which were previously considered to be necessary. Kate Stone thought so, for she was quite as interested in, and sensitive to, changing fashions as the struggle for possession of the city. In her diary she briefly noted that she could hear the sound of the Vicksburg guns, then she wrote:

> Clothes have become a secondary consideration. Fashion is an obsolete word and just to be decently clad is all we expect. The change in dress, habits, and customs is nowhere more striking than in the towns. A year ago a gentleman never thought of carrying a bundle, even a small one, through the streets. Broadcloth was *de rigueur*. Ceremony and fashion ruled the land. Presto-change.

4. Emma Crutcher to Lavinia Shannon, June 8, 1862, Phillip Crutcher Collection, Miss. Arch.

5. *Official Records Army*, Ser. I, Vol, XV, p. 7.

6. *Vicksburg Daily Whig*, May 15, 1862.

7. Winchester Hall, *The Story of the 26th Louisiana Infantry, in the of the Confederate States* (n.p., 1890), p. 13.

Now the highest in rank may be seen doing any kind of work that their hands find to do. The men have become "hewers of wood and drawers of water" and pack bundles of all sorts and sizes. It may be a pile of blankets, a stack of buckets, or a dozen bundles. One gentleman I saw walking down the street . . . had a piece of fish in one hand, a cavalry saddle on his back, bridle, blankets, newspapers, and a small parcel in the other hand; and over his shoulder swung an immense pair of cavalry boots. And nobody thought he looked odd. Their willingness to fetch and carry is only limited by their strength . . . . Broadcloth is worn only by the drones and fireside braves. Dyed linsey is now the fashionable material for coats and pants. Vests are done away with . . . . A gentleman thinks nothing of calling on half a dozen young ladies dressed in home-dyed Negro cloth and blue checked shirt . . . .

Then Kate, a member of the planter class, summed it all up: "In proportion as we have been a race of haughty, indolent, and waited-on people, so now are we ready to do away with all forms and work and wait on ourselves."[8]

Winchester Hall could have seen the same sight in Vicksburg, but if he did it did not register in his mind. He thought that Vicksburg was a desolate place, for he was an urbane Louisianian and was accustomed to New Orleans' brilliant face, but another soldier received an entirely different impression of the city under attack.

William Chambers had grown up in the piney woods of Mississippi and his railway trip through Jackson to Vicksburg had been his most adventurous and lengthy journey. When he arrived in Vicksburg he spent the first Sunday of June, a misty, rainy day, walking through the city. He thought Vicksburg was a lovely city. When he returned to camp he opened his journal and wrote: "The City itself is a study . . . . The streets are located and houses are built [along the hills], the side walks of one street often being on a level with . . . the roofs of the houses on the next street below. The most beautiful yards and gardens I [have] ever seen [are] here, generally arranged in terraces, with stone stairways between, and I also saw finer buildings than I [have]

8. Stone, *Brokenburn,* pp. 109-10.

ever seen before. The court House . . . has a much more imposing appearance than the Capital at Jackson."[9]

So war, even a focal point of attack, is like all things, relative. One man arrived in Vicksburg and saw desolation, another came and found beauty. Both desolation and beauty were in the city. Empty houses stood dark and shuttered, while behind them in their gardens flowers and grass were brilliant in the sun. Simple things such as grass and sunlight seemed to take on added meaning and interest for some of the people. Perhaps it was because nature was immutable and its certainty was a pleasant contrast to the precariousness and pall that the gunboats had brought. At any event May 25 was warm and bright, and this in itself was enough to cause comment and pleasure.[10]

The same day, on the river, the gunboat captains met with Farragut and General Williams to discuss the feasibility of landing troops and assaulting the town. Williams believed that with the number of soldiers he had, he could not successfully attack the city. Captain De Camp thought at least a naval attack should be made, as the Confederates had "insultingly" answered Lee's demand for surrender. Captain Alden alternately voted for attack, then against it, finally hid his face in his hands, agreed with the majority, and proposed that the vote should be made unanimous—no. Farragut, sick and fidgety, reluctantly agreed. The risk of running the boats close under the shore batteries, without troops to attack and spike the guns, was too great. Instead of assaulting Vicksburg, Williams would set to work digging a canal which was designed to channel the Mississippi through a by-pass around the city and away from its guns. Farragut would send the fleet below the city, blockade the river, occasionally lob a shot at the town to harass the defenders, and wait for the coming of the northern (or upper) fleet which was steaming down from Memphis. No mention was made of the ironclad ram being built on the Yazoo—the destruction of which Farragut had previously said was of "the first importance."[11]

9. William P. Chambers, "My Journal," ed. Ruth Polk, *Publications of the Mississippi Historical Society,* V (1925), 241.

10. Stone, *Brokenburn,* p. 112.

11. "Private Diary of Commander H. H. Bell," *Official Records Navy,* Ser. I, Vol. XVIII, p. 706.

The people of Vicksburg knew of the boat. Rumors concerning the ram had come drifting out of the delta country, but the people did not take them very seriously. The Navy Department could not even find a crew for the boat and advertisements in the *Whig,* offering a fifty-dollar bounty and pay of twenty-five dollars a month for seamen and even landsmen, failed to attract much interest, though there were experienced rivermen in the city without work.[12]

During the latter part of May a naval lieutenant slipped into town. He remained for a few days, receiving on May 28 a telegram from the Navy Department ordering him to his new command—the *Arkansas.* Isaac N. Brown did not waste any time; the same day he received the order he boarded a little river steamer bound for Greenwood, Mississippi. He was paid little attention and left Vicksburg without fanfare.

When he arrived at Greenwood and saw his ship, Brown's heart sank. The river was up, backwaters flooded far over the banks of the Yazoo, and the hulk of the *Arkansas* floated four miles from dry land. Brown's command was an unfinished hull with no engines, no armor, no gun carriages, few crewmen, and the railroad iron intended to be the armor lay sunk on the bottom of the Yazoo.

The iron was fished up and the *Arkansas* was towed to Yazoo City, fifty miles from Vicksburg. Brown had his wits, his ingenuity, a good executive officer, and very little else to turn the hulk into a fighting ship. He borrowed over two hundred soldiers to augument his crew; he scoured plantations for forges to use with the iron work; he found abandoned and unused railway tracks to supplement his existing stock; he selected trees to be used in the construction of gun carriages; and all the while he kept an apprehensive eye turned downriver, for he feared a surprise attack on the unprepared vessel.

May slipped into June, then June into July. The summer sun leached the unprotected workers. When the sun set and the evening coolness settled on the delta, banks of mosquitoes rose from the swamps to torment the men; and in the distance they could hear the guns at Vicksburg. The only consoling

12. *Vicksburg Daily Whig,* May 15, 1862.

The *Arkansas,* being built by Isaac Brown and his crew from scrapped rails and boilerplate, worked in forges requisitioned from surrounding plantations. (From *Battles and Leaders of the Civil War*)

thought Brown could muster was that Oliver Hazard Perry, under much the same circumstances, had cut a ship out of the forests in ninety days.

Slowly Brown's masterpiece of improvisation, cajoling, begging, and inspiration took shape. The deck lay almost at water level; amidships the superstructure, slant-sided and capped by a smokestack, arose like a box. The box was made of wood a foot thick. Iron rails were bolted over the wood and were supposed to be curved around the rear of the box, but there was no machinery to bend the rails and the stern was left unprotected. Ten guns were mounted inside the box, three to a broadside and two forward and aft. The engines, set deep in the hull, drove two propellers which had the frustrating habit of rarely stopping at the same time, thus pushing the *Arkansas* round in a circle. There was no paint, but the iron rails took care of that. Their rust, streaked and run down the sides, gave the ship some color, and Farragut later described the *Arkansas* as being chocolate-hued.[13]

13. Isaac N. Brown, "The Confederate Gun-Boat 'Arkansas,'" *Battles and Leaders,* III, 572.

While Brown was commencing his work the last link in the river defense chain above Vicksburg was shattered on June 6, when Memphis fell to the northern fleet. Now the Union navy could navigate the river between the Gulf of Mexico and Vicksburg, and from the headwaters of the Mississippi south to Vicksburg. The city stood alone. Its little arc of cannon and the rusty boat, still abuilding on the Yazoo, were all that separated two Union fleets. The pincers had almost snapped shut.

On June 24, 1862, Colonel Alfred W. Ellet, a soldier commanding the Union fleet of rams north of Vicksburg, sent his son, his nephew, and two other men to locate Farragut, who was south of the city. The little party splashed through sloughs and swamps, sometimes up to their necks in water, slipped by Confederate pickets, and finally got to Farragut. Ever so tenuously the pincers had closed around Vicksburg.[14]

Mortarboats had already been brought up from the south, and their lazily arching shots were falling into the city.[15] Now the northern fleet added their weight of metal, and the people of Vicksburg, no longer uninterested, asked for news of the *Arkansas* and anxiously awaited the moment when she would come out of the Yazoo for a try at the Union fleet.[16]

The people were also asking other questions. The queries were chiefly about food, and how to get it. Food became scarcer and prices climbed. A bushel of corn meal sold for two dollars and a bushel of field peas was priced at $2.50. Salted fat pork, the cheapest of meats and formerly used for slave rations, was forty cents a pound—when it could be bought. Yet at the same time there was waste and carelessness in the handling of food as large stores of molasses were allowed to ferment and spoil under the sun.[17]

High prices were merely a manifestation of shortage, not the cause. The cause lay with the bombardment, for the range of the Union guns marked a line separating scarcity from abund-

14. *Official Records Navy,* Ser. I, Vol. XVIII, 584, 750.

15. Martin L. Smith to Earl Van Dorn, June 2, 1862, Van Dorn Papers, Library of Congress.

16. Edward G. Butler to Ann Butler, July 18, 1862, Butler Family Papers (E), Department of Archives and Manuscripts, Louisiana State University.

17. Allen, Plantation Book, p. 69.

ance. In the country early crops were beginning to ripen and there was plenty of food, yet it remained on the farms and plantations and only an insufficient trickle found its way into the city. The planters refused to expose their slaves, who ordinarily brought the produce to market, to the danger of shellfire and the stores remained partially empty. Even the people who camped just beyond the rim of the danger zone found difficulty in obtaining enough to eat. In the *Whig,* Marmaduke Shannon appealed to the "patriotism and humanity" of the planters to supply food to the hungry people camped on the edge of the city, as it could be done "without danger." He did not even attempt to persuade them to bring their produce into the city and run the risk of being subjected to "the annoyance we daily experience from the enemy"; perhaps he thought he would be wasting his ink.[18]

Those who remained tightened their belts and went underground. Until the mortarboats came the people had found safety behind the reverse slopes—the sides away from the river—of the hills. The flat trajectoried naval guns could not reach over the hills and down the far sides. The mortars could. They fired a shot high into the air, which fell almost perpendicularly and left no backside hill, gully, or creekbed safe. Now the only place for shelter was beneath the earth's surface, and the people started digging. Vicksburg began to be turned into a city of caves.

The caves measured the ebb and flow of war around the city. In the beginning they were simple affairs, usually a little hole scooped out of a hillside. There were not many of them as there were few people in the city and the bombardment was not severe. Then for nine months, the time between the lifting of the naval siege and the combined assault of the Union army and navy, no new shelters were built—there was no need for them—and the erosion of wind and water worked on the existing ones. When Grant with all his fury swept in behind the city, cave building became big business. Caught in a cross fire between the artillery and the naval guns, the people honeycombed the hills with elaborate tunnels in which they could live for days, and in

18. *Vicksburg Daily Whig,* July 1, 1862.

doing so even developed a cave psychology. But that was all to come. In June 1862, the simple shelters served the purpose.

The movement underground was just one of the many aspects of a people changing their way of life to accommodate themselves to attack. In the early days of June the Sisters of Mercy closed their convent school. After the students were dismissed the sisters opened the convent to the sick and wounded, and for a while stayed to nurse them. At the outbreak of the bombardment the sisters were given the choice of leaving the city or remaining to do what good works they could; seven sisters left immediately, but three of the seven soon returned. As June wore on, and the attack showed no indication of abating, plans were made to move the order. In late June 1862, all of the sisters left. They went first to the military hospital at Mississippi Springs, then to hospitals at Jackson and Oxford. They would not return to Vicksburg until May 28, 1865.[19]

Sick and wounded troops were also taken into the homes of the citizens. Winchester Hall's Twenty-sixth Louisiana Regiment was hard hit with measles and the military medical service was incapable of caring for them. By a few discreet inquiries and hints Hall found places and nurses for the stricken men, though sometimes they had to be content to lie on bare floors rather than beds.[20]

The military authorities began to clamp travel restrictions on the civilians. Persons desiring to leave the city had to obtain proper military authorization and passes before they could move. A provost marshal's office was established in the center of town to issue the passes, though they were not difficult to obtain and the authorities probably sought merely to keep account of who was moving rather than seriously to curtail travel.[21]

Transportation was more affected by the gunboats than by Confederate military regulations. It was now risky business to venture out on the river. A few steamboats still sneaked down along the Yazoo and the Big Black, then darted into Vicksburg; but they did not run on schedule, and they came into the city

19. Register, Convent of the Sisters of Mercy, Vicksburg, unnumbered pages.

20. Hall, *26th Louisiana,* pp. 14-15.

21. *Vicksburg Daily Whig,* May 15, 1862.

only when their captains thought they might be able to slip by the Union vessels. Train service was still available to the east, but it was haphazard, and Emma Crutcher wrote her mother that "the cars pass [Clinton] irregularly."[22]

Despite the strictures the people still moved and communicated, though sometimes not in the direction which appears at first glance. Some persons found safety in the country; others fled to the Union fleet. Perhaps they had taken all of the pounding and shortages they were able to absorb; perhaps now that United States forces were close, latent Unionism could more safely show its head; whatever the reasons contacts were opened with the Federal navy.

On the afternoon of June 23, the officer of the deck aboard the *Richmond* was surprised by a sight on the riverbank. A woman stood there with a small boy. She waved a white handkerchief to indicate that she wished to come aboard; when she was questioned she said simply that she was a refugee from Vicksburg.[23] The attackers were able to learn as much about conditions inside the city as the defenders themselves knew. Union sympathizers along the river supplied the fleet with Vicksburg newspapers—one officer on the *Richmond* reported that they received the papers every day.[24] Farragut was in constant touch with refugees, and they gave him detailed accounts of happenings within the city, though they often exaggerated the suffering and destruction.[25]

The trail of Unionism stretched all the way from Washington to Vicksburg. On June 25, R. A. Watkinson, an employee of the Navy Department, wrote to Flag Officer Charles H. Davis suggesting contacts which might be established inside Vicksburg. Watkinson said that he had "lived a long time in the region," and knew that "there must be in the town a large element of latent Unionism." He believed that William C. Smedes and "a Burwell, of Virginia . . . belonged to this class." He also said that A. B. Reading, one of the foundry owners, was a "traitor by force of circumstance."[26]

22. Emma Crutcher to Lavinia Shannon, June 8, 1862, Crutcher Collection.
23. *Official Records Navy,* Ser. I, Vol. XVIII, 749.
24. *Ibid.,* p. 750.
25. *Ibid.,* Ser. I, Vol. XIX, 81.
26. *Ibid.,* Ser. I, Vol. XXIII, 227.

The implication of Watkinson's letter was this: here is a list of persons who are Union men, all that must be done to turn them to use is to communicate with them. But it was not that simple. In the security of his Washington office the issue of loyalties might be clear-cut to Watkinson, but in Vicksburg it was a complex tissue of many considerations—the chief one being living in peace. Smedes had long since given up the struggle and had written a lengthy defense on the right of the Southern states to secede.[27] Burwell was still a deep-dyed Unionist, but would remain silent until the city fell; then he would feel safe to open communication with United States authorities. Reading's foundry continued to cast arms and ammunition for the Confederacy until Grant marched into the city. Watkinson's suggestion came to a dead end, and in doing so indicated something of the Unionists' situation in Vicksburg.

Their position, in a place which was under attack by the nation they espoused, was manifestly precarious, and silence was their greatest protection. Alexander Arthur, an unbending Unionist, kept his own counsel, went about his business, and was left unbothered. When a young Unionist couple from New Orleans came to Vicksburg they too remained silent. They tried to fit themselves into the life of the city, and gave no outward sign that they were opposed to the Confederacy. The price of overt opposition was high; a friend of Arthur's named Wesson found it to be so. He refused to join the army, talked too much about the strength of the United States, and was forced to exile himself for a while.[28]

The fact that some of the men still refused to enlist in the army, choosing instead to take membership in the home guard, rankled some of the women. They took to satire to spur into field service those whom they considered to be laggards and circulated this broadside in the city: "To Arms! To Arms!—There will be a meeting of the young ladies of Warren county, to be held . . . for the purpose of forming themselves into a Home

27. William C. Smedes, *In Vindication of the Southern Confederacy* (Jackson, Mississippi, 1861), *passim.*

28. Alexander H. Arthur to Joseph Holt, May 26, 1865, Joseph Holt Papers, Library of Congress.

Guard, for the protection of those young men who will not volunteer for the country's cause."[29]

The city government finally showed a flicker of life when, on June 16, the council managed to obtain a quorum and held their first meeting since May 5. The civil affairs of the city had already passed from their control by default if for no other reason, but they did manage to appropriate $318.75 to be used to defray the costs of moving indigent families from the city. Other than this single action they made no attempt to govern or care for the people, preferring to leave that responsibility to the provost marshal. The meeting of June 16 was the council's sole session while Vicksburg was under attack.[30]

The county government, seated in the city, also ground to a halt. Public officials as well as private citizens scattered before the enemy, seemingly without a thought or qualm about abandoning their offices. The county clerk's office closed on June 19 and did not reopen until long after the bombardment had ceased. Yet before the office closed enough people had registered property transfers to indicate that the wave of fear-caused selling initiated by the fall of New Orleans was still strong.[31]

Now the city seemed empty and silent. William Allen came to town, looked about, then returned home and wrote: "Vicksburg is deserted . . . no one [is there] except soldiers."[32] This was an overstatement for Shannon still published his paper, a few shops were open, the post office and depot were open, but it was as though an air of expectancy, of waiting, hung over the city. Anyone could look across the river to the Louisiana shore and see Union soldiers and impressed slaves digging at the ground, trying to cut a new channel for the Mississippi which would isolate Vicksburg and render her guns harmless. Anyone could look out on the river and see the *Oneida,* the *Richmond,* the *Brooklyn,* the *Hartford,* the *Miami,* and the swarm of supporting ships, as they conducted the slow bombardment; and between the reports of the guns the strains of the "Star Spangled

29. Reprinted in the *New York Sunday Mercury,* June 18, 1862, quoted in *The Rebellion Record: A Diary of American Events,* ed. Frank Moore (New York, 1867), II, 57.
30. Council Minute Book, p. 166.
31. Warren County Deed Book CC, entries for June, 1862.
32. Allen, Plantation Book, pp. 78, 85.

Banner" came drifting faintly from the boats, which was something not calculated to improve the morale of the defenders.[33] The initiative rested with the Federal fleet. In Vicksburg all anyone could do was wait, and watch, and see what would happen.

On June 24, the tempo of action increased. Just before sundown Ellet's little party of messengers reported to Farragut, and rockets announcing the approach of the upper fleet blazed in the night sky north of Vicksburg. An officer aboard the *Richmond* noted that "great excitement prevails in the city on account of the two fleets meeting."[34] The civilians as well as the military men knew that the only way the two fleets could rendezvous was for one of them to run the Vicksburg batteries, which was an entirely different proposition from standing to one side of the city and haphazardly lobbing shells at fortifications and homes. When the attempt to pass the batteries was made every gun on both sides would come into fast and furious action.

The Confederates would have their first real opportunity to deal Farragut's fleet a crippling blow, for the boats would have to pass the city broadside, their speed would be cut by the current of the river, and their lightly armored decks and cabin tops would be exposed to the plunging fire of the batteries sited high on the bluffs.

The best chance for success for the fleet lay in slipping by the batteries in the dark when it would be difficult for the Confederate gunners to see their targets and in bringing every gun they could to bear on the defenses, thus smothering the batteries with a blanket of fire. The consequence of this was that the city as well as the batteries would receive an onslaught of shells.

For two days Farragut worked to prepare his fleet. Splinter nets were hung over the sides of the ships, barrels of sand were stacked around the engines, chains and bags of coal were piled on the decks, and mortarboats were towed into positions which gave them "a good view" of the city.[35] In the city the people waited; there was nothing else they could do.

33. *Official Records Navy,* Ser. I, Vol. XVIII, 750.
34. *Ibid.* 35. *Ibid.*

June 26: the sky was clear and the sun was hot. In mid-afternoon the mortarboats opened a rapid fire on the city. They continued the action until sundown and the Confederate guns scarcely fired a shot in return. The next morning the mortars commenced the bombardment at daybreak. Later in the day the gunboats moved in to add their metal to the shelling. The firing continued all day and on into the night. No Confederate gun answered. The pounding began to shake the defenders, civilian and soldier alike, and the silence of their batteries began to grate on their nerves. William Chambers was afraid and was not ashamed to admit it: "I confess I was uneasy and nervous, in fact was badly demoralized . . . . One feels utterly defenseless, unless there is a chance to strike back. . . ."[36]

Rowland Chambers' reaction was quite different. After they had finished supper, he and his brother went outside and sat unprotected on a horseblock watching the shelling. Chambers, undisturbed, thought it was "a most grand display of fireworks." At 10:00 P.M. the firing ceased and with nothing else to see he went to bed. He lay in bed and listened to the "deadly stillness" which had fallen over the river.[37]

There was no moon in the sky; the city sat shrouded on the bluffs, and the dark, silent hours passed by.[38] Then at 3:00 A.M. the sound of anchor chains being raised rattled up the river. Farragut's fleet was in motion. The *Oneida* led the way, the other boats in line behind her with gunports open and cannon rolled out. Slowly they came abreast of the sleeping city and there was still no sign of alarm. Then the mortars opened fire, the captains of the ships ordered full steam, the broadsides lashed out at the city, and the Confederate cannon began to answer.

The unsuspecting people were routed from their sleep by the explosions. This was the first night attack and the first concentrated bombardment they had experienced, and they tumbled from their beds groggy and panicked. In the light of the ex-

36. Chambers, "My Journal," *Publications of the Mississippi Historical Society,* V, 240.

37. Chambers, Diary, June 27, 1862.

38. *The Confederate States Almanac for . . . 1862* (Nashville, Tennessee, 1862), p. 9.

plosions Marmaduke Shannon watched their terror: "Men, women and children, both black and white, went screaming through the streets . . . some dressed and others almost nude . . . . One man [carried] his wife in his arms—she having fainted with fright."[39] They stumbled to whatever shelter they could find, gaining what comfort they could from the sound of their own guns giving as good as they got.

At first the fight was in the dark; stabs of light were the only targets. Though he was busy at a cannon, a simile popped into Hugh Moss's mind: ". . . the shells fell so fast that they looked like stars falling from the heavens—it was a sublime, but dangerous scene—the flashes of the cannon were that of lightning and its rumbling was that of thunder."[40] Aboard the *Richmond* an officer looked toward the shore and it appeared to him that the batteries surrounded the city with "one line of flame."[41]

But the gauntlet was long, and before the last ships had run it they lay exposed in the sunlight. The firing was heavy and sustained, the ranges easier to compute, and on the *Richmond* "brains and blood [were] flying all over the decks." Then it was over. At 5:40 A.M. the last ship passed the batteries, but below the city the mortars and the *Brooklyn* hammered away for two more hours until, at 8:00 A.M., they too fell silent.[42] In the city one woman was dead and several people were wounded. Shells had struck homes, and the Methodist and Catholic churches.[43]

Swashbuckling Major General Earl Van Dorn, always seeking glory but already defeated at Pea Ridge, was newly appointed commander of Confederate forces in southern Mississippi. He had been in Vicksburg only one day when the Federal fleet ran the batteries. After the action he telegraphed Jefferson Davis: "Bombardment heavy yesterday and this morning. No flinching. Houses perforated; none burned yet . . . . All sound and fury and to brave men contemptible."[44]

Rowland Chambers would never express himself through words such as Van Dorn's, but he lived the spirit of the general's

39. *Vicksburg Daily Whig,* July 1, 1862.
40. *Diary of A. Hugh Moss* (n.p., 1948), p. 19.
41. *Official Records Navy,* Ser. I, Vol. XVIII, 751.
42. *Ibid.*
43. *Vicksburg Daily Whig,* July 1, 1862; Allen, Plantation Book, p. 75.
44. *Official Records Army,* Ser. I, Vol. XV, 14.

report. He did not allow the shelling to interrupt his social activities, for even on the days of heavy bombardment he made his way through the city to visit friends and also received them in his home. On June 30, as the bombardment slackened, Chambers noted in his diary that there was "occasional fireing," but this did not deter him from working in his garden. He spent most of the day setting out sweet potato slips, unmindful of the shells which were exploding in the city.[45]

The heavy attack did, however, affect some of the civilians. Dr. Emanuel finally admitted that the danger to his trains and to passengers gathered at the depot was too great to continue to bring the trains into the city. He posted notice that for the duration of the attack the trains would stop two miles outside the city; both passengers and freight would be loaded and deposited at that point, and service was curtailed to one eastbound train a day. The travelers were also inspected to insure that they had obtained passes permitting them to leave the city.[46] Two other public services were moved with the railroad terminal. The telegraph station and the post office were also relocated outside the city, and as they were moved the people's feeling of isolation increased.[47]

Marmaduke Shannon's printers began to complain of the danger and the editor was forced to agree with them. On July 1, the *Whig* suspended regular publication, because, said Shannon, "With the enemy's shot and shell falling around us . . . we cannot ask the printers to work." He did not venture to guess the length of the suspension; perhaps it would be "a few days—perhaps months." At any event, Shannon would not quit entirely; he promised to print a paper when he could manage to do so, or "publish the news in extra form."[48]

Shannon was reluctant to suspend publication of his paper; for, as he counted them, there were "many families . . . still living in town," and he thought it was his duty to supply them with the news. The people who remained fell into three groups:

45. Chambers, Diary, June 29, 30, 1862.
46. *Vicksburg Daily Whig,* July 1, 1862.
47. Edward G. Butler to Ann Butler, July 12, 1862, Butler Family Papers (E).
48. *Vicksburg Daily Whig,* July 1, 1862.

those who absolutely refused to be frightened from their homes; those who could not find a place to which to move; and those who could not afford to move. Their reasons for remaining to suffer the bombardment were varied, but they faced common hazards and problems.

The scarcity of food became more acute, yet if the inhabitants so desired they could purchase stoves, wagons, pistols, plows, carpets, and even Italian marble in the city's stores.[49]

The problem of obtaining enough to eat faced the soldiers as well as the civilians, and as a consequence the soldiers became almost as unpopular as the Union navy. The vicissitudes connected with being part of a fortress began to multiply as the people discovered that living in a beleaguered city meant not only that they should suffer at the hands of the enemy, but also that their defenders were a mixed blessing, as some of the soldiers seemed to think that private property should be regarded as community property. Anything in the city that was eatable was considered to be fair game. Rowland Chambers' food stock suffered because of the soldiers. In the space of a few days his ripening peach crop was looted and a large pig was stolen.[50]

Even the loss of valuable food did not sour Chambers, for he was something of a philosopher at heart. He wasted little time with recrimination and found pleasure when he could. On the Fourth of July he wrote: "This is a lovely morning perfectly cloudless with a gentle breze and not too hot to be pleasant, everything quiet and a person could hardly Realiz that he was in the center between two large armies intent on nothing but death and destruction of every thing within their reach."[51] Little did he realize as he wrote these words that they would be equally true a year later.

That afternoon as the bombardment recommenced, William Chambers counted the shells as they fell into the city. He tallied 150 explosions, then laconically wrote: "In commemeration of Independence Day, I suppose." That night he and others watched as the fleets gave a fireworks display.[52]

49. *Ibid.*

50. Chambers, Diary, July 3, 9, 1862.

51. *Ibid.*, July 4, 1862.

52. Chambers, "My Journal," *Publications of the Mississippi Historical Society,* V, 243-44.

Earlier that day General Van Dorn issued an order which was as pyrotechnic as the Federal fireworks. In General Order Number 9, which would be denounced from private homes in Vicksburg to the capitol in Richmond, he declared martial law in a band of river and coastal counties. Martial law was defined as "the will of the military commander" and was imposed to curb disloyalty. *"Disloyalty,"* the order read, *"must and will not be countenanced . . . . The seeds of dissention and dissatisfaction shall not be sown among the troops. Speculation and extortion upon soldiers and citizens will not be tolerated . . . ."* Anyone who attempted to trade with the enemy would be sentenced to death. Anyone who refused to accept Confederate money, who published information regarding troop movements, who sought to impair confidence in commanding officers, or who charged exorbitant prices would be subject to fine, imprisonment, and property confiscation.[53] Reaction was violent and instantaneous, but the *Whig,* on July 11, circumspectly carried no mention of the order. George W. Randolph, Secretary of War, did not wait for Congress to complete the debate concerning the issue—he rushed Van Dorn a countermanding order and, on September 5, Van Dorn publicly apologized for his unauthorized action.[54] Civilians who had been convicted for violating the order were released from jail and the people of Vicksburg retained the right to live under civil jurisdiction.

On July 11, when neither side fired, Shannon kept his promise to supply the news by publishing an issue of the *Whig.* The paper reminded the people that they were fighting a two-front war—casualty lists from the Seven Days Battle in Virginia were printed with comments concerning casualties at Vicksburg. Shannon devoted a column to a summing up of almost two months of attack in which he gave the lie to accounts of widespread destruction: "The terrace[d] hill'd city . . . presents today a desolate yet . . . sublime appearance . . . . No buildings have been destroyed, and the city at a distance presents its wonted appearance. There have been no casualties since [June 28] and those citizens remaining appear to have become 'used to it.' "

53. *Official Records Army,* Ser. I, Vol. XV, 771-72.
54. *Ibid.,* Vol. XVIII, Pt. 2, 694.

Though the buildings stood relatively undamaged, the heart had been cut out of the city: "Our streets which of old teemed with the tide of business, now echo the tread of the sentinel as he paces his weary rounds . . . . Had a simoon fresh from a Upas grove blown its destructive and poisonous blast over our city, the effect could scarcely be more appaling than that caused by the presence of the enemy . . . ."[55]

Shannon did find one brief item which he inserted to add a touch of levity to the somber picture he had painted. He reported the capture of a single sailor, "a real live Yankee," who was sent through Vicksburg on his way to prison. Shannon thought the man's political inclination "seem to be of the Greely school."[56] This was the best humor he could muster.

Though Shannon and other citizens might mourn their city as being desolate, it nevertheless seemed a haven to some people—especially those who lived in occupied territory. While the guns pounded away, refugees from Louisiana filtered into town. Charles Allen saw one man, an old acquaintance, making his way toward Vicksburg. He had been three weeks coming from New Orleans and had walked the entire distance. He carried a coat, cravat, and carpet bag, which was all that he had managed to salvage from his estate. Allen told the man that Vicksburg was under attack, but that made no difference for he continued on his way.[57]

After the ferocious hours of June 28, a certain sameness characterized the passing days. The fleets returned to their practice of a harassing bombardment, occasionally answered by the Confederate batteries. The Fourth of July fireworks and a complete day of safety, July 11, when neither side fired, stood out as singular events, but other than that a tedium settled over the city.

As the people became used to the shelling they began to study their assailants; they learned the names of the individual ships and the type of guns they carried. In the people's minds the ships and the fleets began to assume definite human characteristics. Edward Butler thought that the upper fleet was lazy and

55. *Vicksburg Daily Whig,* July 11, 1862.
56. *Ibid.*
57. Allen, Plantation Book, p. 88.

cowardly. Behind the protection of a bend in the river, its ships indiscriminately peppered the city, and, wrote Butler: "They have never done anything else since they came and not one of [the ships] has ever come within sight of any of our batteries." The lower fleet was quite different. It was considered to be composed of "brave and daring men [who] fight like brave men. They have only shelled the town once or twice when they had reason to believe we were bringing troops through, and their vessels have twice passed our batteries."[58] In this manner much of the impersonality of the battle was dissipated and the civilians, like soldiers, learned to regard their enemies as human beings, rather than mere fighting machines.

The turning point of the naval siege came on July 15, when the rusty *Arkansas* steamed out of the Yazoo. An abortive start was made on the fourteenth, but leaky boilers blew steam into the powder magazine and Brown had to stop his ship, lay out tarpaulins, and spread the powder upon them to dry. Helpless and only a few miles from the Federal ships, the crew spent most of the day turning and sifting the drying powder.[59]

Early on the morning of the fifteenth Brown was ready to try again. He hoped to catch the Union fleet at sunrise, but the *Arkansas* ran aground and dawn broke long before the enemy was sighted. As the *Arkansas* pushed out into the Mississippi she was twelve miles from the support of the Vicksburg batteries with at least thirty-seven Union vessels lying in her path.

The *Carondelet* made the first pass at the rusty boat, followed by the *Tyler* and the *Queen of the West*. The *Carondelet* was disabled, and the *Tyler* and the *Queen* fled downstream to the safety of the massed fleet. The *Arkansas* followed, with Brown wounded and the temperature in the engine room standing at 130°. As the ironclad rounded a bend the massed might of the Union navy in the west, "a forest of masts and smokestacks," confronted her and still Vicksburg was not in sight. The *Arkansas* lurched ahead, her wheezing engines aided by the push of the river current. The range closed and the Union can-

58. Edward G. Butler to Ann Butler, July 18, 1862, Butler Family Papers (E).

59. The following account is based upon Brown, *Battles and Leaders,* III, 573-76.

non began to reach out for her. The banging of shells off her armor was unceasing, and Minie balls and shrapnel slapped through gunports and cracks in the iron. It seemed to Brown that he was in the middle of a "volcano."

The sound of the gunfire roused the people of Vicksburg. They were not able to see anything, but the crescendo of explosions could mean only one thing—the *Arkansas* was coming. They stopped whatever they were doing and lined the hilltops, unmindful of the risks. To the north the sound of gunfire slackened and after a bit they could see a single ship limping toward them. Pandemonium broke loose. The people cheered, they sang, they danced and hugged one another. Edward Butler said that he would not even attempt to describe their excitement.[60]

As the *Arkansas* tied up, the civilians gathered along the wharf to welcome the crew. They crowded about the boat and pushed aboard, then recoiled when they peered into her gundeck. Acting Master's Mate Wilson watched them "retreat hastily," for when they looked inside the *Arkansas* they saw "blood and brains bespattered every[where], whilst arms, legs, and several headless trunks were strewn about." Evidently, even in their beleaguered city, they were not used to the sight of gore; and the crew were left alone to carry off their dead and wounded and to patch up the ship.[61] A vicarious thrill of victory was enough for the people; they would take their naval battles from a vantage point on the hills. But they wanted more—even Charles Allen, out at Nanachehaw, planned to come in to watch the renewal of the battle.[62]

The battered *Arkansas* threatened to ruin the Union naval offensive. She could menace either fleet, forcing them to keep up steam day and night in order that they might be prepared for a sudden sortie. Occasionally Brown would have the boilers lighted and smoke blown through the stacks as though the *Arkansas* was preparing for attack, but this was only a ruse because the boat was so riddled that Brown did not think that she

60. Edward G. Butler to Ann Butler, July 18, 1862, Butler Family Papers (E).

61. *Official Records Navy,* Ser. I, Vol. XIX, 133.

62. Allen, Plantation Book, p. 89.

would have a chance against the superior Union ships. The suspense began to eat at the attackers' nerves: maintaining a constant state of preparedness was wearing; the crews began to suffer from the heat, which was often 100° in the shade; and malaria struck both the sailors and Williams' canal diggers.

Farragut decided to make one last try for the *Arkansas.* The *Essex,* fresh from dry dock and with a new crew, had recently joined the fleet and was given the task of destroying the *Arkansas.* On July 22, supported by the *Sumter* and the *Queen of the West,* the *Essex* dashed in under the batteries to strike at the ram. Aboard the *Arkansas* there were men enough to man only two of her guns and for a while Brown thought that the *Essex* would take him, but finally the attackers were driven away.

The next day General Williams wrote Flag Officer Davis that he was finished—malaria had reduced his forces from 3,200 to 800, and besides that the river had fallen so much that it scarcely trickled through his canal. Davis, in turn, wrote Gideon Wells, Secretary of the Navy, that he too was in a difficult situation—the crews on the mortarboats were cut from 130 to 30 by sickness, and one-half of the gunboat crews were ill. And he did not believe that conditions would improve, for "the most sickly part of the season is approaching; and the Department would be surprised to see how the most healthy men wilt and break down [in] this pernicious climate." But, he continued, the defenders were in an equally riddled condition, therefore he would continue the attack and he did not want Williams to leave.[63]

Farragut, however, agreed with Williams. The navy alone would never take Vicksburg, especially with the *Arkansas* there. The operation must be suspended, but not before the city was given a final mauling.

On the morning of July 24, the last bombardment commenced and the missiles landed so fast that Rowland Chambers was driven to his cave. He sat in the hole, his diary with him, as the shells shook the ground. The explosions were so close, he wrote, "that we can feel the shock very sensibly; this is the first time I have felt alarmed my nerves are completely unstrung

63. *Official Records Navy,* Ser. I, Vol. XIX, 49-50.

I can scarcely write."[64] So at last, after sixty-one days, his nerve cracked and he must have been relieved when he realized that he had suffered the final bombardment—at least for a while.

On the river the mortarboats were unmoored, the gunboats were turned around, the canal diggers were embarked aboard their transports, and Farragut cautioned the captain of the *Essex,* which was bringing up the rear, to keep a sharp eye open for the *Arkansas.*[65] At two o'clock in the afternoon the signal was given to get underway; by five o'clock the *Essex* had disappeared downstream. Van Dorn watched them steam out of sight, then telegraphed Jefferson Davis: "The whole of the lower fleet and all of the troops have disappeared down the river. The upper fleet [is] in motion . . . ."[66]

This was a terse message, shorn of elation, yet interlined by a note of military triumph. It was sent by a general who had thwarted the enemy's will and who was justifiably proud of his success. If there was a corresponding throb of triumph among the civilians, it is not recorded. They had not won; they had merely survived. The upper fleet had not moved far—it was now anchored off the mouth of the Yazoo—and the ships could easily slip downstream to recommence the bombardment. Van Dorn had won, but the people of Vicksburg received only a breathing space; and they knew it. Rowland Chambers guessed that the city would be safe "until the yankeys pays us an other visit."[67]

There was no instant quickening of the pulse of Vicksburg. It had taken months to uproot families and business and to dislocate the patterns of life. It would take longer even partially to restore them. River traffic was still almost at a halt, though there was a tenuous reopening of communications across the Mississippi; houses and stores remained shuttered; and the

64. Chambers, Diary, July 24, 1862.

65. *Official Records Navy,* Ser. I, Vol. XIX, 54. Almost immediately after the naval siege was lifted, while Brown was sick and away from Vicksburg, Van Dorn ordered the *Arkansas* to support an attack upon the Union forces at Baton Rouge. Just before the boat reached Baton Rouge, with Brown in hot pursuit, the engines quit for the last time, leaving her helpless before a Union fleet. At this point the *Arkansas* was scuttled, less than two weeks after she had driven Farragut from Vicksburg.

66. *Ibid.,* p. 75.

67. Chambers, Diary, July 28, 1862.

streets were empty. James D. B. De Bow, the peripatetic editor, visited Vicksburg during the closing days of July and the city appeared almost lifeless to him. He wrote this report for his *Review*: "City deserted and desolate; only sentinels and darkies to be seen, and very attenuated cats and dogs. Houses are closed, and though a large number were struck by the shells . . . no dwellings seem to be much injured. A few stores, an engine-house, and the Methodist Church, are the only severe sufferers, and these may be readily repaired." After the stories which he had heard describing the destruction in the city, De Bow was surprised by what appeared to him to be slight damage.[68]

Yet at least one of the inhabitants took a different view of the battered city. Rowland Chambers who, day by day, watched the mounting destruction wrote: "The principal part of the town has been much damaged scarcely a house has escaped."[69]

There is closer agreement concerning the number of persons who were killed by the naval guns. Charles Allen was told that "2 women, [a] negro & a few artillerymen" were casualties. Alexander S. Abrams, on the staff of the *Whig,* knew of only "one female and a negro" who were killed.[70] The July 11 issue of the *Whig* reported that, up to the time of its publication, only one woman had been killed. At any event, the number of casualties was remarkably low, especially when the duration and the intensity of the bombardment are considered.

As the days passed and the fleets did not return, the scattered refugees began to drift back into the city. The trains once again unloaded passengers and freight at the depot, wagons and carriages headed for Vicksburg passed by the outlying plantations, shutters were taken down, homes and shops were reopened. Charles Allen, watching the people passing by Nanachehaw, took the stream of returning refugees to be a good omen. He wrote: "What will they say [in the] North now about opening the Mississippi River; huzzah for Vicksburg & 9 groans for New Orleans."[71] Allen's huzzahs for Vicksburg were the

68. *De Bow's Review,* New Series, II (August, 1866), 193.
69. Chambers, Diary, July 20, 1862.
70. Allen, Plantation Book, p. 93; A. S. Abrams, *A Full and Detailed Account of the Siege of Vicksburg* (Atlanta, 1863), p. 7.
71. Allen, Plantation Book, p. 93.

Refugees camped in the woods on the outskirts of the city, just beyond naval gunfire range. As seen by the special artist for the *Illustrated London News.*

reactions of the South in microcosm; throughout the Confederacy, editorials, orators, and general orders heaped lavish praise on the beleaguered city and her defenders. Charles Allen himself was in many respects the Southerner, and especially the Mississippian, in microcosm—he cheered success at Vicksburg, but he had done absolutely nothing to help insure that success.

Inside the city Rowland Chambers watched the returning people, but he was not as jubilant as Allen nor did he think the refugees augured much good; their presence was no insurance that the gunboats would not renew the attack, and if they did Chambers was certain that the people would flee again.[72]

There was probably some resentment manifested toward the refugees by the people who had stayed through the attack. Their trial had been a singular one and their suffering was a badge which those who had fled could not claim. The refugees, in turn, might retort that they too had been subjected to trials and tribulations, and they thought that their vicissitudes had been bad enough.

72. Chambers, Diary, July 29, 1862.

One woman said that her railway trip to Jackson was "indescribable." Instead of fleeing the war she thought that she "seemed to be right back in the stream [of it], among officers, soldiers, sick men and cripples, adieus, tears, laughter, constant chatter, and . . . sentinels posted at the locked car-doors demanding passports . . . . Every moment [she] saw strange meetings and partings of people from all over the South. Conditions of time, space, locality, and estate were all loosened." Food was little better or more plentiful than in Vicksburg. In Jackson she had a meal consisting of "tough steak, heavy, dirty-looking bread, [and] Confederate coffee," which was made from sweet potatoes. When she arrived at the home of her friends, deep in the middle of Mississippi, she found that she had still not escaped "the trials of war." There were no matches in the house and when a servant let the fire go out a man had to ride mule-back three miles to a neighbor's home to get a pan of live coals. The crockery was broken, even the bottoms of the tin drinking cups were rusted out, and they made drinking glasses by cutting bottles in half with a heated wire. Vicksburg was no worse than this and before the month was past she was traveling back toward the city.[73]

Other refugees did not choose to return to the city and face the dangers of the inevitable recommencement of attack. William and Emma Crutcher left Clinton when the bombardment was lifted, stopped at their home long enough to arrange their affairs and gather their belongings, and then crossed the river toward the west. They did not stop until they reached Palestine, Texas, where they leased a ranch and waited out the war.[74]

A tense atmosphere still clung to the city; the upper fleet, at the mouth of the Yazoo, posed a constant threat and the people were skittish and jumped at every rumor. Some of those who had returned could not stand the tension of never knowing if the coming day might bring the gunboats again—almost as soon as they had settled themselves they repacked and left.[75]

73. "War Diary," *The Century Magazine,* XXXVIII, 944.

74. Emma Crutcher to Marmaduke Shannon, February 1, 1863, Crutcher Collection.

75. *De Bow's Review,* New Series, II (September, 1866), 324.

The city council, already proven unstable and bereft of leadership, reflected the difficulties involved in attempting to reconstitute a semblance of normality in the war-touched city. A meeting, the first since June 16, was called for August 18. Those in attendance sat and waited far beyond the appointed hour, but there was no quorum and they disbanded. They tried again on September 1, on the second, then again on the fourth, all with the same results. Finally on September 8, forty-six days after the last shell had landed in the city, enough members gathered together to constitute a quorum and the council went into session. In the meeting they disposed of three items of business: two councilmen were given thirty days' leave; the Washington fire engine was moved from its damaged building; and property owners were scolded for not keeping their gutters in repair. While surrounded by a damaged city, homeless people, and meagre food supplies, the councilmen addressed themselves to trivia. The chief thing which they did during the meeting was to re-affirm their uselessness.[76] Alone, the people grouped toward the re-establishment of their lives.

As the people returned, the business of the city slowly increased. When a woman from New Orleans arrived in Vicksburg on September 7, she was impressed by two things: the thick layer of dust that coated the entire city, and the fact that the stores were open. Though the shops were open the choice of merchandise was limited, but from time to time a merchant would put out scarce articles for sale. Pearl buttons, a truly dear commodity, were available, as were shoes and umbrellas. Slave trading also continued. Some persons questioned the trade as being "impolitic," especially at a time in which the capture of the city was a distinct possibility, but that condition did not prevent the sale of Negroes. There were, however, new factors to be taken into consideration when slaves were purchased. One man said that he would buy only young slaves, preferably females, as they would be less likely to run away if a Union army approached.[77]

76. Council Minute Book, p. 171.
77. "War Diary," *The Century Magazine,* XXXVIII, 945.

Food was still another matter. The cessation of attack did not alleviate the food problem. Prices remained high and the presence of the large number of troops, competing with the civilians for supplies, compounded the problem. Butter, for example, sold in Vicksburg for $1.50 per pound, while in Clinton, only thirty miles away, it was priced at forty-five cents.[78] The planters, sitting in the midst of plenty, were loath to cut into their own stores to help feed the city dwellers. Outside Vicksburg one planter had an abundance of fruits and vegetables and plenty of beef, mutton, sugar, milk, butter, honey, and pigs. Yet he made no effort to ship even a portion into the city.[79] In Vicksburg one woman said that there were only two topics of conversation: "the question of food alternated with news of the war."[80]

Housing, too, was scarce. The Washington Hotel was jammed, the army had occupied what houses there were for rent, and the boarding houses had been "broken up." In September only one boarding house was open to civilians, and one couple looked for a home for two weeks without success.[81]

Shortages of food and housing, as acute as they were, were taken in stride by the citizens. In the lack of food and clothing the people were not alone—there were such scarcities throughout the South—and the knowledge of this gave them some comfort, however meagre; they shared a common plight with other members of the Confederacy. In another respect they were unique—they lived in the midst of an army.

Early one morning Mahala Roach was called to her door to be told that an artillery battery would be emplaced in her front yard. She sat in her house and watched the work: fences were torn down, walks dug up, shrubbery cut away, and before long she had several cannon practically in her lap. She admitted that at first she "felt very badly about it" but then decided that resentment would do no good. By the end of the day she had come to this conclusion: "I must bear my part of annoyance and trouble, as much as anyone else."[82]

78. William Crutcher to E. C. Crutcher, August 14, 1862, Crutcher Collection.
79. "War Diary," *The Century Magazine,* XXXVIII, 945.
80. *Ibid.,* p. 946.
81. *Ibid.,* p. 945.
82. Roach, Diary, p. 227.

William Merritt lost a fine stand of timber as the ring of defenses was closed about the city. On his property at the outskirts of town the engineers cut down one and a half miles of hardwood so the cannon might have clear fields of fire. Merritt wrote his father that his aunt "took it very much to heart to see the timber cut," but he wasted no ink lamenting the loss—it was necessary.[83] Even Charles Allen relented in his adamant refusal to help with the defense. Throughout October and November he uncomplainingly sent his field hands to work on the fortifications.[84]

It was difficult to feel much rancor toward something as impersonal as cannon or hacked-up stands of timber, which were imposed as regrettable but unavoidable preparations for defense—a defense as much to the interest of the individual citizen as to the Confederacy. The people realized this and they bore these tribulations with patience. Mahala Roach's reaction was typical. She did not care to have the cannon in her yard, complained a bit, then finally admitted that she must accept them as her duty.

But the depredations of individual soldiers were not impersonal actions, and they grated on the civilians. Some of the people could never accept the fact that so long as they lived in a garrison they would have to expect trespassing and thievery from the troops. They could not understand that in war, regard for private property diminishes in direct proportion to the size of an army and the nearness of the enemy. The people complained first to the local military officials and then to the War Department. John A. Campbell, Assistant Secretary of War, looked at the letters and wrote General John Pemberton, who had replaced Van Dorn as commander in Mississippi, that the citizens showed "a good deal of temper and irritation."[85]

The military authorities tried to control the troops in the city—a provost marshal's guard of one hundred men was detailed to do nothing but police the town. But over seventy-five of the men selected for this duty were Creoles who spoke no English,

83. William Merritt to Alexander Merritt, November 20, 1862, W. H. E. Merritt Papers, Duke University.

84. Allen, Plantation Book, p. 111.

85. *Official Records Army,* Ser. I, XV, 864.

and the efficiency of the guard probably left something to be desired.[86]

Sometimes the troops could not be blamed for the forays they made against the people's property. Good drinking water was difficult to obtain—the city depended upon cisterns for its water supply—and the soldiers' supply came from creeks which had filth in them. Private S. R. Martin readily admitted that he never drank the creek water if he could help it but instead "would beg . . . or steal Cistern water" when he was able.[87] Pure water was equally precious to the civilians, and petty squabbles often erupted when a soldier was caught helping himself to a citizen's supply.

There was something tangible about stealing a pig or helping oneself to a bucket of water which made outrage and annoyance a clear-cut matter. There was no question about thievery: if something was stolen that was all there was to it and the resulting rancor was very logical. Yet there was more to the problem than that, for the relationships between soldier and civilian were further colored by factors which were vague and subtle and depended upon the curious twistings of the Southern mind. The result—conflict between civilian and soldier—was the same, but the causes were quite different. It was a matter of the mind: a tangled web of parochialism, States' Rights, war-weariness, and human perversity. Somehow for the wary provincial consciousness there was something unsettling in registering the faces of the swarming soldiers but not recognizing a single familiar one. Vicksburg was home, ran this thought train, and it was a shame that "the old familiar faces are away fighting in Virginia and Tennessee and strangers are defending their city."[88]

A Tennesseean, Captain John J. Blair, felt the sting of this sentiment and during the cold winter he transferred some of the venom to his diary: "How ungrateful the citizens of Vicksburg are to Tennesseans who are defending their firesides for them . . . . No accommodations extended to us by Mississippians

86. Chambers, "My Journal," *Publications of the Mississippi Historical Society,* V, 250.

87. S. R. Martin, Recollections of the War Between the States, 1861-65, p. 46. Owned by John S. Hoggatt, Vicksburg.

88. Stone, *Brokenburn,* p. 142.

. . . . Now denied the privilege of sleeping before the fire because I was a Tennessean."[89] The feeling of exclusiveness was manifested on a larger scale when four thousand paroled prisoners passed through Vicksburg. No preparations had been made for their arrival and the soldiers were cast on their own to find food to eat and a place to sleep; many of them wandered through the streets begging for meals. Kate Stone commented on the warmth of their reception: "The ladies of Memphis gave them a heartfelt and enthusiastic welcome, kisses were as plentiful as blackberries, but there was nothing of that kind in Vicksburg."[90]

Yet to write off all of the people as callous and indifferent is a mistake, for time after time they responded to the needs of their defenders. The creeks and backwaters were already skimmed with ice when Winchester Hall went into town to beg. His men were barefoot and without blankets, and Hall had been rebuffed by quartermaster sergeants when he requested shoes and blankets from them. There was only one place to turn: to the people. Hall spent several days in Vicksburg, going from door to door asking for shoes and blankets—anything which could be used for protection against the cold. When he finished there was no doubt in his mind about the generosity of the people—one woman had pulled the carpet up from the floor, a slave had given him the quilts from her bed. His haul was rag-tag and motley, but his men were warm.[91]

Many of the women worked in the hospitals to supplement the over-taxed medical service. Lavinia Shannon, unaffected by the groans and filth, went day after day to the City Hospital and every once in a while received a note such as this in return:

Kind and Generous Lady

Since leaving the City Hospital and my return to camp I have been prostrate with chills and fever, and therefore, have been unable to visit you and return my thanks for the kindness you manifested towards me while confined in the Hospital. Please accept my warmest thanks and may Heaven bless you . . . .[92]

89. John J. Blair, Diary, Tennessee State Library and Archives, pp. 1-2.
90. Stone, *Brokenburn,* p. 142. 91. Hall, *26th Louisiana,* pp. 24-25.
92. Philip A. Vanderdoes to Lavinia Shannon, October 8, 1862, Crutcher Collection.

The women's war spirit carried their activities far beyond nursing and such gentle things. When ammunition supplies ran low they became munition makers and without hesitation, once the stores' stock of flannel was exhausted, stripped off petticoats, tore down curtains, and cut up table linens to roll cartridges in.[93] Some of them doubled in brass as unofficial quartermasters as they ransacked tool sheds and closets for saws, augers, planes, axes, and hatchets to give to the troops.[94]

Then there was a lighter side to the business of living in the middle of an army. There were parties in the officers' homes, sight-seeing trips to the batteries, and even jaunts to the jail where the Yankee prisoners crowded at the gate to watch the passers-by, who in turn stopped and peered and wondered if they were so inhuman after all.[95]

There was not much pattern to the social life in the city; it was catch-as-catch-can for each individual. Kate Stone, who visited for three weeks during the autumn, thought Vicksburg was "dull . . . so deadly dull." Besides that she was squeezed out of one house and finally found a bed in another where she felt like a "sardine"; worst of all she knew no eligible men.[96] Other girls had no difficulty in this respect—there were plenty of officers to go around, and they set up a form of military etiquette in which they would receive passes to visit the fortifications in return for passes which would admit the officers into their homes.[97]

The enlisted men got short shrift. Most of the camps were on the outskirts of Vicksburg and permission to enter the city was difficult to obtain. When the men did come into town they usually sought out persons who kept no records and the soldiers' activities, except when they were startling enough to cause general comment, went almost unrecorded. Only an occasional glimpse

93. "Southerner" to Marmaduke Shannon, August 29, 1862, Crutcher Collection.

94. Unsigned note to Elizabeth Eggleston, August 29, 1862, Roach-Eggleston Papers, Southern Historical Collection, University of North Carolina.

95. Daniel Beltzhoover to Elizabeth Eggleston, October 21, 1862, Roach-Eggleston Papers; Stone, *Brokenburn,* p. 150.

96. Stone, *Brokenburn,* pp. 142-43.

97. Daniel Beltzhoover to Elizabeth Eggleston, October 21, 1862, Roach-Eggleston Papers.

of the enlisted man survives, usually through his own diary or letters.

When he wangled a pass, William Chambers eschewed the city's flesh-pots and, instead of following his comrades to the dark places Under-the-Hill, browsed through the tombstones in the city cemetery where he "saw many things that [were] of interest" to him.[98] Another soldier, Granville Alspaugh, a private in the Skipworth Guards, wrote his mother that he thought Vicksburg was "a very nice place," but he did not explain why.[99]

These things—the thievings, the petty bickerings, the unstinting, gladly-given gifts, the light kisses in requisitioned homes, the solitary soldier wandering in a graveyard—were all particulars of the whole. The whole was a whetting, shaping, and fitting of the lives of the people with that of the army. The fall of 1862 was the first time the citizens had really felt the soldiers' presence, for when the first detachments arrived in May the people, scattered and frightened by attack, were somewhat insensitive to the tugs and grindings of the troops in the city. Throughout the bombardment the contentiousness was set aside in the face of the common danger. Now, however, as the people refilled the city and the ways of peace were partially restored, the attitudes of a people at peace were also restored and autumn was a time in which these attitudes had to be modified to accommodate the soldiers. This is the sum of the autumn of 1862 in Vicksburg and, though the people did not realize it, fall was, like the summer, a time of preparation for what was to come.

There were other troublesome things that were not necessarily related directly to the army, but which stemmed merely from the fact that the people lived in a beleaguered land. Mail service became erratic and some persons began to suspect that the mails were being robbed.[100] Shortages of clothing, as well as of food, led to a slave problem. William Merritt wrote his father in Virginia that his seventeen Negroes had become "a great annoyance," and he asked for shoes, linsey, and jeans be-

98. Chambers, "My Journal," *Publications of the Mississippi Historical Society,* V, 252.

99. Granville L. Alspaugh to Mrs. A. E. Alspaugh, undated, J. P. Knox Papers, Department of Archives and Manuscripts, Louisiana State University.

100. William Merritt to Alexander Merritt, October 15, 1862, W. H. E. Merritt Papers.

cause he could not buy them in Vicksburg. Most any place but Vicksburg seemed to offer better opportunities for the use of slaves, and Merritt toyed with the idea of sending them to Georgia, to Texas, or to Virginia, but finally admitted that he was "at a loss what to do." Then to compound his difficulties he was inducted into the army. He tried to obtain a discharge but complained that he had "no organic disease"; next he sought to hire a substitute but wailed: "That can hardly be done in Miss. Substitutes are very hard to find and $5000—is the common price."[101] As a result he waited with the Vicksburg garrison, his problems unsolved.

A few minutes after six o'clock on the evening of October 4, a crimson comet streaked across the Mississippi sky, and some people who saw it thought that it was a portent of victory.[102] For a while it seemed that this was a shallow hope.

On the same day the comet appeared, Van Dorn smashed into the Union forts at Corinth and reeled back in defeat. A little later, Grant, up in north Mississippi, worked out the plans for a two-pronged thrust at Vicksburg. He would move down the center of the state along the Mississippi Central Railroad, which would ultimately put him behind Vicksburg, while Sherman, with a detached corps from Memphis, came sailing down the Mississippi to strike at the city's northern flank, a finger of bluffs lining the Yazoo River.

In Vicksburg the only reverberation felt from the impending action was the halting of civilian travel on the Southern Railroad. This order was immediately protested, for the trains were the best and fastest way of escape should that become necessary. After three days of argument, Dr. Emanuel, whose engines and cars they were, managed to obtain permission to run one train a day for the civilians.[103] At best, rail travel was now a hazardous undertaking. War's erosion had eaten into the once reliable Southern railway, and rickety engines, sprung rails, and washed roadbeds began to take their toll. Engine failures and derailings

101. *Ibid.,* October 15, November 20, 1862.

102. *Natchez Daily Courier,* October 8, 1862.

103. Morris Emanuel to John J. Pettus, December 2, 1862, Governors' Correspondence, Ser. E, Vol. LVIII, Miss. Arch.

became common occurrences and once a train jumped the tracks and killed thirty-one passengers.[104]

Brandy was a good barometer for measuring conditions at the close of the year. On December 3, it was $40 a gallon; by December 29, when Sherman was knocking on the gates of the city, the price had risen to $60.[105] Between these dates the people ran a gamut of emotion from placidity to fear.

Early in the month Kate Stone's mother crossed the river to shop in Vicksburg. She had no difficulty finding finery in the stores, and she returned to Brokenburn laden with packages. Among other things she bought some grey silk, which would be made into a dress for Kate, though it had "cost a pretty penny."[106] Even precious salt, long a scarcity, was offered for sale.[107] With luxury items in the stores, it seemed as though the city was at last breathing easier.

Then things began to tighten up. H. C. Clarke sensed some danger, or perhaps it was merely foresight on his part, for he moved his printing offices from Vicksburg to Georgia. Now his *Diary of the War For Separation* and the *Confederate Household Almanac* carried an Augusta, Georgia, imprint rather than that of Vicksburg. The women in the city began to feel uneasy—rumors of Sherman's advance had drifted down the river—and they circulated a petition calling for a day of fasting and prayer. When the city council met on December 20, they adopted the petition and proclaimed a day of "Humiliation, Fasting, and Prayer to Almighty God, that Vicksburg may be spared from the Hand of the Destroyer, that our beloved Home may be preserved to us, that the insolent invader who would take from us our Property, our Children, and our Servants may be driven back, and that we may once more live free from the Cares and Foes that beset us . . . ."

The council also appropriated $3,500 (ten times the amount they had raised in June) to move the poor families out of the city in case of bombardment. Their last bit of business was to

104. *Vicksburg Daily Whig,* January 1, 1863.

105. Stone, *Brokenburn,* pp. 159, 164.

106. *Ibid.,* p. 162.

107. Cobb and Manlove to John J. Pettus, December 9, 1862, Governors' Correspondence, Ser. E, Vol. LVIII, Miss. Arch.

see to the collection of ad valorem and wharf taxes, which was a fitting note with which to end the meeting for the city was a river town and had drawn its strength from the wharves. It was even more fitting, though touched with irony, that the council should look to the river in the closing minutes of their meeting. Just as the river was their strength, it was also the cause of their destruction, and December 20 was the last time they would gather together.[108]

The next day, December 21, Jefferson Davis, with Joseph Johnston and his staff in tow, visited the city. The soldiers were drawn up in ranks to be reviewed, and by the time Davis trooped the line the men "did not feel as enthusiastic as they did in the early morning," for they had been standing for seven hours. Davis' appearance was brief. Apparently he did not even make a speech, but nevertheless some of the people were anxious to get a look at him. To one person he appeared to be "a spare made man, and . . . a rather ugly one. His complexion . . . sallow and his face . . . on the 'hatchet' order."[109]

This time the city council made no mention of the President's presence, much less organize a reception for him. Perhaps they remembered the cost of the music and fireworks after his last visit and thought that enough gunpowder had been expended in the city to satisfy any man. Maybe Davis sensed this; at any event he waited until he had returned to Jackson to declare the suspension of habeas corpus in Vicksburg and in "the adjoining and surrounding country to the extent of ten miles."[110]

The military authorities began to clamp a little harder on the civilians. A notice appeared on December 22 stating that all persons arriving in the city would be required to register their names and business at the post headquarters, and there would be patrols on the streets to arrest anyone who failed to register.[111] All things considered, it looked like a bleak Christmas.

108. Council Minute Book, p. 177.

109. Chambers, "My Journal," *Publications of the Mississippi Historical Society*, V, 253.

110. *Official Records Navy*, Ser. I, Vol. XIX, 821. This action was taken on December 23, 1862.

111. *Vicksburg Daily Whig*, December 30, 1862.

Sherman made it bleaker. In the early hours of Christmas morning a bedraggled messenger pushed his way through the dancers at a ball to inform General Smith that Sherman was landing at Milliken's Bend and Young's Point, across the river and somewhat north of the city. As the messenger remembered it, Smith turned pale, and said in a loud voice, "This ball is at an end; the enemy are coming down the river." Then he advised all non-combatants to leave the city.[112]

When the news of Sherman's landing reached him, Rowland Chambers did not even bother with Christmas. He called his wife and daughter and put them on the train for Clinton. When he brought his diary up to date he wrote: "After a family consultation we thot prudence the better part of vallor . . . and started to Clinton . . . . I remained at home to try and take care of the place as best I could under the circumstances."[113]

General Pemberton added the weight of his authority to General Smith's advice to the civilians to leave the city. On December 27, he had this notice published:

> It is earnestly recommended that all the noncombatants, especially the women and children, should forthwith leave the city . . . . The places of supposed protection with which I am informed many have provided themselves during the progress of a battle here, may prove wholly insufficient for their safety. When the city becomes crowded with the soldiery, it will be impossible to afford the helpless those aids and facilities which humanity might seem to demand. It is therefore hoped there will be no delay or reluctance . . . to leave the city, while there is time to . . . find places of safety outside the city limits.

Then he became frank: ". . . all . . . persons are hereby notified that their presence will not be allowed under any circumstances to interfere with the defense of the city."[114]

The persons who heeded Pemberton's advice (or subtle threat) were helped by advertisements such as this: "A few nice persons, who come well recommended, can get board at my

112. Stephen D. Lee, "Details of Important Work by Two Confederate Telegraph Operators," *Publications of the Mississippi Historical Society*, VIII, 54.

113. Chambers, Diary, [December 26, 1862?].

114. Proclamation dated December 27, 1862, published in *Vicksburg Daily Whig*, December 30, 1862.

house one mile from Bovina . . . . Boarders must furnish themselves with lights and bedding. Board can be had only while the enemy threatens Vicksburg . . . ."[115]

Sherman was not yet a name that conjured up spectres in the minds of Southerners, but his name was synonymous with an army of attackers, and that in turn was equated with fear. Some of the merchants were so frightened that they dumped long hoarded stocks of food on the market. One man offered thirty thousand pounds of salt for sale—salt which had become so scarce that planters had long since dug up smokehouse floors to try to recover some of the precious stuff which had dripped from their curing meats. A druggist advertised that he had "quantities" of quinine and morphine, and they were almost worth their weight in gold.[116] In his ledger, the county clerk measured the extent of the fear. In December, he recorded almost as many property sales as had been entered during the previous four months.[117]

For three days Sherman probed into the Confederate right flank, and the sound of cannon fire which drifted into Vicksburg had an ominous roll to it. On December 29 (the day the price of brandy rose twenty dollars) Sherman tried to break the flank. It was a difficult position to attack—low, swampy, dank ground overwatched by bluffs on which the Confederates sat with rifles and artillery. The Northerners wallowed through the muck and tried to climb the bluffs while the Confederates swatted them back like flies. When it was over the defenders counted two hundred casualties and the attackers had lost almost ten times that number. But Sherman was not finished yet. He pulled back and waited for the sound of guns at Vicksburg's rear, which would mean that Grant had carried out his part of the plan.[118]

Grant had never gotten started. Van Dorn had swept in behind him to destroy his supply center at Holly Springs, and

115. *Vicksburg Daily Whig,* December 30, 1862.

116. *Ibid.*

117. Warren County Deed Book CC, entries for December, 1862. Cf. entries for August-November, 1862.

118. George W. Morgan, "The Assault on Chickasaw Bluffs," *Battles and Leaders,* III, 467-69.

Forrest had swung deep into Tennessee and Kentucky to lacerate his rearward communications. While Sherman waited for the sound of his superior's guns, Grant was moving back into Tennessee.

Shannon's printers were glad to set the type for the December 30 issue of the *Whig,* for it had exultation written all over it: Sherman whipped at Chickasaw Bluffs and Grant retreating out of the state. And there were still victory reports from the Army of Northern Virginia at Fredericksburg. The paper also carried Pemberton's notice advising the citizens to evacuate the city.[119] Some who read it probably snorted.

Sherman made one last try. On January 1 he started his men around the extreme right flank of the bluffs, but before the movement was well underway a blanket of fog drifted over the bottom lands and the column was halted in confusion. That stopped him—he loaded his corps on their transports and backed out of the Yazoo.

The Confederates following him turned around and went back to Vicksburg. They marched in the rain, muddy but happy, playing tricks on one another. William Chambers wrote: "The whole way was lined with newly arrived soldiers, who amused themselves, near the *real* slippery places by calling to some imaginary person *up a tree* and seeing some fellow lose his footing, as he looked upward while walking along."[120] The people watched this horseplay and were equally elated. It seemed that those who had looked up at the comet and had seen victory were right.

119. *Vicksburg Daily Whig,* December 30, 1862.

120. Chambers, "My Journal," *Publications of the Mississippi Historical Society,* V, 257.

Chapter VII

"HOW CAN WE EVER BE CONQUERED?"

VICTORY was bittersweet. As Sherman's whipped corps steamed out of the Yazoo, and the jubilant Confederates marched into Vicksburg, the cancerous growth eating deep into the city was laid open. The Southerners wore Union overcoats, the pockets stuffed with Union money, and some of them, said Jared Sanders, a Louisiana soldier, carried over $100 in Northern currency. They had looted the bodies of the dead Federals for one reason—in Vicksburg they could exchange ten Union greenbacks for fifteen Confederate dollars. And they knew where the money would go once it left the Vicksburg speculators—to "smugglers . . . to trade off to the enemy for contraband goods."[1] Like a malignant organism that gnaws its way into the tissues of a healthy body and rots it away, scarcity worked in Vicksburg.

The city had made its wealth from trade, and once its normal peacetime trade was ruptured new slender lines of illegal commerce took its place. Profit knew no patriotism, and profit lay in scarcity. Now the *Whig*'s advertisements of flour, salt, coffee, and sugar were punctuated by exclamation marks. The Unionist bride from New Orleans wrote: "I got with difficulty two chickens . . . . An egg is a rare and precious thing."[2] Yet Vicksburg sat in the midst of some of the richest farming land in the world—land still relatively untouched by the enemy's armies.

The shortage of food could be laid to cotton, which in turn pointed in only one direction—human greed. The Confederacy's

1. Jared Sanders to "Friend," January 4, 1863, Jared Y. Sanders Papers, Department of Archives and Manuscripts, Louisiana State University.
2. "A Woman's Diary," *The Century Magazine,* XXX, 767.

cotton diplomacy had backfired. The government had gambled that blockaded cotton (and empty mills in England and France) would bring European intervention on the side of the South. Instead, it brought hunger to Southerners. The mills of the North and Europe were slack, there was a glut of cotton in the South, but the planters kept their broad fields planted in it. Cotton that could be smuggled through the Union lines was worth $1.00 per pound, and some of the planters took the chance that their bales would find an illegal way through the lines. Why, they asked, should we grow corn and vegetables when the price of cotton stands at $1.00? The planters in the ten counties and parishes surrounding Vicksburg raised nearly one-seventh of the South's cotton crop and, with the glittering lure of windfall profits from smuggled cotton, they would not stop to cultivate food for their people and their armies. This was "the most potent of all causes of demoralization and decay of the war spirit in the river country—more effective than all [others] combined."[3]

In editorial after editorial Marmaduke Shannon implored and threatened the planters in an effort to get them to raise food instead of cotton: "The man who plants anything but grain or vegetables renders himself liable to be suspected of disloyalty."[4] But Shannon's pleas and threats were lost on deaf ears, and in the city if there was not actual hunger there was at least want. "As the spring comes," wrote a woman, "one has the craving for fresh, green food that a monotonous diet produces . . . . An onion salad, dressed only with salt, vinegar, and pepper seem[s] a dish fit for a king." Yet there was little variety to her austere diet, and a little bed of radishes and onions, "that were a real blessing," was raided by soldiers.[5]

The shortage of food was the largest area in which the war rot worked, but other things were equally symptomatic of the cost of the hollow victory at Chickasaw Bluffs. The hardware dealers no longer advertised that they had metal products—stoves, knives, axes, plowshares—for sale. When wine was prescribed for a typhoid patient, only six bottles could be found

3. J. S. McNeily, "War and Reconstruction in Mississippi: 1863-1890," *Publications of the Mississippi Historical Society,* II (1918), 77.

4. *Vicksburg Daily Whig,* March 25, 1863.

5. "A Woman's Diary," *The Century Magazine,* XXX, 768.

in the city and the doctor had to certify that his patient's life depended upon having two of the six bottles.[6] The druggists posted notice that they could no longer extend credit "in consequence of our inability to procure supplies, except for CASH . . . ."[7] There was no question from where their cash purchased drugs came. Even the *Whig* refused to credit advertisers.[8] Paper was scarce. Envelopes were made by cutting and folding sheets of coarse, colored stock. The *Whig,* said one woman, "shouts victory as much as its gradually diminishing size will allow." She tried to buy some books, found only one bookstore open, and the sole volume in stock was Harriet Beecher Stowe's *Sunny Memories of Foreign Lands,* which was offered at a discount because the people refused to buy her books.[9]

The communication systems began to fail. The postal service was almost completely broken down. More and more the practice increased of sending letters by travelers instead of through the mails. Marmaduke Shannon ceased accepting subscription payments through the postal system at his risk. He notified his subscribers: "So much is being stolen from the mails that now the policy is for the subscriber to send [money] at his own risk."[10] Another communication link failed as the ferryboat service between Vicksburg and the Louisiana shore was discontinued; now only skiffs plied back and forth across the river.[11] The Southern Railroad had almost succumbed to the heavy military traffic on its ramshackle equipment. Dr. Emanuel admitted that his road was "impracticable" and asked General Pemberton for permission to stop all trains until they could be inspected and repaired.[12] The railroad came under severe criticism from the newspapers. The *Whig* reported one accident after another and finally said: "The pen hardly dries in chronicling accidents on the Southern railroad."[13] The Jackson

6. *Ibid.,* p. 767.
7. *Vicksburg Daily Whig,* January 1, 1863.
8. *Ibid.*
9. "A Woman's Diary," *The Century Magazine,* XXX, 767.
10. *Vicksburg Daily Whig,* February 11, 1863.
11. *Ibid.,* January 13, 1863.
12. C. L. Stevenson to John J. Pettus, February 2, 1863, Governors' Correspondence, Series E. Vol. LIX, Miss. Arch.
13. *Vicksburg Daily Whig,* March 11, 1863.

Crisis called the railroad the "meanest of them all," and said there was "less risk in fighting a battle than in traveling a short distance on that road."[14] Even Pemberton, while busy trying to stop Grant's push through the delta, telegraphed Emanuel: "Nine-tenths of the difficulties I have to contend with are due to your R. R."[15] This was not very flattering to Dr. Emanuel, but it was equally uncomplimentary to Grant.

The decay—both material and moral—had eaten into practically every facet of the people's life. "A Drunken soldier," wrote Rowland Chambers, "went in to Arthurs hooping & yelling at the top of his voice among the women Run them into the house he bolted after them and they came [out] again screaming the man after them and the dog after him he got a club and roved round until he was arrested . . . and marched off."[16]

Robbed dead men, traffic in stolen money, cotton planted instead of corn, smuggled drugs, looted mails, wrecked trains, assaulted women—this was the price the people of Vicksburg were paying for the victory at Chickasaw Bluffs and for the passionate words Jefferson Davis had rolled off his tongue on a flare-lit night in November 1860. But there was little looking back and recriminating over what might have been; the present pressed too hard for attention.

On January 19, Sherman was back across the river and, on January 29, Grant, patient and unruffled by his previous failure, joined him. As the winter days passed Grant puffed on his cigar and worked up one scheme after another to get into Vicksburg. He started his troops digging at Williams' abandoned canal; he sent a corps swinging deep through a labyrinth of waterways in Louisiana, hoping that they could get south of the city without being exposed to its batteries; he tried to work through the web of sloughs and little delta rivers, so he might ease in behind the city. As spring came he was still trying.

The people could sit in their homes and watch the little specks that were Union troops across the river. The *Whig* printed

14. *Jackson Crisis,* March 9, 1863.

15. John C. Pemberton to M. Emanuel, March 9, 1863, Letters and Telegrams sent, Department of Mississippi and East Louisiana, Chapt. II, Vol. LVII, 514. National Archives, Record Group 109. Hereinafter cited as NA (RG).

16. Chambers, Diary, March 2, 1863.

daily summaries of the enemy's activities: "The Yankees were all quiet along the peninsula yesterday," though occasionally a shell would be lobbed in the city.[17] River traffic was choked off during the last of January. On January 21, Josephine Clare arrived in Vicksburg aboard the last boat which came from Alexandria, Louisiana. She was on her way north to join her husband who had fled Confederate conscription officers. Weary and with a sick child, she finally found a room at the Washington Hotel. There was little comfort in Vicksburg for her. "It was useless," she said, "for me to plead for attention: the rebs . . . would sooner administer to the wants of a negro than one whom they supposed to be their enemy." Yet other travelers did not think that their reception would be so grim, for, noticed Mrs. Clare: ". . . refugees from New Orleans are arriving daily."[18]

In addition to refugees and transients another group of people appeared in the city who in the long run would exert a great amount of pressure on the city's already over-taxed resources. These persons were the families of officers who chose, even at the risk of being subjected to attack, to join their husbands and fathers. Major Winchester Hall's family—his wife and four children with carriage and horses—crossed through the Union lines in Louisiana and settled in Vicksburg.[19] Housing, food, and fodder had to be procured for them. As this sort of situation multiplied, the strain on necessities, already pronounced, was increased.

In mid-February the city's butchers went on half-schedule. There was no profit to tending the almost empty markets all day, and they opened them only in the afternoon.[20] But shortened hours did not mean more food and Rowland Chambers said: "I went to market but could get nothing."[21] Word of the city's plight was spread throughout Mississippi and Louisiana, and private citizens began to send donations for the relief of the poor and the hungry. One man came to Vicksburg with 375 dozen

17. *Vicksburg Daily Whig,* February 12, 1863.

18. Josephine Clare, *Narrative of the Adventures and Experience of Mrs. Josephine Clare* (Lancaster, Pennsylvania, 1865), pp. 10-12.

19. Winchester Hall, *26th Louisiana,* p. 57.

20. *Vicksburg Daily Whig,* February 18, 1863.

21. Chambers, Diary, March 6, 1863.

eggs, 400 pickled pigs' feet, 5 dozen chickens, a keg of sausage, 3 boxes of fruit, and 2 barrels of crackers, which were donated by the women of Shreveport, Louisiana. Another group of Louisianians sent Marmaduke Shannon $1,300 which was to be used "for the needy families in your city."[22]

Shannon administered the fund, saw that it did not begin to alleviate the want, and turned to the columns of the *Whig* to protest: "We think that Vicksburg has always been neglected in subsistence, as well as everything else. Notwithstanding the government had full control of the railroad and steamboat transportation all last summer and fall, but little provision was made for a siege, and many of the articles that were brought here remained exposed to the rain until they were unfit for use."[23] For the first time the critical word "siege" appeared. It was stuck there, almost lost in the context of complaint, but it was registered—almost in passing, almost as an afterthought.

The county board of police, the governing body of Warren County, and now the sole operative local civil authority also turned its thoughts toward the possibility of a siege. The board was anxious about the city's water supply. A committee was appointed to advise the military officials of "the insufficiency of cistern water in the city during the summer months." The board wanted the tin gutters repaired and the cisterns cleaned

22. *Vicksburg Daily Whig,* January 13, March 11, 1863.

23. *Ibid.,* March 5, 1863. Shannon's statement concerning the military's requisitioning of transportation is substantially correct, but it appears that military use was not absolute. For example, on January 24, 1863, Pemberton impounded every vessel at Vicksburg, even skiffs, and directed that they could not leave the city without his permission. Yet the following day, Dr. Emanuel was authorized to run his trains for civilian purposes upon his "positive assurance that it will not in any way interfere with . . . the transportation of troops or supplies . . . ." Letters and Telegrams sent, Department of Mississippi and Eastern Louisiana, Chapt. II, Vol. LVII, 355 NA (RG) 109. Also, on January 26, the Vicksburg Commissary Officer reported that enough corn had been shipped to the city to make 1,500,000 rations. *Ibid.,* 354. By March 31, shortly after Shannon's criticism, the Commissary Officer reported these amounts of rations on hand: Bulk Pork 302,400; Bacon 319,728; Lard 22,720; Wheat Flour 109,139; Rice Flour 12,175; Corn Meal 46,086; Rice 3,003,500; Peas 4,003,500; Sugar 280,500; Salt 3,170,266; Molasses 120,000. Correspondence Relative to Supplies for Vicksburg, Commissary Department, Department of Alabama, Mississippi, and East Louisiana, Box No. 7, NA (RG) 109. On the basis of these reports, Shannon's criticism seems to be too harsh, probably stemming from a lack of appreciation of the difficulties facing the military officials and a refusal to accept the realities of war.

in order that they might be prepared to catch the spring rains, and they hoped that the "government [would] order" this action to be taken; but the "government" failed to heed the committee.[24]

More and more there was merging and interaction between the civilians and the soldiers. Occasionally it was of an official nature, as in the case of the communication between the board of police and the "government," but usually it was a personal affair; and these relationships ran the course of human behavior, from lovemaking to bitter enmity, with accolades, charges, and countercharges freely given on both sides.

Rowland Chambers had his first bout with military officialdom when an army surgeon ordered him out of his house in order that it might be used as a hospital. Chambers refused to leave until General Smith ordered him to, and then, grumbling, he moved into his servants' quarters. The experience must have soured him, for he made this general accusation: "The soldiers are all the time annoying us in some way." A few days later he was more specific: "The soldiers came in and stole some of our cabage last night."[25]

The *Whig* protested the behavior of an officer who went into a hospital, drank the medicinal whiskey, and reeled out. Then the paper made the suggestion, a tacit admission that the civilians themselves were not simon-pure, that the hospitals should be relocated outside the city in order that "the convalescents would be out of the reach of the unavoidable temptations that beset them in the city."[26] From time to time the *Whig* would rise from bland protests to righteous indignation: "We regret exceedingly having to notice the disgraceful conduct of some of our soldiers . . . . Yesterday a soldier knocked at the door of a respectable lady . . . and requested her to give him some milk. On the lady's replying that she regretted her inability to oblige him, he abused her in the most obscene language. No male protector being present . . . he escaped the punishment he richly merited."[27]

24. Minutes of the board of police of Warren County, March 21, 1863, reprinted in the *Vicksburg Daily Whig,* March 24, 1863.
25. Chambers, Diary, February 10, March 9, 25, 1863.
26. *Vicksburg Daily Whig,* January 30, February 14, 1863.
27. *Ibid.,* March 26, 1863.

As self-appointed critic the *Whig* pulled no punches. It criticized privates and generals alike. The privates were flayed for their lack of regard for Southern womanhood; the generals and other officers were chastised for appreciating the company of the ladies too much. Shannon thought that the officers were paying too much attention to parties and not enough to war. On March 7 he printed: "The very night the 'Indianola' passed our [batteries], some of the high officers were tripping the light fantastic toe with some of the ladies who have not [left] town . . . . Piping and dancing have been the order of the night for every night this week."[28] Criticism of privates went unanswered, but Shannon received scalding protests for this article from both officers and women.[29]

This was the contentious side of the people's garrison life, but the whole was Janus-faced. For every grate and rub there was a corresponding lilt, which also ran from private to general. Granville Alspaugh (who must have received his two white shirts) found a sweetheart. He wrote his mother that his sweetheart was a nice girl, and she had given him a ring; but he was not going to be swept off his feet, and he reassured his mother that he would never marry Mollie Price.[30]

For several months James Brotherton, a second lieutenant from Georgia, had been complaining about Mississippi. Then his letters lost their querulousness, and he wrote his father: "Tell Mat that I have found me a Mississippi Sweet Heart tell him that she is very pretty and accomplished her name is Maggie."[31]

Even generals were susceptible. On a rainy day in January, General Smith sent this note to Elizabeth Eggleston: "I am . . . glad the day is stormy, for she who brings joy and comfort to

28. *Ibid.,* March 7, 1863. The *Indianola* ran the batteries on the night of February 13, without suffering a single hit. *Official Records Navy,* Ser. I, Vol. XXIII, 403.

29. *Vicksburg Daily Whig,* March 17, 1863.

30. Granville Alspaugh to Mrs. A. E. Alspaugh, March 15, 1863, J. P. Knox Papers, Department of Archives and Manuscripts, Louisiana State University.

31. James M. Brotherton to Levi Brotherton, February 11, 1863, William H. Brotherton Papers, Emory University.

all others might well let a ray of sunshine come into my apartment."[32]

Most of the people's contacts with the military fell somewhere between the limits set by General Smith's billet doux to Elizabeth Eggleston and his expulsion order to Rowland Chambers. By now the people had accustomed themselves to the army, which had begun to withdraw from the camps on the outskirts and take up quarters inside the city. Winchester Hall's regiment was scattered in various places—vacant warehouses, private homes, and Hall himself lived in the Masonic Hall.[33] James Brotherton's cavalry company was quartered in one home: ". . . a splendid house," he wrote his father, "with 5 rooms and 3 fire places . . . . We have a table and chairs in fact it's just like living at home."[34] This movement threw the people and the soldiers even closer together, and they learned to work together as well as bicker. For several days the *Whig* devoted advertising space to a joint project of the civilians and the soldiers:

APOLLO HALL!
GRAND VOCAL AND INSTRUMENTAL
CONCERT!

Prof. G. A. Gnospelius and E. H. Baldwin, assisted by several amateurs, residents, and Col. Withers' Light Artillery Brass Band, will give a Concert for the benefit of our NEEDY SOLDIERS . . . .[35]

Then, too, the civilians worked alone to supply some of the needs of the troops. The *Whig* advertised for women volunteers to knit clothing for the men: "There are a few more socks to finish yet for the soldiers. All who will assist in finishing them are requested to call at Mrs. Edwards' . . . . The yarn is there."[36] And in other ways the citizens and the soldiers found common interests, purpose, and even objects of derision. Some of the regimental chaplains began to preach in the city, and they invited the civilians as well as their men to attend the services.[37] When

32. Martin L. Smith to Elizabeth Eggleston, January 19, 1863, Roach-Eggleston Papers, Southern Historical Collection, University of North Carolina.
33. Hall, *26th Louisiana,* p. 58.
34. James M. Brotherton to Levi Brotherton, March 27, 1863, William H. Brotherton Papers.
35. *Vicksburg Daily Whig,* January 23, 1863.
36. *Ibid.,* February 12, 1863.
37. *Ibid.,* February 28, 1863.

conscripted soldiers arrived in the city their white woolen uniforms set them apart from the volunteers and they were treated contemptuously, their white clothing a badge of reproach. Then the volunteers were issued white uniforms and it became impossible to single out the conscripts for abuse.[38] Yet at the same time the poor conscripts walked the streets, unsure when a barbed comment would be aimed at them, there were still men in the city who sought substitutes for military service—they would pay $5,000 to avoid the white uniform, or any uniform for that matter.[39]

Even with Grant across the river and with the soldiers moving in their homes and with their city turned into a fortress, there was a part of the people's life which remained separate from the military and occasionally seemed almost incongruous when set inside the war context in which they lived.

Spring came early to Vicksburg. In mid-February the weather was warm and bright. Peach trees were covered with white blossoms; roses and spirea were blooming.[40] Rowland Chambers, his house taken by the army, thought that at least the yard remained his own and he set out trees in the garden. They were to be for his daughter.[41] Valentine's Day did not go unnoticed. Little Grace Shannon received a card, cut from rough paper and clumsily lettered:

> A veil is round thee
> And thy heart is like a hidden flower,
> But could we see thee, as thou art,
> We should confess thy power.[42]

Some persons, keenly aware that they were the actors in a tortured segment of history, kept these little scraps of makeshift and put them away "to look at when we are old."[43]

The clerks in the county offices, probably unaware of what they were doing, pinned their accretions to the record of a people

38. Hall, *26th Louisiana,* p. 58.
39. *Vicksburg Daily Whig,* March 10, 1863.
40. R. L. Howard, *History of the 124th Regiment, Illinois Infantry Volunteers* (Springfield, Illinois, 1880), p. 59.
41. Chambers, Diary, March 3, 1863.
42. Unsigned Valentine, Crutcher Collection.
43. "A Woman's Diary," *The Century Magazine,* XXX, 768.

hanging on to the apparatus of peace in a battle situation. The county board of police, unlike the city council, continued to function. The board was re-organized early in January, and later in the month an election for various county officials gave the local politicians an opportunity to brush up their long unused vote-getting techniques. The school system, such as it was by then, was still operative, and by late March the political structure remained stable enough to allow an election of school trustees. The county clerk's office was open, though the number of property transfers recorded in January, February, and March did not equal the December total—an indication of the people's returning confidence.[44]

Francis Clewell, adjutant of a Missouri cavalry company, thought the people were confident. "The citizens," he wrote his mother, "are quite contented, and are waiting patiently to see the next move of the enemy. They do not fear an attack and say if they should be attacked, they are not afraid of the result. Every body goes about their business as if there was not a yankee in a thousand miles of them. In fact Vicksburg is the fastest place I have been in for two years."[45]

The people's resolution stemmed from two sources: from Grant's seeming inability to move, and from their own knowledge that they had withstood the best that Farragut and Sherman could throw at them. They had become inured to the "shells . . . thrown in at intervals." "The slow shelling," wrote the woman from New Orleans, "goes on all the time, and we have grown indifferent. It does not at present interrupt or interfere with daily avocations, but," a shadow of apprehension flickered across her mind, "I suspect they are only getting the range of different points; and when they have them all complete, showers of shot will rain on us all at once."[46]

Yet at this time the bombardment did not cow or enervate, it excited and exhilarated. On Sunday, February 22, the gun-

44. Supervisors' Minute Book, 1853-67, Courthouse, Vicksburg, pp. 592-93; *Vicksburg Daily Whig*, January 7, 13, March 21, 1863; Warren County Deed Book CC, cf. entries of March 1863, with those of December 1862.

45. Francis C. Clewell to Mother, February 15, 1863, Gertrude Jenkins Papers, Duke University.

46. "A Woman's Diary," *The Century Magazine*, XXX, 767.

boats at the mouth of the Yazoo commenced a rapid fire, and the people thought that an engagement of some sort was beginning. There was "considerable excitement"; the courthouse hill, the "Sky Parlor," and Hansford's hill—the city's vantage points —were crowded with people. Then the firing ceased. There was something anti-climactic about the whole thing. "It turned out," reported the *Whig,* "that the Yankees were only celebrating the 22nd of February—the anniversary of Washington's birthday."[47]

The Sky Parlor, one of the highest hills two blocks from the waterfront, was the rendezvous for the "upper circle families." A driveway on one side and a "dizzy flight of wooden steps" on the other led to the top of the hill. At first there was just a bare hilltop, but then some officers took up quarters there and a band and a telescope were installed, and the elite could watch the shelling in style if not in safety.[48]

Mary Loughborough, visiting in Vicksburg, said: "Almost every day we walked up the Sky Parlor Hill, and looked through the glass at the Federal encampment," at the gunboats, and at the steamers. She was at breakfast one morning when the conversation turned to the possibility of locating a concealed battery at the mouth of the canal, and the family spent most of the morning sweeping the opposite shore with a telescope. Mrs. Loughborough also noted: "Crowds of people collected at the Sky Parlor when any movement was made on the river."[49]

On the night of March 19, the Unionist couple from New Orleans climbed the hill to watch the shooting. The woman did not care for the Sky Parlor—she thought the view was better from a "quiet" hill nearer her home. Her attention wandered to the other persons on the hill, and she overheard a woman say to an officer: "It is such folly for them to waste their ammunition like that. How can they ever take a town that has such advantages for defense and protection as this? We'll just burrow into these hills and let them batter away as hard as they please."

"You are right madam," replied the officer, "and besides,

47. *Vicksburg Daily Whig,* February 24, 1863.

48. [Mary A. Loughborough], *My Cave Life in Vicksburg* (New York, 1864), p. 86.

49. *Ibid.,* p. 20.

when our women are so willing to brave death and endure discomfort, how can we ever be conquered?"

"The only drawback," the woman said, looking squarely at the Union couple, "are the contemptible men who are staying at home in comfort, when they ought to be in the army if they had a spark of honor."

The next day when the diarist described the incident she concluded: "I cannot repeat all, but it was the usual tirade. It is strange I have met no one yet who seems to comprehend an honest difference of opinion, and stranger yet that the ordinary rules of good breeding are now so entirely ignored."[50] What she said was true, but what she forgot was that she was living in the midst of a people who were fighting for their lives.

The slow shelling which some persons thought exciting and colorful struck fear in the hearts of others. They gladly would have left the city, but they could find no place to go. Marmaduke Shannon commented on their plight: "We learn that several families are here now who would willingly leave but don't know where to go. Others can get places but the price of board or the amount demanded for rent per month is so exhorbitant that they find themselves unable to pay it."[51] The path to safety was still paved with depreciating Confederate currency.

Whatever their reasons for remaining in the city, through choice or circumstance, the people began one activity in common. They started digging. Cave building became big business, with set prices depending upon the size and elaborateness of the excavation. For twenty dollars a simple, one room affair could be dug. A deeper thick-roofed, several-chambered cave, shored up by timber and with shelves cut into the earth, cost fifty dollars. Great single-roomed caverns, which could hold close to one hundred persons, were also hollowed out of the hills. By mid-March, said a woman in a morbid but descriptive simile, the city was "so honeycombed with caves that the streets look[ed] like avenues in a cemetery."[52]

50. "A Woman's Diary," *The Century Magazine,* XXX, 767-68.

51. *Vicksburg Daily Whig,* February 5, 1863.

52. "A Woman's Diary," *The Century Magazine,* XXX, 767; Reed, "A Woman's Experiences," *ibid.,* LXI, 924; Loughborough, *Cave Life,* p. 17.

As much as the people tried to improve the caves—by bringing in furniture and carpets and lamps—they were still utilitarian affairs, dark and dank, and many of the civilians, especially the women, avoided them as much as possible. On March 20, after her first trip to a cave, one woman wrote, "When we went in this evening and sat down, the earthy, suffocating feeling, as of a living tomb, was dreadful to me. I fear I shall risk death outside rather then melt in that dark furnace."[53] Even after Grant encircled the city and the rain of shells had begun, Emma Balfour refused to go underground where "the sense of suffocation . . . the certainty that there was no way of escape, that we were hemmed in, caged" bore so heavily on her that she "perferred to risk the danger" in her house.[54] Yet she would learn to live in a hole cut out of the earth. It merely took her a little longer than most people—they were learning in February and March.

Grant was also learning during February and March. He learned that the old canal would not work, that the tortuous water route through Louisiana would not work, that the delta sloughs and streams were a horrendous trap. He was at his wits' end.

In Vicksburg, Jared Sanders had already turned to his Bible, found an appropriate reference and said: "I think it will long be a question of old Abe's—'Who will bring me into the *strong* city.' "[55] In the March 4 issue of the *Whig,* Shannon reported that the crew of the captured *Indianola* (whose successful passage of the batteries still rankled him) was lodged in the city jail, that "our lower batteries sent a number of iron messengers over to the Yankees," and that the enemy "was all quiet on the peninsula."[56] He sounded almost smug. The number of property sales trickled down to the lowest number since the beginning of 1862.[57]

If there was a growing sense of security, it was not reflected in an easing of shortage. General Pemberton approved a citi-

53. "A Woman's Diary," *The Century Magazine,* XXX, 767.
54. [Emma] Balfour, Diary, p. 6.
55. Jared Sanders to "Friend," January 23, 1863, Jared Y. Sanders Papers. The reference is to *Psalms* 60:9.
56. *Vicksburg Daily Whig,* March 4, 1863.
57. Warren County Deed Book CC, entries for February 1863.

zens' petition asking that they be allowed to travel into the Tallahatchie-Yallobusha river region, some 120 miles away, to seek food.[58] The foundries ran short of coal for their war work, and not even Pemberton was able to find any.[59] Rowland Chambers, a dentist, learned to make shoes.[60] But conditioning had blunted the edge of scarcity, and there was little grumbling. In fact, the people began to take pride in their ability to turn scraps and odds-and-ends into usable articles. One woman wrote:

> I have learned to darn like an artist. Making shoes is now another accomplishment. Mine were in tatters. H—[her husband] came across a moth eaten pair that he bought me, giving ten dollars . . . and they fell into rags when I tried to wear them; but the soles were good, and that has helped me to [have] shoes. A pair of old coat-sleeves saved—nothing is thrown away now—was in my trunk. I cut an exact pattern from my old shoes, laid it on the sleeves, and cut out thus good uppers and sewed them carefully; then soaked the soles and sewed the cloth to them. I am so proud of these home-made shoes, think I'll put them in a glass case when the war is over as an heirloom. H—says he has come to have an abiding faith that everything he needs to wear will come out of that trunk while the war lasts. It is like a fairy-casket.[61]

The *Whig* printed instructions for turning hems in order that worn spots would not show, and the women darned, turned, mended, and improvised "while the shells . . . leisurely scream[ed] through the air."[62]

James De Bow made his last visit to the city during the latter part of March. On Sunday, March 29, the telegraph wires were down, there was no news, and he turned his attention to church and to the people:

> It is remarkable considering the . . . scarcity . . . how well everybody manages to dress. To look at the ladies bonnets and robes, no one could imagine that a blockade of two years has shut us off from the world of fashion. Silks, laces, ribbons, flounces, [and] frills . . .

58. John C. Pemberton to L. Lindsay, March 16, 1863, Letters and Telegrams sent, Department of Mississippi and Eastern Louisiana, Chapt. II, Vol. LVII, 559, NA (RG) 109.

59. John C. Pemberton to Mr. Paxton, March 10, 1863, *ibid.*, p. 521.

60. Chambers, Diary, February 27, 1863.

61. "A Woman's Diary," *The Century Magazine,* XXX, 768.

62. *Ibid.*

have kept wonderfully well. The ladies are good economists and perform marvels in cleaning, cutting up, turning inside out and refitting. Everything looks neat and tidy. Even their feet show no evidence of neglect. The gentlemen are not quite so well off, but still do very well. With them there is no motive to dress. Army clothes and colors are in fashion. The everlasting grey suit [is] everywhere . . . .

What De Bow saw was Sunday-best. He put his finger closer to the pulse of the city when he jotted down a few cold facts and figures. "Prices," he observed, "are still advancing." Board at the hotels was $8 per day, double the price of two months previous. Flour was $125 per barrel, meat 75¢ a pound, broadcloth $50 per yard, shoes $30 a pair, boots $75, sugar $1 per pound, coffee $5 per pound. Furniture was scarce, and it sold for "fabulous prices." A pitcher and washbasin was worth $20 and "the most common negro bedstead" cost $25. Real estate was also caught in the spiraling prices. City property brought "enormous prices," and the only property which had not "advanced much" was farm land. It, said De Bow, "may be bought at 25 to 50 per cent above old prices."[63]

Fancying himself an economist, De Bow recorded what he believed to be the economic aspects of a people two years blockaded and close to war. Though prices were inflated and food and consumer goods were difficult to obtain, De Bow, with his comments and figures, left the impression that all things considered the people were not doing too badly. But his concrete figures reflected something more than inflation and scarcity. They pointed up an intangible—the working of the mind.

The will to victory was a fragile thing; it could stand just so much external buffeting and internal doubting before it started to crack. These destructive bangings and gnawings had begun with the fall of New Orleans, and they had never really let up, though they had been momentarily lessened from time to time. The gunboats had sailed away, but they had returned; Sherman had been whipped, but he was back with reinforcements; Grant had been stymied, but he was still across the river; and the people themselves had already applied the word "besieged" to their city. Each event did not necessarily vitiate the will to victory,

63. *De Bow's Review,* New Series, III (January, 1867), 104.

but each left a scar on the people's consciousness, a scar that deepened and widened with the passage of time. What De Bow recorded during the last of March 1863 was the accumulation of doubt of ultimate victory. The people, perhaps barely conscious of it, had begun to hedge their bets on the Confederacy when they put such premium on real property—pitchers, bedsteads, lots, and houses—which would retain their value regardless of the outcome of war.[64]

Then, for some persons, the doubt of victory was not unconscious, but one which brought certainty and relief. On April 2, the Unionist couple had to give up their home to the returned owner, who said that he intended to bring his family back into the city. "That," said the woman, "means that he has got tired of the Confederacy and means to stay here and thus get out of it."[65]

But these things worked beneath the surface. The only widespread, conscious acknowledgement of them was another day of "Fasting, Humiliation, and Prayer," which was proclaimed by Jefferson Davis to be observed throughout the Confederacy. Mayor Lindsay thought the situation in Vicksburg warranted that he "specially call the attention of our citizens" to the day. On March 26, all of the city's churches held services, and many prayers must have been uttered for the deliverance of the city from Grant's grasping army.[66]

This quiet day was probably the same day that Mary Livermore, a volunteer nurse, stood on the levee opposite the city and looked across to the beleaguered place. Even with a telescope she could see "no sign of inhabited homes"—no children playing

64. This interpretation is not completely "hind-sight speculation." That doubts had begun to arise is undeniable for, on March 1, Pemberton telegraphed General Carter L. Stevenson: "Prevent today's *Mississippian* being circulated in Vicksburg and let not the matter [unknown, but obviously considered detrimental to the war effort] be published by the *Whig* . . . . Prevent circulation of today's issues of *Appeal* and *Crisis* in Vicksburg as well as the *Mississippian*." John C. Pemberton to C. L. Stevenson, March 1, 1863, Letters and Telegrams sent, Department of Mississippi and Eastern Louisiana, Chapt. II, Vol. LVII, 506, 509, NA (RG) 109. Also, property sales began to edge upward during March (double the February total), and in April over four times as much property was sold as in February. Warren County Deed Book CC, entries for March-April, 1863.

65. "A Woman's Diary," *The Century Magazine,* XXX, 768.

66. *Vicksburg Daily Whig,* March 26, 1863.

in the streets, no women walking or shopping. Vicksburg appeared desolate to her.[67]

Mrs. Livermore watched at the wrong time, for there was plenty of life and gaiety in the city—especially at night. A waxing moon swung high in the night sky; on April 3, it was full, and officers and their ladies began to take moonlight rides in the pleasant, quiet evenings.[68] Beneath the moon on dirt roads the hooves of horses were muffled, and the murmur of quiet voices was contrasted with the silent, shadowed hulk of cannon and fortifications. On the bright nights the riders could push back the present, find peace in the plans and dreams they wished for, and war was very far away.

Then, too, the secret plans and dreams had a way of backfiring that provided the entire city with snickers and good belly-laughs. The *Whig* reported that several young ladies had received invitations to a moonlight ride with some officers, then waited in vain long past the set hour. They later discovered that "rival belles" had sent the invitations.[69] One officer found the spring nights ripe for courtship and pressed his suit almost to success (and pressed his luck too far)—wedding plans and arrangements had been made when the news arrived that the officer's wife and children were on their way to Vicksburg. "He hastily departed," observed the *Whig,* "leaving the girl to breathe:

> Oh, that a dream so sweet, so short enjoyed,
> Should be thus sadly, cruelly destroyed."[70]

Moonlit nights affected enlisted men as well as officers. Granville Alspaugh told his mother of a conscript who "make[s] out he is sick [and] lays up all day and runs about at night with the girls."[71]

Grant gave them plenty of time to run with the girls, and in doing so heightened the illusion of peace. He sat across the river,

67. Mary A. Livermore, *My Story of the War: A Woman's Narrative of Four Years of Personal Experience* (Hartford, Connecticut, 1892), pp. 335-36.

68. *Clarke's Confederate Household Almanac for the Year 1863* (Vicksburg, Mississippi, 1863), p. 8; *Vicksburg Daily Whig,* April 4, 1863.

69. *Vicksburg Daily Whig,* April 4, 1863.

70. *Ibid.,* April 2, 1863.

71. Granville Alspaugh to Mrs. A. E. Alspaugh, April 6, 1863, J. P. Knox Papers.

quiet and seemingly immobile. The *Whig's* daily summaries of the enemy took on an almost placid tone. On April 10, the paper reported: "There was an unusual quietness among the Yankees across the river yesterday. There was no stir among the troops, and but one arrival at the landing." On April 14, the *Whig* printed: "Dispatches received . . . indicate that the [attack on] Vicksburg is virtually ended—that the majority of Grant's army and the heaviest of the iron-clads will soon be found on the Tennessee river." By April 16, the paper was lulled into a sense of security. It suggested that the streets be repaired "now that there is no immediate danger here." Even a concentration of Union shipping was explained away: "We do not regard the fleet's coming down as at all pointing to an attack here. The boats are all more or less damaged, the men dissatisfied and demoralized." The paper made no mention of the waned moon and the dark nights.

Grant was waiting for the dark moon. He had tried every way of getting into Vicksburg except a suicidal frontal assault and a swing south across the river which would put him behind the city; and he needed the transports to ferry his army across the Mississippi. He could move the army overland to the point south of the city, but the boats would have to pass the Vicksburg batteries to get there. So he waited for a dark night for them to try to slip by.

On the morning of April 16, the people of Vicksburg picked up their copies of the *Whig* and read: ". . . there is no immediate danger here." As the day passed Major William O. Watts decorated his home for a ball planned for that night, throughout the city women laid out their party dresses, and officers gave dress uniforms and boots to servants to be cleaned. Several miles north of Vicksburg, at Millikens' Bend, Grant's staff planned a party too—celebrating the beginning of what they hoped would be the final phase of the Vicksburg campaign, for that night the first elements of the fleet would run the batteries.

When the sun set the Union ships dropped down to the "Lower Landing," four miles from Vicksburg. They tied up in a cluster, thirty boats surrounding the *Von Phul* which Grant was aboard. Franc Wilkie, correspondent for the New York

Tribune, was on the *Von Phul* watching Grant, Mrs. Grant, the still honeymooning John McClernands, and other officers and women. Nothing indicated that deadly business was at hand—the couples popped champagne corks, sang, gossiped, and wandered off for light love-making. In the distance the lights of Vicksburg twinkled along the bluffs.[72]

In the city Major Watts's ball was underway. Mary Loughborough was there, dancing with one officer after another, amid a galaxy of women in silks and laces and officers in dress uniforms. The night was placid, starlit but moonless.

About ten o'clock the gaiety subsided aboard the *Von Phul.* The party-makers turned quietly to look out on the river as a line of dark shapes slid slowly by toward Vicksburg. In Major Watts's home a brigadier general lightly held a young girl in his arms as they whirled about the ballroom floor.

When the first shell's explosion ripped through the night the girl clasped her hands and asked: "Where shall we go?" The brigadier jestingly replied: "To the country for safety." Out into the dark she ran, falling into the dust, party dress and all, when she heard a shell whining overhead. Mary Loughborough said that there was nothing but "confusion and alarm" when the shelling started, and there was much scurrying by high officers to get to their posts.

The fight lasted for over an hour. The Confederates burned wooden buildings along the waterfront to illuminate the river, and they sank one transport. But the first wave of the fleet was past, the second would follow in a week, and Grant had the transports necessary to cross the river.[73] The noose had begun to close.

The lull was past. On April 28, a woman wrote:

72. The following account is based upon these sources: Loughborough, *Cave Life,* pp. 23-24; Hall, *26th Louisiana,* p. 60; Franc B. Wilkie, *Pen and Powder* (Boston, 1888), pp. 313-14.

73. *Harpers' Weekly Magazine,* May 16, 1863, p. 315; James R. Soley, "Naval Operations in the Vicksburg Campaign," *Battles and Leaders,* III, 566. Lavinia Shannon thought that the timing of the ball was fortunate because "the battery officers were all at large party . . . and so were up and ready." Lavinia Shannon to Emma Crutcher, April 22, 1863, Crutcher Collection.

The first phase of Grant's final move against the city. Union transports run the Vicksburg batteries, April 1863. (From *Harper's Pictorial History of the Civil War*)

For many nights we have had but little sleep, because the Federals gun-boats have been running past the batteries. The uproar when this is happening is phenomenal . . . . One of the batteries has a remarkable gun they call "Whistling Dick," because of the screeching, whistling sound it gives, and certainly it does sound like a tortured thing. Added to all this is the indescribable Confederate yell, which is a soul-harrowing sound to hear. I have gained respect for the mechanism of the human ear, which stands it all without injury. The streets are seldom quiet at night, even the dragging about of cannon makes a din in these echoing gullies.[74]

Rowland Chambers noted: "People are leaveing town," then he returned seemingly unconcerned to his garden, where he was planting cabbage and peas.[75] Yet there was no headlong rush from the city. Lavinia Shannon wrote her daughter: "A good many families still remain in town and some have moved back."[76] With Grant on the move there was no telling where he might appear, and, if a person fled, he might well run right into the Union army. There were other hazards too. Marmaduke Shannon had sent eight members of his family to Raymond, where he hoped they would be safe. Instead, diphtheria struck them all, from

74. "A Woman's Diary," *The Century Magazine,* XXX, 768.
75. Chambers, Diary, April 20, 27, 29, 1863.
76. Lavinia Shannon to Emma Crutcher, April 22, 1863, Crutcher Collection.

mother to baby, and within the space of four weeks Shannon buried four of his children.[77] The survivors stayed in Raymond and Shannon remained in Vicksburg to edit the *Whig*. Once again the printers complained of the danger, but this time instead of suspending publication Shannon moved his offices to his home and the printers set type in Mrs. Shannon's bedroom. The paper still had to be printed in the pressroom, but the editorial work and the typesetting were done in Shannon's home "as the shelling disturbed them so much at the office."[78]

The shells interdicted the stretch of railroad that lay exposed to the river, yet the trains continued to run into the city. The unprotected depot was shunned, and most of the passengers boarded the trains in the shelter of hillsides and cuts.[79] A passenger, James Pugh, long-time resident of Vicksburg who had fled to Shreveport, was summarily taken from a departing train, led to the Provost Marshal's office, and searched. His searchers were seeking $30,000 in gold specie, which Pugh was alleged to have stolen. Only $2,800 was found, which Pugh said he had dug up from its hiding place upon the request of the owner, another Vicksburg refugee living in Shreveport. He was released and sent on his way, but his arrest was indicative of a closer scrutiny of the civilians and a mounting incidence of crime.[80]

When the Cobb-Manlove Company warehouse was looted of three thousand pounds of sugar the authorities suspected a gang of soldiers and civilians. A few days after the robbery the Provost Marshal's patrol caught the thieves—a slave, two members of the patrol itself and several citizens.[81] Some of the soldiers were also disposing of military stores on the black market. One man brought a sack of meal home and told his wife that it was "a case of corruption." He said: "A soldier who was hauling some of the Government sacks to the hospital offered me this for five dollars, if I could keep a secret."[82] A tailor shop was also looted, and the *Whig* commented: "Stealing seems

77. *Ibid.* 78. *Ibid.*
79. Loughborough, *Cave Life,* p. 21.
80. *Vicksburg Daily Whig,* April 11, 1863.
81. *Ibid.,* April 9, 22, 1863.
82. "A Woman's Diary," *The Century Magazine,* XXX, 769.

to be carried on here on a pretty extensive scale."[83] The situation became so bad that the people were warned: "The city is patroled every night, and both black and white who cannot give proper vouchers or satisfactory reasons for their being out, will find themselves in 'limbo' in the morning."[84]

A twinge of uneasiness concerning the slaves flicked across the city. All owners were urged to keep their Negroes at home after dark; those who were caught out at night were to be jailed. "Some seven or eight of these 'snuff-colored' individuals," reported the *Whig,* "were picked up by the police . . . and a little wholesome admonition, administered to them. This may prove a warning to others."[85] The system had begun to crack. In Vicksburg the fissures were just appearing; hard by the city the slave structure was in shambles.

Across the river Kate Stone's family, cowed by marauding Negroes, abandoned Brokenburn after "a night and day of terror."[86] In the delta the slaves were leaving the plantations by droves and flocking toward the Union army. Franc Wilkie, aboard the *Silver Wave* on the Yazoo, saw "throngs of negro families" waiting to be taken away. Some were already aboard flatboats and rafts. One raft loaded with Negroes was tied to the stern of the *Silver Wave,* then the stern-wheeler began to move downstream. The paddlewheel threw back waves which washed over the raft, and, as the *Silver Wave's* speed increased, the bow of the raft dipped and bit into the water. Before Wilkie's horrified eyes the raft sliced under the water. Its human cargo vanished from sight. Nothing—not a single head, rag or fragment or any kind—bobbed to the surface.[87]

Within the sight of Vicksburg, Edmund Newsome, an Illinois volunteer, heard the Negroes sing of their masters:

> He saw the smoke 'way up the riber,
> Whar' the Linkum gunboats lay;
> He tuck his hat an' he lef' berry sudden,
> I's 'spec' he's ran away.[88]

83. *Vicksburg Daily Whig,* April 22, 1863.
84. *Ibid.,* April 10, 1863. 85. *Ibid.*
86. Stone, *Brokenburn,* pp. 194-97.
87. Wilkie, *Pen and Powder,* pp. 307-10.
88. Edmund Newsome, *Experience in the War of the Great Rebellion* (Carbondale, Illinois, 1879), p. 18.

Tensions began to mount and, on April 28, as Grant readied his army to cross the river below the city, a woman in Vicksburg wrote: "I have never understood before the full force of these questions—what shall we eat? what shall we drink? and wherewithal shall we be clothed?" Her first question was double-edged: a soldier whom she had brought into her house to feed had robbed her cupboard; and the recipes, all based on rice flour, which she had copied from the newspapers, resulted "in brick-bats, or sticky paste."[89]

Grant momentarily took her mind from food worries. On April 30, without opposition, he crossed the Mississippi, at Bruinsburg, his intentions quite clear—to strike for Vicksburg. Two Confederate armies, hundreds of square miles of hostile country, and self-severed supply lines separated him from the city. Yet on May 1, when Grant was many miles away, the woman wrote: "It is settled at last that we shall spend the time of siege in Vicksburg." She and her husband laid their beds in their wine cellar and gathered in what food they could find: a hogshead of sugar, a barrel of syrup, ten pounds of bacon, four pounds of wheat flour, a small sack of cornmeal, and some spices. They ruefully looked at the imbalance—a hogshead of sugar and a small sack of flour and thought that perhaps when the flour was gone they could "keep alive on sugar." In the flickering, sputtering light of a home-made candle the woman sat in the cellar and mused over "the accumulated bottles [which] told of 'the banquet hall deserted,' the spirit and glow of the festive hours whose lights and garlands were dead, and the last guest long since departed." Her reverie passed, her mind returned to the present, and her only consolation was the thought: "a city besieged is a city taken—so if we live through it we shall be out of the Confederacy."[90]

89. "A Woman's Diary," *The Century Magazine,* XXX, 768-69.
90. *Ibid.,* p. 769.

CHAPTER VIII

"THE DAY OF OUR DOOM"

EVENTS had moved full circle. A year before, the people in their panic had awaited the first approach of Farragut's gunboats. Now, a year later, almost to the day, they awaited the approach of Grant's army. Eighteen days would pass before Grant would stand before Vicksburg; but, unlike the May days of 1862, there was little violent fear in the city. Instead, it seemed that the people knew that Grant must come and that the intervening hours must somehow be lived and marked off. Life was confused and incongruous, but not fear-stricken.

Clerks enrolled voters for a coming election, while Rowland Chambers wrote day after day of "great excitement and alarm."[1] The board of police went through the motions of a meeting, but conducted no business and for the last time the county clerk registered and validated property transfers with Confederate revenue stamps.[2] A. B. Reading telegraphed Jefferson Davis, urging him to come at once to the threatened city.[3] Junius Browne, a captured newspaperman, was "lionized" by the people; at the jail he received "calls every hour in the day," and he left Vicksburg feeling like an honored guest instead of a prisoner.[4] Somewhere a merchant found a thousand yards of golden lace, which he offered for sale; and another man dumped sixty-five thousand pounds of sugar on the market.[5] The *Whig* tried to pump confidence into the people, but its columns could not match the pace set by those of Grant. Two days after the Grand

1. *Vicksburg Daily Whig,* May 2, 1863; Chambers, Diary, May 3-16, 1863.
2. Supervisors' Minute Book, 1853-67, p. 598.
3. *Official Records Army,* Ser. I, Vol. LII, Pt. 2, 467.
4. Junius H. Browne, *Four Years in Secessia* (Hartford, Ohio, 1865), pp. 243 ff.
5. *Vicksburg Daily Whig,* May 5, 1863.

Gulf detachment had been brushed aside the *Whig* printed: "The utmost confidence is felt in our ability to defeat this movement on Grand Gulf."[6] The paper would not chart Grant's progress much further—within the week a naval shell blew the printing office into a smoldering shambles.[7] The post commander published an order (which no one obeyed) prohibiting everyone except generals and staff officers from congregating on the hilltops and at the railway depot.[8] The railroad was shuttling frightened people out of the city and bringing frightened people into the city. At the Jackson station, Mary Loughborough was caught in a "living stream that flowed and surged along . . . seeking the Vicksburg cars." She had joined a family that, in a supreme sort of irony, was moving to Vicksburg, "as the safest place," for Grierson's Raiders, taking a leaf from the tactics book of Forrest and Van Dorn, had cut a swath lengthwise across the state to throw Pemberton into confusion and to touch the civilians with a fear of "the rabble that usually followed a large army . . . who might plunder, insult and rob."[9]

Grant, in the wake of the confusion caused by Grierson, was moving swiftly. On the night of May 12, he thrust a column athwart the railroad at Clinton and, with the railway and telegraph cut, there was no more news.[10] Shortly before the telegraph went dead Rowland Chambers outlined a heavy, black rectangle in his diary, and inside the black lines wrote: "Stonewall Jackson Died yesterday."[11] As he wrote this he recorded one of the last bits of information which came into the city. From then on the people had to rely on the rumors that filtered in with the refugees.

Grant made plenty of refugees and rumors. Port Gibson, Raymond, Jackson, and Champion's Hill—at each place a victory, and at each place refugees and stories. Anne Martin, one of Marmaduke Shannon's daughters, was at Raymond when the Union army marched past. Unlike some other people, she did not try to run ahead of the advancing Federals, but instead stayed

6. *Ibid.,* May 2, 1863.
7. Chambers, Diary, May 9, 1863.
8. *Vicksburg Daily Whig,* May 8, 1863.
9. Loughborough, *Cave Life,* pp. 26-27.
10. Newsome, *Experience,* p. 26.
11. Chambers, Diary, May 11, 1863.

in the house and hoped that locked doors would protect her. Shortly after the army had marched on she wrote her sister:

> For a week that immense army continued to pass through . . . pouring into town, flaunting their star spangled banner, playing Yankee Doodle, and, oh the desecration! the Bonnie Blue Flag . . . . All night the fife and drum was heard as fresh regiments passed . . . . I prayed most earnestly for protection during the night for we could hear them tearing down fences, shooting cattle, shouting and going on and we expected every minute to be broken in on . . . . The doors were locked but they broke them open and took everything but one sidesaddle, even pulled the curtains down and tore them in strings. The remaining sidesaddle was taken by one of these fancy yellow girls, an especial pet of one of the officers. The morning after the battle [he was] standing in the kitchen door assisting at her toilet by pouring water on her hands from the sugarbowl . . . . She was a dreadfully affected piece. Spying the sidesaddle, she took a fancy to it and on leaving sent a soldier to get it for her. So she rode off with the best sidesaddle on the pacing pony and I suppose that hussy is capering around on it now . . . . We could see them bringing all kinds of plunder, showing around silverware and jewelry they had stolen . . . . If you are ever invaded, Emmie, don't bury anything. Everything that has been hidden in that way has been found. Hearing that . . . Mrs. Robinson . . . had buried her silverware, they dug up every foot of her garden until they found it. Near Vicksburg . . . Martha Durden's baby was buried in the yard and would you believe it: that child's remains were dug [up] no less than three different times in search of treasure . . . . [This is] how we fared at the hands of the Yankees.[12]

Like a great scythe, Grant's army hooked into central Mississippi, then cut back westward toward Vicksburg. In the city all the people could do was wait, and they had to wait without news. They sat there, dumb and frightened, but not without hope. As Lida Lord remembered it, she was dismayed when she learned of the loss of Jackson, but she did not "doubt either the valor or the wisdom of our generels, but felt confident [of] the speedy surrounding and utter annihilation of Grant's army."[13] Rowland Chambers felt the gnawing of ignorance. On May 16, he wrote: "Great excitement & alarm prevailes we can get no

12. Anne Shannon Martin to Emma Crutcher (May 15 to July 1, 1863?), Phillip Crutcher Collection, Miss. Arch.

13. Reed, "Woman's Experiences," *The Century Magazine,* XLI, 921.

new[s] from the army, Jackson is cut of[f] at this time."[14] The same day Chambers lamented the lack of news, Emma Balfour expressed the same thoughts: "All has been uncertainty and suspense. No news from any quarter—not a word from our army. It is terrible when we know that events so fraught with deep interest to us, are transpiring . . . ." That night she continued: "We have just heard that Jackson is in the hands of the enemy . . . . This looks ominous, but I still have hope."[15]

Her hope was shattered. The following morning McClernand's corps broke through the line of the Big Black, the last defensive position outside Vicksburg. The William Lords, who had taken refuge on a plantation on the Big Black, were so close to the action that they could smell the gunpowder. In a panic, they packed servants and provisions in a wagon and the family in a carriage, and set out for Vicksburg. They arrived in the city that night; behind them thousands of campfires twinkled and glowed, and Lida Lord thought that it was a beautiful sight, but the family "did not linger to admire it."[16] They had to make their way through jammed streets, and when they reached their house had to pick their way through the soldiers sleeping on the front porch. They finally got to bed, and Sunday night ended with the sound of caissons and wagons rumbling through the streets.[17]

Sunday had begun quite differently. It was a pleasant morning, bright and clear and quiet when Mary Loughborough went to church. The pastor was at the Big Black tending the wounded, then as the visiting preacher delivered his sermon the sound of cannonfire drifted in from the east. He interrupted the service to ask the women to meet to prepare bandages for the wounded and the people left the church to the accompaniment of the unceasing cannon. As Mrs. Loughborough walked home she noticed that the city was very quiet—"sullen and expectant."[18] The people were waiting—that was all they could do.

14. Chambers, Diary, May 16, 1863.
15. [Emma] Balfour, Diary, Miss. Arch., p. 1.
16. Reed, *The Century Magazine,* LXI, 921.
17. Journal Kept by Mrs. W. W. Lord During the Siege of Vicksburg, Library of Congress, p. 2.
18. Loughborough, *Cave Life,* pp. 40-41.

Mrs. Winchester Hall was one of the first to hear the news (or rather see it). Before breakfast she watched as some stragglers came limping in along the Jackson Road—an infantry squad, a horseman, cannoneers with a single gun; no order, no discipline.[19]

About noon the flood started. A lieutenant, tears streaming, told Emma Balfour that they were whipped. She wept too; but, she said: "Not only for him, indeed all individual feeling seems merged in grief and interest for my country. Oh will God forsake us now? I cannot believe it. He may chasten us but I will not be disheartened or discouraged!"[20]

A man rapped upon the door of the house of the Unionist couple from New Orleans.[21] "Well," he said, "they are upon us; the Yankees will be here by this evening . . . . Pemberton has been whipped at Baker's Creek and Big Black, and his army are running back here as fast as they can come and the Yanks after them, in such numbers nothing can stop them. Hasn't Pemberton acted like a fool?" Then he left to try to find his parents who had fled to the Big Black.

The couple thought that this was a strange performance for a Confederate—that there "was the absence of that concern to be expected, and a sort of relief or suppressed pleasure."

Shortly after noon, to some soldiers sitting under her window, the woman called: "What is the news?"

"Ritreat, ritreat!" they replied in broken English—they were Creoles.

Through the rest of the day and on into the night the army poured into Vicksburg. Emma Balfour thought that her heart would break as she watched them pass by, and a Unionist woman felt no exultation when she saw the battered troops. Instead she thought they were a "woeful sight . . . humanity in the last throes of endurance. Wan, hollow-eyed, ragged, footsore, bloody, the men limped along unarmed . . . followed by siege-guns, ambulances, gun-carriages, and wagons in aimless confusion. At twilight two or three bands on the court-house hill

19. Hall, *26th Louisiana,* p. 66. 20. Balfour, Diary, p. 2.

21. The following account is drawn from: "A Woman's Diary," *The Century Magazine,* XXX, 771.

and other points began playing *Dixie, Bonnie Blue Flag* . . . and drums began to beat."[22]

Emma Balfour put her family and servants to work carrying pails of water to the street for the men to drink, and she set out all of the food she had on the porch and invited the men to eat.[23]

Other women merely berated the passing troops:

"Where are you going?"

"We are running."

"Oh, shame on you! Why don't you stand your ground."[24]

Rowland Chambers, who had lost his house as a hospital, now lost his shed as wounded were piled into it. Chambers helped bandage and amputate, and before the day was past declared that he had witnessed "more human suffering than I ever saw at one site before."[25]

Slowly some sort of order was made from the confusion, or perhaps it was merely that tired bodies and minds refused to be confused any longer and sank into exhausted sleep. Past the sprawled figures on the pavements marched fresh troops from Warrenton, and to the women's entreaties for protection they dipped their hats and yelled that they would die for them.[26]

Finally the noise died away and the city was silent; only the occasional clatter of hooves or rumble of a wagon broke the stillness. Yet sleep did not come easily for the civilians. Mary Loughborough lay awake late into the night, and she said that many others did too, wondering what would happen to them. Every defense they had erected had been swept aside, and the echoing sounds in the night were hollow sounds of defeat. A crushed army slept in their midst, and the will to victory lay equally crushed.

Rowland Chambers gave up hope: "The day of our doom appears close at hand, only the God of heavan can save us and in him I trust."[27] Emma Balfour, who earlier in the day had declared her dauntlessness, made this last entry before closing her diary: "My pen almost refuses to tell of our terrible defeat

22. *Ibid.*
23. Balfour, Diary, p. 3.
24. Loughborough, *Cave Life,* p. 41.
25. Chambers, Diary, May 17, 1863.
26. Loughborough, *Cave Life,* pp. 46-47.
27. Chambers, Diary, May 17, 1863.

. . . . I cannot write more—but oh! there will be a fearful reckoning somewhere. This has been brooding, growing and many fears have been felt for the result. Gen. Pemberton has not the confidence of officers, people or men judging from all I am compelled to see and hear. I would rather not have heard if I could have helped it. What is to become of all the living things in this place when the boats begin shelling—God only knows. Shut up as in a trap, no ingress or egress—and thousands of women and children who have fled here for safety . . . ."[28] She closed the diary and laid aside her pen. Out in the night were the sounds of a defeated army shuffling through the streets. East of the city Grant's army slept by glittering, dancing campfires.

The next day things looked little better. There was very little gunfire, but there was a lot of jostling and movement for the city had suddenly absorbed over thirty thousand soldiers. Emma Balfour thought the situation was little better than before: "Still all seems confusion."[29] If he had known that Mrs. Balfour thought this, Rowland Chambers would have agreed with her. He said: "We are almost over run by the soldiers they have three hospitals on the place and them full of sick wounded and shirks and lofers . . . the army see[ms] to be more and more demoralized . . . ."[30] Mrs. William Lord thought that the people, like the army, were despondent and afraid—a fear which stemmed not so much from a dread of personal harm but, instead, from a belief that General Pemberton was a traitor.[31] Emma Balfour's husband was not apprehensive of Pemberton but of livestock. He watched as the army's horses and mules and "all of the stock of all kinds for . . . twenty miles around" were herded into the city, and he was afraid of a stampede. His wife was more practical: "We can live on them, for I fear we have not the provender to feed them for long."[32]

Whatever the reason—military defeat, distrust of Pemberton, personal injury, property damage, starvation, stampede—everyone was afraid, and the only way their fears would be allayed would be through Grant's defeat; thus countless rumors—straws

28. Balfour, Diary, pp. 3-4.
29. *Ibid.*, p. 4.
30. Chambers, Diary, June 1, 1863.
31. Lord, Journal, p. 2.
32. Balfour, Diary, p. 4.

to be eagerly clutched, repeated, and set in diaries—darted through the city. Joseph Johnston marching into Grant's rear, Bedford Forrest down from Tennessee cutting through Grant's army, Southern gunboats made in England forcing their way up the Mississippi—these were some of the fanciful hopes that mounted as the day progressed.[33] Yet the only certainty was set down by Emma Balfour: "We are cut off from all knowledge of the outside world." When General Stephen D. Lee asked her if she had a "rat-hole" (a cave), she replied that it seemed that they were all caught in a rat-hole.[34]

Slowly Grant felt his way toward the high ground surrounding the city. Late in the afternoon the people could hear the sound of firing, and they were told that a battle would be fought at daybreak. During the night the city was lighted by the lurid glare of burning buildings—homes built along the outskirts, destroyed by the engineers to clear avenues of observation and fire. Emma Balfour watched them burn: "A grand and awful spectacle . . . . It was sad to see. Many of them we knew to be handsome residences put up in the last few years as country residences . . . but the stern necessity of war has caused their destruction."[35]

As the night passed the wings of Grant's army spread around the city. The Confederates were locked in, and Grant thought that he had them trapped. He wanted to get it over with: he did not have enough troops on hand to invest the city and conduct wearing siege operations; and in addition he knew the defenders were worn out and demoralized. He ordered a quick assault against the Confederate lines and asked Admiral Porter's support with gunboats and mortarboats. Porter told his captains: "Fire heaviest charges and long ranges, and scatter your shot around the forts and town."[36]

At daybreak the firing began, then welled up to a crescendo as the assault was mounted. Anne Harris listened to the swelling roar. She thought it "resembl[ed] the sound of a vast canebreak on fire with its crackling noise and rumbling under-tone."[37] Emma Balfour described the attack:

33. *Ibid.;* Moss, *Diary,* pp. 25, 36.

34. Balfour, Diary, p. 4.

35. *Ibid.*

36. *Official Records Navy,* Ser. I, Vol. XXV, 18.

37. Anne Harris Broidrick, A Recollection of Thirty Years Ago, Southern Historical Collection, University of North Carolina, p. 15.

It was terrific! [The assaulted] part of the town is . . . very near so we had the full benefit. It is just where the railroad crosses our lines. I was up in my room sewing and praying in my heart, oh so earnestly for our cause, when Nancy rushed up actually pale, exclaiming, "Oh Mistress, the Yankees are pouring over the hill and our men are running. Just come to the gallery and you can see!" It brought before me forcibly what a state of excitement we were living in when I found that this coincidence did not startle me . . . . I went to the back gallery with my glass and [saw] men pouring over the hill . . . negroes were darting through the shells, [and] a brigade [was] running past towards this point so I thought it might not be so bad as she thought and I quieted her a little. I found out that I was right . . . . [There was] hot and heavy firing . . . all day . . . . About nine o'clock in the morning the gunboats towed some mortars into range, and there was a rushing into caves . . . . We went into a cave for the first time . . . . Just as we got in several machines exploded . . . just over our heads, and at the same time two riders were killed in the valley below us by a twenty-four pound shell from the east side, so . . . we were between two fires. As all this rushed over me and the sense of suffocation from being underground, the certainty that there was no way of escape, that we were hemmed in, caged—for one moment my heart seemed to stand still—then my faith and courage rose to meet the emergency, and I have felt prepared ever since and cheerful . . . .[38]

The numbing shock of defeat and terror had begun to wear off, and as the Union assault was beaten back the spirits of the people began to rise. If the minds of thousands of persons can pivot on a single point, that particular point came to the people of Vicksburg on the afternoon of May 19, when Grant called off his assault. For the first time in three weeks he had been halted—he was not beaten, just stopped, but that was enough for the people; this slender success was enough to clutch and build into the hope that somehow they would be rescued.

Two days previously Rowland Chambers thought he was doomed; now he began to take new hope and he found time to gibe persons who were more afraid than he: "During the day it was laughable to see the skulking of some cowardly men they were hiding in the hollows and behind trees 7 or 8 cralled into our old cave and lay thair all day just like so many scared

38. Balfour, Diary, pp. 5-6.

dogs."[39] Another man noted: "Everything opened bright and cheerfully; full and universal confidence was now entertained . . . that the place could be held until succor arrived."[40] Hugh Moss, in an ambiguous but truth-laden statement, made the keenest analysis of the mind of the people: "The enemy still continue to sharpshoot us. The people here seem to be in great suspense, some are sanguine of success, others are exceedingly doubtful and I think all are hopeful."[41]

The fleet continued to pound away and, to the jeering calls from the soldiers of "rats, into your ratholes," the people went into their caves for the night; but as they sat there, the shells shaking the ground, they were no longer bereft of hope.

This hope, expanded by some people into an article of faith, would last throughout the siege. It would be doubted and distorted, but it would never be entirely discarded. And a supporting structure of what the people thought to be evidence—rumors of relief; beliefs that God was punishing them, but not wholly deserting them; reaffirmations of confidence in Pemberton—was erected to buttress the hope. This hope was born in the last convulsive shift of thought, and, as the subtle chemistry of the mind reacted, the legend of Vicksburg began.

Within the framework of that legend lies the real story of the pounded days and nights at Vicksburg; but the reality was quite often drab and sullied and far removed from the lustered legend. Even as most of the people decided to stand fast and wait for relief, others were passing through the entrenchments and crossing to the Federal lines, until General Smith ordered the lines closed to the civilians.[42] As much by the action of their own generals as by Grant the people were shut up within the city.

Now they were part of total war. Admiral Porter had ordered his naval gunners to fire their heaviest charges at the city, and a correspondent for *Harper's* said the army would match

39. Chambers, Diary, May 19, 1863.

40. "Diary of a Citizen in Vicksburgh During the War," *Rebellion Record,* VII, 163.

41. Moss, *Diary,* p. 22.

42. M. L. Smith to R. W. Memminger, May 19, 1863, Papers of Various Confederate Notables, Box 18, NA (RG) 109.

the navy's effort. He reported: "General Sherman seems to have a determined propensity to carry on the . . . war in a manner most offensive to the rebels. The last instance of his beneficence is a continued shelling of the 'Virgin City of Vicksburg'!"[43] But just how close they came to total war the people never knew, for General Stevenson had requested permission to arm all men in the city and put them in the trenches.[44]

As it was, the people thought they could not get closer to war. Lida Lord said that her family's troubles began on the twenty-first. After a quiet night, they gathered for breakfast around a table set with china and silver; the windows were open and Lida could smell the scent of roses in the fresh air. "Before sunset," she said, "a bombshell burst in the very center of that pretty dining-room, blowing out the roof and one side, crushing the well-spread teatable like an eggshell, and making a great yawning hole in the floor, into which disappeared supper, china, furniture, and the safe containing our entire stock of butter and eggs."[45] The family moved to the basement of Christ Church, and little William Lord, Jr., was left with an indelible picture of that night embedded in his memory. Doctor Lord sat on a barrel, smoking his pipe; the servants were in the coal bin praying and moaning; and Mrs. Lord and the children were huddled on a coal heap. As the shells shook the ground, Lida began to cry. Mrs. Lord, trying to comfort her, said: "Don't cry my darling. God will protect us."

"But, momma," sobbed Lida, "I's so 'fraid God's killed too!"[46]

The bombardment became so intense that Emma Balfour had to stop writing up her diary—the explosions made her "involuntarily jump from [her] seat." Yet she was not frightened enough to go to her cave. She and her husband "sat or stood in front of the house until eleven o'clock knowing that it would never do to go to bed . . . . We concluded as we had to be up,

43. *Harper's Weekly Magazine,* May 16, 1863, p. 315.

44. C. L. Stevenson to J. C. Pemberton, May 19, 1863, Papers of Various Confederate Notables, Box 18, NA (RG) 109.

45. Reed, "Woman's Experiences," *The Century Magazine,* LXI, 923.

46. William W. Lord, "A Child at the Siege of Vicksburg," *Harper's Monthly Magazine,* CXVIII (December, 1908), p. 44.

it was well to see all that was going on so we went . . . to [the Sky Parlor] and stayed there until one o'clock . . . . It was not in the usual way we walked down the street, but [we] had to take the middle of the street, when we heard a shell . . . and this was every half minute . . . . It took both of us . . . to keep a proper lookout." The rule of thumb regarding the shelling was: "If you see a shell burst above you, stand still, unless it is very high; if it be the sound of a Parrott, the shot has passed before you heard it . . . and so on."[47]

If a person kept a sharp watch, being outside during a bombardment was not exceedingly hazardous. Most of the shells were set with burning fuzes; in the daylight they left a trail of smoke and at night a trail of fire. Against a dark sky the flight of a shell was visible almost from the moment it left the muzzle of the cannon, and the people could watch its path and have sufficient time to dodge if it seemed headed toward them. Even if a shell exploded overhead, they learned, they would be safe, for the fragments fell forward and ahead of the person beneath. The only real danger, said Emma Balfour, "is that sometimes while watching one—another comes and may explode or fall near you 'ere you are aware."[48]

On May 22, Grant attacked again, and again his troops were beaten back. The following day Seth Wells, a private in the Seventeenth Illinois Regiment, was digging in a trench and carrying on a "sensible chat" with the defenders, only a few yards distant. The Confederates called to Wells and told him that they were confident of holding the city, but that they were tired of the war and wished "Old Abe and Jefferson Davis had to fight it out." The chief thing the defenders wanted was coffee. At this point, said Wells, the "conversation became too general and our batteries opened and put a quietus on it."[49] "For an hour or more, as fast as the guns could be worked, [we] pour[ed] it into them . . . Columbiads, Dahlgrens, Parrotts, Howitzers,

47. Balfour, Diary, pp. 8-9; "A National Account," *Rebellion Record,* VII, 164.

48. *Ibid.,* p. 9.

49. Seth J. Wells, *The Siege of Vicksburg from the Diary of Seth J. Wells* (Detroit, 1915), p. 69.

and James rifles, all mixed together . . . 'Giving them their coffee,' this was called."[50]

The attack of May 22 also put the quietus on Grant's plans to take the city by assault. Whether he liked it or not he was stuck with a siege, and the Union army settled in its lines and began waiting. The waiting, however, was not a passive exercise. The Columbiads, Parrotts, Dalhgrens, and James rifles gave the defenders "their coffee" day and night, and Porter added his naval guns and mortars.

Mary Loughborough summed up the civilians' reactions to the first days of heavy mauling. To a friend's question of how she managed to live, she replied: "After one is accustomed to the change, we do not mind it; but becoming accustomed, that is the trial."[51]

Her statement was a masterpiece of generalization; it rolled up thousands of particulars and lumped them together under one word—trial. And trial was an ambivalent word—it meant the same thing to everyone, and, at the identical moment, different things to different people. When it meant inconvenience, dread, and hope, the word applied to everyone. When it meant that which touched each person separately, it was singular and unrepeated. It was Doctor Benjamin Lay begging Elizabeth Egleston to make room in her cave for his two young sons; Lewis Guion walking into town bearing the body of Felix Gibbs to his unsuspecting mother; Major Edward Higgins' gentle report to a mother that her son was neither captured nor killed, but his whereabouts unknown. It was Emma Balfour's teasing admonition to General Lee not to allow Grant to shoot so near because the shells might break her flower pots; and Rowland Chambers' onomatopoetic observation: "The whurrur of the paret shells is frightful the whize of the minie ball has an undescrubeable affect where you heer on you know it has passe you, but heave a dread of the next one." It was a woman's articulated terror: "We are utterly cut off from the world, surrounded by a circle of fire. Would it be wise like the scorpion to sting ourselves to death?" Trial was the sight of bloody Union prisoners carried

50. Howard, *History of the 124th Regiment,* p. 111.
51. Loughborough, *Cave Life,* p. 12.

into the city, heads laid open and brains oozing from the wounds; it was a child playing in the street gathering unburst shells, extracting the powder, and having one of them explode in his face; and it was Hugh Moss finding comfort during a Sunday morning cannonade as he thought: "How little they respect the laws of the Great I Am, and it is not reasonable that they can be successful under such circumstances."[52] Trial was, for each person, a touch of blood, and death, and raillery, and hope. And so, as the attackers settled in their trenches and sapped and mined and bombarded, the people settled in their caves and homes and accustomed themselves to the ways of siege.

Mary Loughborough said that they did acclimate themselves to the "trial." But she made her generalization so glibly that it was as though she had forgotten the intensity that each particular bore. Perhaps she had forgotten—maybe her mind had mercifully blotted out the memory of scenes ranging from unpleasantness to stark horror. Yet at the time they occurred there was no blotting out, only the steady accretion of one day's torment after another. Somehow, though, the burden was hefted and shouldered and held to. Even in the early days of the siege the resilience and tenacity of the human body and mind were apparent. When he thought of sleeping soundly in the midst of the explosions of the heavy guns, Doctor Balfour said he believed that people could become inured to anything. Then his wife punched a hole in his theory: "Poor Mrs. Crump does not get used to it and it is pitiable to see her at every shell jumping up and crouching with fear."[53]

Mrs. Balfour herself charted the flexibility of the mind. Within the space of a few hours her thoughts could sweep from despair to a keen appreciation of beauty (though laden with paradox). When she saw several thousand horses and mules, for which there was no feed, driven into the Federal lines, she believed that it was a sign that they were a lost people. Then

52. Benjamin Lay to Elizabeth Eggleston, May 17, 1863, Edward Higgins to Elizabeth Eggleston, May 17, 1863, Eggleston-Roach Papers, Department of Archives and Manuscripts, Louisiana State University; Lewis Guion, Diary, May 20, 1863, Department of Archives and Manuscripts, Louisiana State University; Balfour, Diary, p. 15; Chambers, Diary, May 24, 1863; Ephraim McD. Anderson, *Memoirs* (St. Louis, 1868), p. 325; Moss, *Diary,* pp. 28-29.

53. Balfour, Diary, pp. 12-13.

several hours later she wrote: "In the midst of all this carnage and commotion, it is touching to see how every work of God, save man, gives praise to Him. The birds are singing as merrily as if all were well, rearing their little ones, teaching them to fly and fulfilling their part in nature's program as quietly and happily as if this fearful work of man slaying his brother man was not in progress . . . . The flowers are in perfection, the air heavy with perfume . . . and the garden bright and gay with all the summer flowers . . . . Nature is all fair and lovely—all save the spirit of man seems divine."

Another woman, however, saw more despair than hope in nature: "A pair of chimney-swallows have built in the parlor chimney. The concussion of the [shells] often sends down parts of their nest, which they patiently pick up and reascend with . . . . I think all the dogs and cats must be killed or starved, we don't see any more pitiful animals prowling around." The phrase "killed or starved" opened another line of thought—one which constantly preyed upon her mind: "We are lucky to get a quart of milk daily from a family near who have a cow they hourly expect to be killed. I send nearly five dollars to market each morning, and it buys a small piece of mule-meat. Rice and milk is my main food; I can't eat the mule-meat . . . . I am so tired of corn-bread, which I never liked, that I eat it with tears in my eyes."[54]

Yet for many people the specter of starvation still hung in the distance. Emma Balfour, who had no qualms about the food supply, delighted in serving meals to visiting officers. On May 25, General Pemberton took lunch with her and assured her that there was enough food in the city to last sixty days, and even longer if the rations were reduced,[55] though with mule meat being eaten, some persons thought that they were already on starvation rations. The chief complaint, however, stemmed not from eating mule meat, but instead from the bread made of pea meal. One man swore that the longer a loaf was baked the harder it became on the outside and the softer it became on

54. "A Woman's Diary," *The Century Magazine,* XXX, 771.
55. Balfour, Diary, pp. 13-14.

the inside, and "one might have knocked down a full-grown steer with a chunk of it."[56]

But food was not yet paramount in the minds of the people. The sense of isolation and the lack of news were the main sources of complaint and foreboding. Day upon day Rowland Chambers noted that there was no news from the outside and wished that some word would come through the lines.[57] J. M. Swords continued to publish the *Citizen,* but it was merely "a rehash of speculations which amuses a half hour."[58] So starved for news were the people that when the gunboat *Cincinnati* was sunk some personal letters found in the debris were eagerly passed from person to person.[59] The craving for news stemmed not only from the fact that the people were isolated, but also from the belief that when news was brought to the city it would be that Johnston was moving to their relief. But until that information arrived (and most people were sure that it would), they had to shift for themselves. Emma Balfour said: "Last night Mrs. Higgins and myself sat up until after eleven o'clock making cartridges. We get no help from the outside world now and have to help ourselves."[60]

And so they helped themselves, but at the same time anxiously awaited information from Johnston. On May 28, after being shut up for ten days, the first courier from Johnston slipped into the city. Emma Balfour invited General Pemberton and other officers to come "to lunch and . . . a thanksgiving for this good news and [for] the sinking of the [*Cincinnati*] the day before." Previously Mrs. Balfour had chided Pemberton for "being gloomy and told him the ladies were not despondent." Now Pemberton told the group that "things look brighter" and said: "The Yankees, if they could look in, would not think that we minded the siege very much." Mrs. Balfour thought that they were very merry and hopeful.

They probably were, for the courier's dispatch said that Johnston, with forty thousand men, and Bragg, with his Tennessee army, were marching to their relief, and also that Robert E.

56. Anderson, *Memoirs,* p. 337.
57. Chambers, Diary, May 27, 1863.
58. "A Woman's Diary," *The Century Magazine,* XXX, 771.
59. Balfour, Diary, p. 17.
60. *Ibid.,* pp. 7-8.

Lee, giving tit-for-tat, was laying siege to Washington.[61] Now all they had to do was wait until Johnston's and Bragg's armies united and assailed Grant in the rear.

But hope was a slender bulwark against the mounting pressures and tensions of siege; waiting became more difficult with the passage of each day. Even after the arrival of the courier's heartening message Mrs. Balfour watched Pemberton and thought: "He is inclined to be rather despondent." Perhaps he knew the sheer military impossibility of what the dispatch promised. Other persons were despondent too, and the unceasing pounding and shortages bore heavily upon them. The streets were now "literally plowed up," the hotels had been requisitioned and filled with wounded, and many of the homes had wounded in them. All of the civilians' shovels, spades, and picks were appropriated for military use, fences were torn down for firewood, houses were rocked "like cradles" by the shock of the explosions, and living in caves had lost whatever novelty it might once have held.[62]

Lida Lord began to dread the nights in the caves—"the blessed daylight came like heaven." She had spent a night in a cave with sixty-five other persons, "packed in, black and white, like sardines in a box." There was not much sleep, just constant movement, snuffling, moaning, and crying. Three wounded soldiers lay on the cave floor, a big box lined with blankets held several babies, and a woman writhed on a mattress, her body swollen and in labor. Before the night was past William Siege Green had entered the world.[63]

Emma Balfour still refused to go into the caves unless she was forced, but a night in her home was no better than a damp, crowded, mosquito infested cave, or so it appears from her diary entry of May 31:

> The shelling from the mortars was worse than usual last night . . . . I could hear the pieces falling all around us as the shells

61. *Ibid.*, pp. 16-17.

62. John C. Pemberton to C. L. Stevenson, May 23, 1863; Benjamin Lay to W. H. McCardle, May 21, 1863; Benjamin Lay to F. M. Stafford, May 25, 1863; all in Papers of Various Confederate Notables, Box 18, NA (RG) 109; Balfour, Diary, pp. 13, 15.

63. Reed, "Woman's Experiences," *The Century Magazine,* LXI, 924; Bell, "A Girl's Experience," *Harper's Weekly Magazine,* LVI, 12-13.

would explode, and once I thought our time had come . . . . The mortars [fired] all night. We soon perceived that we could not retire while they fired as they had changed the range and every shell came either directly over us or just back or front of us so we made up our minds to sit up and watch, hoping, however, that they would cease about midnight, as they sometimes do . . . but no all night it continued to add to the horror. At 12 o'clock the guns all along the lines opened and the parrot shells flew as thick as hail around us! . . . . We had gone upstairs determined to rest lying down but not sleeping, but when these commenced to come it was not safe up-stairs so we came down in our dining room and lay down upon the bed there, but soon found that would not do as they came from the southeast as well as east and might strike the house. Still from sheer uneasiness we remained there until a shell struck in the garden against a tree, and at the same time we heard the servants all up and making exclamations. We got up thoroughly worn out and disheartened and after looking to see the damage, went into the parlor and lay on the sofas there until morning, feeling that at any moment a mortar shell might crash through the roof . . . . We have slept scarcely none now for two days and two nights. Oh! it is dreadful. After I went to lie down [after watching the shells] I could see them just as plainly with my eyes shut as with them open. They come, gradually making their way higher and higher, tracked by their firing fuze until they reach their greatest altitude, then with a rush and whiz they come down furiously, their own weight added to the impetus given by the powder . . . .[64]

The pounding became too much for some people to endure. They circulated a petition asking that Pemberton order a cease fire and allow the women and children to leave the city. Pemberton replied that he would not grant the request of a few individuals, but if a majority of the civilians would sign the petition he would allow it. Four persons fixed their names to it.[65]

One woman told Pemberton that she hoped he would not comply with the petition as "we had all been sufficiently warned."[66] Perhaps they had not taken the warning seriously, but for six months they had been asked, almost ordered, to leave the city, and most of those who remained were there of their own volition. This matter of free choice threw another intangible into the crucible of the collective will of the people—it added

64. Balfour, Diary, pp. 19-20.
65. *Ibid.*, p. 21.
66. *Ibid.*

another item to the supporting structure that buttressed the faith in their relief and their determination to survive. This intangible was a matter of personal honor. The people had elected to remain in the city; therefore honor demanded that they not allow the bombardment to cow them, even if they thought the Federals were fighting "the garrison in part, but the city mainly."[67]

Emma Balfour summed it up: "The general impression is that they fire at the city . . . thinking that they will wear out the women and children and sick, and Gen. Pemberton will be [forced] to surrender the place on that account, but they little know the spirit of the Vicksburg women and children if they expect this. Rather than let them know they are causing us any suffering [we] would be content to suffer martyrdom."[68]

Emma Balfour might justifiably be called a member of the local aristocracy—her husband was a successful doctor and she was on close terms with the leading generals—and her statement might be said to reflect the sentiments of only a portion of the population. But if it was a reflection of the mind of the upper class, it was nevertheless valid. The only distinction between Emma Balfour's determination and that of a woman who lived in a rough shack along the waterfront was one of degree.

Alexander Abrams, a staff member of the defunct *Whig* who was now taking his turn in the trenches, was perhaps in closer touch with the various segments of Vicksburg society than Emma Balfour. As he watched and listened to the women, he decided that class distinctions made little difference in the war spirit: "Among the poorer classes of women, the feeling of patriotism was strong, and the desire for a successful defense was apparent in their conversation, while the feeling among the wealthier class of women almost amounted to a wild enthusiasm."[69]

Though Abrams was given to rhetorical splurges and glossed the truth from time to time, he was substantially correct in this assessment of morale. Hugh Moss, who tended a cannon in one of the river batteries, said: "The women here, although exposed

67. Edward S. Gregory, "Vicksburg During the Siege," *The Annals of the War Written by Leading Participants North and South* (Philadelphia, 1879), p. 116.

68. Balfour, Diary, p. 21.

69. Abrams, *Full and Detailed History,* p. 48.

to much danger, encouraged the soldiers in their daily duty and peril, cooking for them and even sending provisions to them on the battlefield, attending to their wounds and administering every comfort within their power. May they receive due reward by seeing victory perch upon their standard."[70] Osborn Oldroyd, on the opposite side of the trenches, seemed to sense the defiance that Emma Balfour set into her diary. As he peered over the top of his trench and studied the city, he was struck by two things: the courthouse where "there is a Confederate flag waving . . . defiantly"; and by the sight of women, which brought from him this unadulterated praise, "The women . . . did not all leave the city, and I suppose they have determined to brave it out. Their sacrifices and privations are worthy of a better cause, and were they but on our side how we would worship them."[71]

Class and caste distinctions were blurred in the face of common adversity. Inside one of the large caves which held several dozen persons, William Lord ate and slept with slaves, planters, overseers, slave traders, business and professional men and their families, who lived "side by side, in peace if not in harmony."[72]

As slave owners noticed that their servants behaved well under fire, there was a further lapsing of caste barriers. Mary Loughborough was one such owner who came to have new respect for her Negroes. She thought they possessed "more courage than is usually attributed to negroes," for her "boy" George slept at the entrance of her cave with a pistol, declaring, said Mrs. Loughborough, "dat anyone dat come dar would have to go over his body first." He also had no qualms about carrying food and messages to Mrs. Loughborough's husband, who was in the trenches; and on one occasion George picked up a smoking Parrott shell which landed in the mouth of the cave and threw it outside.[73]

As May drew to a close a new quality, timelessness, crept into the city. Hours and days were no longer measured by the clocks or calendars. One day merely blended into the next, then

70. Moss, *Diary,* p. 31. 71. Oldroyd, *Soldier's Story,* p. 52.
72. Lord, "Siege of Vicksburg," *Harper's Monthly Magazine,* CXVIII, 46.
73. Loughborough, *Cave Life,* pp. 65, 74.

that one into the succeeding one until, said one man, "It can scarcely be said that one day differs much from another." Instead of the ticking of a clock, the passage of time was marked by "the chop, chop, chop, of the sharpshooters . . . which greets the ear from morning till night, and from night till morning."[74] Events were set in time by the slackening or the intensification of the bombardment, and the routines of life revolved about the number of shells dropping in the city.

At the caves, meals were prepared when the shelling abated. The cooking had to be done outside and the risk was too great to try to cook in the open with shells landing close by. One woman described the scene at suppertime: "At all the caves I could see from my high perch, people were sitting, eating their poor suppers at the cave doors, ready to plunge in again. As the first shell . . . flew they dived, and not a human being was visible."[75] Occasionally the erratic firing meant that some people went without food for long periods of time. Lida Lord remembered that her family once had nothing to eat for twenty-four hours, and finally when they did get a meal it was because one of their servants walked through the explosions to bring in a "tray of ham and bread and butter."[76] Other people tried to meet this exigency by baking large quantities of bread and subsisting on it and milk, providing their cows had not been killed. This was cold, dreary eating, meal after meal, and as a result any food which was hot was considered to be a luxury, even if it was cornbread and fat pork. Sleeping depended somewhat upon the shelling, not upon the coming of night. Though some persons learned to sleep even in the heaviest bombardment, others did not, and a night during which there were few explosions was also regarded as a luxury. The time for washing and bathing was dictated by the shelling and not by dirt or passage of time. One woman complained that she had not been able to change her clothes for two weeks.[77]

After two weeks of bombardment only two events remained fixed in people's minds. One was Sunday and the other was

74. "Diary of a Citizen," *Rebellion Record,* VII, 168.
75. "A Woman's Diary," *The Century Magazine,* XXX, 771.
76. Reed, "Woman's Experiences," *ibid.*, LXI, 923.
77. Lord, Journal, p. 4.

Life in the Union trenches surrounding Vicksburg, as seen by the special artist of *Harper's,* while waiting for "General Starvation" to defeat the defenders. (From *Harper's Weekly*)

relief. Even the shells would not deter the people from their worship. (Some persons, like their medieval ancestors, clung to the belief that a church was a sanctuary and therefore impervious to, or at least safer from, direct hits.) On Sunday, May 31, the church bells pealed amidst the sound of the cannon.

As she walked to Christ Church, Emma Balfour thought: "It is comparatively quiet . . . how like and yet how unlike Sunday. All nature wears a Sabbath calm, but the thunder of artillery reminds us that man knows no Sabbath—Yankee man at least." There were only thirty people at the service; they had to pick their way through brick and rubble and sweep shattered glass from the pews before they sat, and at times the responses were obliterated by cannonfire, but they found comfort and were determined to continue the services.[78] Most of the people, however, held religious services in the caves. In the large shelters prayer meetings were conducted daily, and white man and Negro alike uttered pleas "for a swift deliverance from the perils of the siege."[79]

78. Balfour, Diary, pp. 19, 23. It appears that only the Episcopal and Catholic churches held regular services throughout the siege.

79. Lord, *Harper's Monthly Magazine,* CXVIII, 46.

Rowland Chambers, who attended no church, got himself closer to God. For the first time since he arrived in Vicksburg he made entries in his diary which indicated that he acknowledged the existence of God. Perhaps he was frightened and, like many of the people, found succor in intensified religious activities. He thanked "the Lord for [H]is great mercies," and allied Him with the relief of the city. "It is believed that we will be able to hold the place with the help of God the decider of all battles."[80]

Now a new factor was added to the problem of survival. It had been brooding in the background since the day the siege began (and even before) but, by the first of June, it was thrust full blown and danger-laden into the beleaguered city. This new factor was the mounting threat of starvation, a peril which came closer with the passage of each day. It sapped the will to victory more than any other single hardship with which the people had to contend. Its vitiating effect was not only measured by the gnawing at empty bellies, but also by the erosion of morale and temper as the hungry people found themselves turned into objects of profit by black marketers and hoarders. As prices spiraled upward and early relief by Johnston failed to come, the people struck back at the profiteers.

On the night of June 1, a fire swept through the business center of the city. Before it was brought under control an entire block of buildings had been gutted. Thus from a single stroke the city suffered more damage than it would throughout the remainder of the siege, and the destruction came not from Grant's artillery or Porter's mortars, but from the matches of some outraged citizens. The gutted block contained several of the city's grocery stores, owned by merchants suspected and accused of profiteering, and it was common knowledge that the fire was set by persons who were incensed by the merchants' speculation on food.[81]

Yet in the long run there was no effective retaliation against speculation. Those who held surplus food and who were inclined to do so squeezed and squeezed. As the profiteers went about

80. Chambers, Diary, May 27, June 4, 1863.

81. Balfour, Diary, p. 23; James H. Pepper, Diary of Vicksburg, Miss. Arch., pp. 5-6; William H. Tunnard, *A Southern Record: The History of the Third Regiment Louisiana Infantry* (Baton Rouge, 1866), p. 244.

their sordid business they left ineradicable loathing in the minds of some of the civilians and soldiers which lasted far beyond the war years. When William Tunnard wrote his reminiscences of the siege he saved his most vitriolic words not for the enemy, but for the Vicksburg merchants: "During the siege . . . there was a class of non-combatants who distinguished themselves in a marked manner. These were the speculators, embracing nearly every merchant within the limits of the city, without distinction of nationality [an oblique way of lumping Christians with Jews who, according to popular belief, would naturally be engaged in profiteering]. These bloodsuckers had the audacity to hold their goods at such prices that it was an utter impossibility to obtain anything from them . . . . Some of these, worse than villains, refused to sell to the soldiers at any price . . . ."[82]

By June 1, food prices reached their highest level since the war began.[83] Yet for those persons who had money or who were close to a source of supply there was no dearth of food. William Drennan ate "good beef, mutton sometimes, ham, flour, rice flour, rice, molasses, etc.," and he rather complacently said he was "well off." He was able to eat well because he lived with a commissary officer who declared that he would "have some [food]—and that . . . of the best kind."[84]

The commissary officer made this statement at the same time the troops in the trenches were calling over to the Yankees "to . . . look out as [we have] a new General . . . . General Starvation."[85] What Drennan did when he recorded the statement of the high-eating commissary officer was in effect to record the attitude of many of the people, soldier and civilian alike, which amounted to "Them that has, gits!"

Charity remained an individual matter and became a relative virtue. Mrs. William Lord said that she would "have been badly off" if it had not been for the "kindness" of a lieutenant. The

82. Tunnard, *A Southern Record,* pp. 141-42.

83. G. R. Elliott, Diary, June 1, 1863, Tennessee State Library and Archives. Some of the items were (per pound): flour $1.50; sugar, 75¢; coffee, $5.00; tea, $15.00; and rice, 40¢.

84. William Drennan, Diary, Miss. Arch., II, 21.

85. Wells, *The Siege of Vicksburg,* p. 75.

lieutenant's kindness consisted of selling her a gallon of molasses for six dollars and "a miserable steak" for three dollars.[86]

Other persons were not able to afford kindness, and they were hungry. On June 6, a group of women and children left the city and crossed the river to the Union-occupied Louisiana shore. Their food supplies exhausted, they "were compelled to seek quarters somewhere else." Hugh Moss, watching as the refugees climbed the opposite bank, breathed the hope that they would "meet with good treatment," which was more than their compatriots in Vicksburg had accorded them.[87]

Summer heat comes quick and searing to Vicksburg. By early June the sun was beating down into the trenches and streets, its heat lending more tarnish to the record of a people struggling for survival. The May rains, thought by some persons to be caused by the heavy cannonade, had ceased and the days marched by, sultry and thirsty.[88] The water supply, as the board of police had apprehensively warned, trickled away as thirty thousand people tried to drink from a water system built to accommodate five thousand. People began dipping water from ditches and mud holes, and other persons, always ready to capitalize on the need of their neighbors, sold fresh water by the bucketful to those who could afford it.[89] One woman, whose house contained two underground cisterns, gave the water from one to the soldiers, but kept the other for her personal use which included nightly baths of cold water as a "nerve-calmer that sends me to sleep in spite of the roar."[90]

The roar continued day after day, night after night. The shelling, said Emmanuel Gebhart, "puts me in mind of the barking of a lot of dogs; the big dogs do some furious barking, but when they stop for breath then you can hear the little

86. Lord, Journal, p. 7.

87. Moss, *Diary,* p. 34. This is the single recorded instance in which women and children successfully passed out of the city. Several other attempts were made, but the refugees were turned back by both the Confederate and Union forces. Men, both soldiers and civilians, came and went by floating on logs. Anne Shannon Martin to Emma Crutcher, June 17, 1863, Crutcher Collection.

88. Jenkins L. Jones, "An Artilleryman's Diary," *Wisconsin History Commission Original Papers, Number 8,* entries for June, 1863.

89. Reed, "Woman's Experiences," *The Century Magazine,* LXI, 926.

90. "A Woman's Diary," *ibid.,* XXX, 772.

Fiste."[91] But the barking of the cannon and rifles had become so familiar that the people began to joke about it. Even when Admiral Porter ordered "Greek Fire" hurled into the city there were, instead of cries of "barbarian," facetious comments about this new instrument of war. O. S. Holland sent his compliments to Elizabeth Eggleston and called her attention to the Greek Fire: "The shells used by 'Professor Porter' in his 'Grand pyrotechnic exhibitions' gratuitously given for the benefit (?) of the women and children of Vicksburg."[92]

This was the indomitable side of the people. Here was no pettiness, no sordidness, no gap in the human soul. Here was the lambent side of their nature, burnished bright by adversity. As the grind of privation and horror brought out the worst in some people's nature, it polished and honed the opposite qualities of generosity, humor, and courage in others.

Accustomed to keeping himself protected as much as possible when he was in the trenches, William Drennan thought that some of the civilians were almost foolhardy in their dauntlessness. "You can see," wrote Drennan, "women gaily dressed promenading the streets—if there is a slackening of shells—and men would give any price for a drink of whiskey—so much do they wish for extra excitement. I saw Mrs. Lum walking the street with a gold laced official and she appeared as thoughtless as any one could be."[93] Behavior such as this also brought admiration from the enemy. A northern newspaperman filed this account of the people of Vicksburg: "One of the most wonderful things of the siege is the fact that ladies, following the example of the men, have actually promenaded the streets in numbers during the bombardment, priding themselves on their ability to dodge the shells . . . . Indeed, the coolness of these people under the terrible fire is most astonishing . . . . No men in the world have ever been called upon to endure so heavy a fire . . . ."[94]

91. Emmanuel M. Gebhart to Noah L. Gebhart, June 11, 1863, Noah L. Gebhart Papers, Duke University.

92. O. S. Holland to Elizabeth Eggleston, June 8, 1863, Eggleston-Roach Papers. Concerning the use of Greek Fire see Porter's report, *Official Records Navy,* Ser. I, Vol. XXV, 518; cf. *Rebellion Record,* VII, 61.

93. Drennan, Diary, II, 18.

94. "A National Account," *Rebellion Record,* VII, 164.

The people would have agreed with the newspaperman. A captain's wife was in her dining room with her two children when a thirteen-inch mortarshell struck the house. The woman pushed the children under the table, dived on top of them, then, after the shell exploded, calmly brushed the dust and debris from herself and the children and went about her business.[95] Another woman was lying in bed reading the *Citizen* when a shell exploded beside her bedroom window. Shell fragments flew into the room and cut plaster from the wall and ceiling. As she was "crawling out of the plaster" another shell exploded close by and she ran to the cellar, but not before she had picked up her brush and comb. She combed and brushed all afternoon before she got the debris from her hair because, she said, "my hands were rather shaky."[96]

This was a rather inverse attempt at humor, though probably the best she could summon at the moment. Other people's humor was more open and heavy-handed. Atop one of the hills there was a deserted house on which someone had charcoaled the sign: "For Rent: Inquire of Davis & Pemberton." One night a mortarshell ripped through the building; in the morning the first sign was marked out and a new inscription put in its place: "Rented, by Grant and McPherson."[97]

The long hours had to be whiled away and some of the more inventive brains created the "Hotel de Vicksburg," on which they lavished the memory of better days, the want of the present, and a fey humor. Cards advertising the Hotel were written in longhand:

> The proprietors of the justly celebrated Hotel de Vicksburg, having enlarged and refitted the same, are now prepared to accommodate all who may favor them with a call. Parties arriving by the river or Grant's overland rout[e], will find Grape, Cannister & Co's carriages at the landing or any Depot on the line of entrenchments. Buck, Ball & Co take charge of all baggage. No effort will be spared to make the visit of all as interesting as possible.

95. J. T. Hogane, "Reminiscences of the Siege of Vicksburg," *Southern Historical Society Papers,* XI (July, 1883), 296.

96. "A Woman's Diary," *The Century Magazine,* XXX, 773.

97. Thomas C. DeLeon, *Belles, Beaux and Brains of the 60's* (New York, 1907), p. 274.

A long menu, emblazoned by the head of a mule, was drawn up, which spoke of an acquaintance with good restaurants, but also of a firm sense of reality:

SOUP
Mule Tail

BOILED
Mule Bacon with Poke Greens
Mule Ham Canvassed

ROASTS
Mule Sirloin
Mule Rump Stuffed with Rice

VEGETABLES
Peas and rice

ENTREES
Mule head stuffed Ala mode
Mule Beef Jerked Ala Mexicana
Mule Ears fricasseed ala Gotch
Mule Hide Stewed New Style Laid on
Mule Spare ribs plain
Mule Liver hashed

SIDE DISHES
Mule Salad
Mule hoof soused

. . . .

Mule tongue cold ala bray

JELLIES
Mule foot

PASTRY
Pea Meal Pudding blackberry sause
Cotton Seed Pies
China berry tarts

DESERT
White Oak Acorns
Beech Nuts
Blackberry leaf Tea
Genuine Confederate Coffee

LIQUORS

Mississippi Water vintage 1492 Superior	$3.00
Lime Stone Water late importation very fine	2.75
Spring Water Vicksburg brand	1.50[98]

Other inventive and idle minds turned to music, or at least the writing of new lyrics for old music. "Listen to the Mocking Bird" was made into " 'Twas at the Siege of Vicksburg":

'Twas at the siege of Vicksburg,
Of Vicksburg, of Vicksburg,
'Twas at the siege of Vicksburg,
When the Parrott shells were whistling through the air—

Listen to the Parrott shells,
Listen to the Parrott shells,
The Parrott shells are whistling through the air.

Oh, well will we remember,
Remember, remember,
Through mule meat, June sans November;
And the minie balls that whistled through the air—

Listen to the minie balls,
Listen to the minie balls,
The minie balls are singing in the air.[99]

William and Lida Lord were taught another song by some Missouri officers who occupied a nearby cave. To the tune of "Then Let the Old Folks Scold if They Will," they sang:

Then let the big guns boom if they will,
We'll be gay and happy still,
Gay and happy, gay and happy,
We'll be gay and happy still.

The officers, usually off duty in the evenings, spent many hours with the children teaching them songs, playing games, and improving the cave by cutting niches into the clay walls for books, vases and candles. Older girls knitted socks and hemmed handkerchiefs for the Missourians, and put blossoms in their buttonholes before they set out for the batteries. There was also time for whist, candy making, and flirtation by candlelight,

98. Thomas N. Waul Papers, Duke University; *Rebellion Record,* VII, 51.
99. William H. Tunnard, "Reminiscences," in Oldroyd, *Soldier's Story,* p. 147.

which made the cave's "gloomy recesses echo with songs and laughter." One of the favorite pastimes was carving bas reliefs of the children's heads in the walls of the caves, though occasionally the shock from a near-miss would shake the ground and cause the knife to slip and ruin the sculpting. Laughter and songs might veneer it, but war was never more than a few feet away.[100]

This was perhaps more apparent to those people who did not desert their homes for the caves. Anne Harris' home was filled with wounded, and the women gave up their beds and slept on the floors. Then healthy troops crowded onto the porch—"many of them disliked tent life"—and Anne said that it was not safe to venture out of doors at night for fear of stepping on some sleeping soldier. She admitted that her family "found it anything but agreeable to be in the midst of so many men," but they did not have the heart to forbid the use of their porch.[101]

Yet there were other people who did not begrudge the soldiers' presence. Private S. R. Martin and a friend named Peers were prowling through the city seeking something to eat when they heard the sound of a piano. Peers walked to an open window and saw a young girl seated at the piano. At his request she continued playing, then invited them both to come in. Peers then sat at the piano and played for over an hour, much to the delight of the entire family, and the two soldiers left the house with full stomachs and full haversacks.[102] Another person who shared her slender food stock with the soldiers was the Unionist woman from New Orleans. As she looked at them she could feel no animosity: "Poor fellows! my heart bleeds for them . . . . They come into the kitchen when Martha puts the pan of cornbread in the stove, and beg for the bowl she mixed it in . . . . When I happen in, they look so ashamed . . . . I know we saved the lives of two by giving a few meals."[103]

100. Lord, "Siege of Vicksburg," *Harper's Monthly Magazine,* CXVIII, 47; Reed, "Woman's Experiences," *The Century Magazine,* LXI, 925.
101. Broidrick, A Recollection, p. 12.
102. S. R. Martin, Recollections of the War Between the States, 1861-1865, p. 57. Owned by John S. Hoggatt, Vicksburg.
103. "A Woman's Diary," *The Century Magazine,* XXX, 772.

Then, too, the giving was not always on the part of the civilians. When a cave was struck by a direct hit, a captain gave the frightened survivors "his cave, bunk & Bedding, [and] consoled them to the best of his ability." James Pepper, who watched as the exchange was made, thought the captain "might strictly be termed a gentleman," but also thought that there might be a secondary motive for his kindness as one of the destitute persons was a "very fine looking young lady."[104]

There was always time for gallantry, but as such it was an empty form unless it was accompanied by a hole in the ground, a piece of bedding, or a scrap of food. The forms of life had long since been discarded and everything was reduced to the most simple terms. There was a time when the acceptance of a stranger's grimy bedding or the begging of an unwashed mixing bowl would not have been thought of. Now it was possibly the difference between living and perishing, and the people scrimped and improvised in every way they knew. Corn cobs were used as a substitute for soda, "Confederate Dye" was made from elderberry juice, strings were dipped in mutton suet to make candles, raspberry and blackberry leaves were used to make tea, and corn beer was brewed, which was said to be "superior to any Cider or Beer [and] innocent for a child, if taken as soon as the gas forms and not permitted to sour."[105]

J. M. Swords improvised and managed to publish the *Citizen,* though no one could predict its size from one day to the next. The June 13 issue was one and a half feet long and six inches wide, and the issue of the eighteenth was printed on wallpaper, which became Swords's standard newsprint. The only thing which remained constant in the *Citizen* was the faith it pinned on Johnston. Issue after issue promised that relief was close by: "The utmost confidence is felt that we can maintain our position until succor comes from outside. The undaunted Johnston is at hand"; then later, "But a few days more and Johnston will be here"; and still later, "Ho! for Johnston!—The most agreeable news now-a-days is to hear from General Johnston. But we have nothing to record of his movements, except

104. J. H. Pepper, Diary of Vicksburg, p. 17.

105. *Clarke's Confederate Household Almanac, for the Year 1863,* pp. 18-20.

that we may look at any hour for his approach. We may repose the utmost confidence in his approach within a very few days. We have to say to our friends and the noble army here that relief is close at hand. Hold out a few days longer, and our lines will be opened, the enemy driven away, the siege raised, and Vicksburg again in communication with the balance of the Confederacy." Some people copied these empty words and set them into their diaries letter for letter, as though the transcription of the words would reinforce their hopes.[106]

Rumor was the stuff that hope was made of. Each day brought a new supply of rumors, stories which were nurtured in hearts and which quickened hopes because the people wanted nothing so much as to believe them. Then as the promised thing, whatever it might have been, failed to materialize the particular rumor passed into oblivion, but its place was quickly filled by another fanciful hope. However flimsy the stories, they supported hope, and as long as there was hope there was tenacity and defiance. Even the wildest fantasies were eagerly clutched at and, as the days passed without the sound of Johnston's guns, they gave comfort to the people. "We are all," wrote Doctor Joseph Alison, "in good spirits and look for help *one of these days.* Our friends outside suffer more in mind, much more than we do. It would surprise anyone not accustomed to shelling to see how cooly we take it."[107]

The Northerners, in much closer touch with fact than the besieged people, ran their own rumor mills. A "mysterious and dreadful beacon that rose out of the earth" was reported to exist in the city, though its purpose was unexplained; one hundred women were said to have been killed during the first day of the siege; and most inexplicable of all, the *Harper's* correspondent reported that the city had been abandoned on May 24.[108]

There was something harmless and pathetic about most of the rumors which seethed in the city and swept through the Union

106. "A Woman's Diary," *The Century Magazine,* XXX, 772; Pepper, Diary, p. 12.

107. Joseph D. Alison, Diary, Southern Historical Collection, University of North Carolina, p. 16.

108. Gregory, *Annals,* pp. 126-27; *Harper's Weekly Magazine,* May 30, 1863, p. 339.

trenches, but there were other stories which were vicious and malign, and which would haunt minds long past the time the guns ceased. These were the tales of atrocity, passed, like the stories of Johnston's advance and the mysterious beacon, from home to home and from trench to trench.

Some of the Yankees had come boiling toward Vicksburg eager to extirpate it as a viper's nest. On the outskirts of the city, so went a story widely circulated in the North, was the plantation of a Mrs. Gillespie where

> Flogging with a leather strap on the naked body is common; also, paddling the body with a hand-saw until the skin is a mass of blisters, and then breaking the blisters with the teeth of the saw . . . .
>
> Another method of punishment, which is inflicted for the higher order of crimes . . . is to dig a hole in the ground large enough for the slave to squat or lie down in. The victim is then stripped naked and placed in the hole, and a covering or grating of green sticks is laid over the opening. Upon this a quick fire is built, and the live embers sifted through upon the naked flesh of the slave, until his body is blistered and swollen almost to bursting. With just enough life to enable him to crawl, the slave is then allowed to recover from his wounds if he can, or to end his suffering by death . . . .
>
> There was a middle-aged [slave] in the family, named Margaret, who had a nursing child. Mrs. Gillespie ordered Margaret to wean the child. The babe was weakly, and Margaret did not wish to do so. Mrs. G. told her that she would examine her breast the next Monday, and, if she found any milk in it, she would punish her severely. Monday came round, and . . . at night the promised examination took place, and the breast of Margaret gave but too convincing proof that, in obedience to the yearnings of a mother's heart, she had spurned the threat of the inhuman mistress. Mrs. G. then ordered the handsaw, the leather strap, and a wash-bowl of water. The woman was laid upon her face, her clothes were stripped up to around her neck . . . . Mrs. Gillespie then paddled her with the handsaw, sitting composedly in a chair over her victim. After striking some one hundred blows she changed to the use of the leather strap, which she would dip into the wash-bowl in order to give it greater power of torture. Under this infliction the screams of the woman died away to a faint moan, but the sound of the whip continued until nearly 11 o'clock. "Jane" was then ordered to bring the hot tongs, the woman was turned over upon her back, and Mrs. Gillespie attempted to grasp the woman's nipples with the heated implement. The

writhings of the mother, however, foiled her purpose; but between the breasts the skin and flesh were horribly burned.[109]

The Confederates countered with their versions of atrocity. Long after the war such stories remained in the people's minds, and they carried them to their graves, but not before they had transmitted them to a new generation; thus the tendrils of hate were grafted onto uninjured minds so that almost one hundred years later the wounds have not completely closed. Ida Trotter, who lived on the outskirts of the city just within the Federal lines, liked to dwell on the stories of horror:

> Two most horrible atrocities . . . took place in our section. Mr. Cook was a planter who was said to be cruel to his slaves. It seems that his negro's had left their Master and gone in a body to the Yankees as most all of them did over the whole country.
>
> It is supposed they reported their Master's cruelty to them and the result was, a squad of soldiers went to the Cook home and overpowered the entire family except one little girl who hid under the house. The father was most horribly mutilated, both arms and legs were cut off—a candle was put into a gun and shot into the Mother—a bayonet was thrust through one child—pinning her to the wall. After the soldiers left—the child under the house heard her father's groans and went to find him—together they made their way to the nearest neighbors—the man just rolling along with both feet and hands gone and lived a short time.
>
> The Watsons were an old couple and he was a paralytic. They had several sons in the . . . army who were noted for their bravery. The Yankees were supposed to have heard this and sought revenge on the parents. They rolled the old gentleman out on his gallery in his rolling chair—they then set fire to the house. The mother they took in the yard—took her own feather bed and cut it open—while some were doing this—others went into her own smokehouse and rolled a barrel of molasses into the yard—after removing all the woman's clothing—they put her in the feathers and emptied the molasses on her—leaving her thus to watch her husband burned to death—sitting on his own gallery.[110]

These stories were part of the mind of Vicksburg; that they were unfounded made no difference, the mind believes what it

109. *Harper's Weekly Magazine,* July 4, 1863, pp. 429-30.

110. Ida B. Trotter, The Seige of Vicksburg, and Some Personal Experiences connected therewith, Miss. Arch., p. 5.

chooses to. Some people dearly wanted the horrors to be true for they buttressed the notion that the enemy was ruthless and inhuman. Other people, more critical and appreciative of truth, found it difficult to know where fact crossed the hairline into fantasy. The mind as well as the body was bludgeoned by the shelling and sometimes the thin line separating truth from fiction was blurred and fuzzed. William Drennan was doubtful of most of the tales, whether they were rumors of succor or atrocity; but he, like most persons, found it comforting to believe some of them. He said: "A man knows nothing. What he hears cannot be believed, as rumor, with her thousand tongues is more busy than ever. A new report is [constantly] in circulation . . . . Of course there is no foundation for any of it—yet I find myself unusually credulous—believing some things that I usually would not think bore a semblance of truth. So much for being enclosed in the fortifications of a city."[111]

Yet the flimsy structure of rumor had to be erected to ease the unceasing grinding. Sometimes the abrasion stemmed from within as well as without. There were little things such as Pemberton's order requisitioning all large pots and kettles to be used in preparing the troops' meals (some people probably wondered what was going to be cooked in the utensils); or the razing of unoccupied houses to obtain lumber to build hospital bunks; or the City Guard's raid on Bazsinky's store to seize sixty-nine bottles of whiskey to send to the hospitals for medicinal use, but which instead got the City Guard drunk; or the continual petty thievery by the troops.[112] Then there were other actions which impinged upon everyone. At the suggestion of a citizen who believed "that a considerable quantity of flour and [other foodstuffs] held by speculators may be hid away," the military forces conducted a house to house search for food. Some persons bore the search with equanimity, others thought that it was an insufferable indignity. Even in the most desperate hour

111. Drennan, Diary, II, 20-21.

112. Thomas H. Taylor to R. W. Memminger, June 13, 1863, Papers of Various Confederate Notables, Box 18; Letters and Telegrams sent, Department of Mississippi and Eastern Louisiana, Chapt. II, Vol. LX, 669; both in NA (RG) 109.

common adversity and suffering could not seal over man's pettiness and greed.[113]

Sometime during the last days of June a final, subtle shift occurred in the people's minds. Perhaps, it was not even a shift, maybe merely a dividing line, or the accumulation of nagging doubt. There was no specific event to pin it upon, for the days characterized only by their sameness slipped by one after the other. Yet it was undeniably there—a lessening of the hope that had sustained the people during the days of battering. As the month lengthened and there was still no sign of Johnston, a plaintive note of anxiety began to creep through the city. The certainty of relief—an article of faith from the beginning of the siege—began to be qualified and doubted. As the siege moved past the fourth week there was a waning of hope which could be halted only by a positive, heartening answer to the question, "Where is Johnston?"

Now the wallpaper *Citizen* began to make excuses for him: "The absorbing question now is where is Johnston, and what time will he be here. All are satisfied he is coming, but seem anxious to know when his victorious columns will march into our city with the 'stars and bars' floating triumphantly before them . . . . Be patient, then, and don't give way to paroxysms of gloom. [Johnston] is a strict believer in the Greek proverb, 'Hasten slowly.' "[114]

James Pepper was not given to "paroxysms of gloom," but he had almost reached the end of his tether: "My patience, as well as many others, are almost worn out. I have been faithful,

113. M. L. Smith to J. C. Pemberton, June 2, 1863, Papers of Various Confederate Notables, Box 18, NA (RG) 109; Chambers, Diary, June 3, 1863. The only indication that foodstuffs were actually confiscated appears in Tunnard, *A Southern Record,* p. 245: "All surplus provisions in the city were seized, and rations issued to citizens and soldiers alike." This statement is not reconciled with his abuse of the merchants. No contemporary document examined supports Tunnard's statement. The author's conclusion is that no systematic attempt was ever made to pool and ration civilian resources. Pemberton's attitude and policy toward the civilians seem to have been those of laissez faire, except when he deemed something necessary for military use, e.g., liquor. It appears that the only civilians who received authorized allowances of government rations were sixteen employees at Paxton's foundry. Letters and Telegrams sent, Department of Mississippi and Eastern Louisiana, Chapt. II, Vol. LX, 670, NA (RG) 109.

114. *Vicksburg Daily Citizen,* June 25, 1863.

and am as *yet* in the belief that [Johnston] would be here in due time. I would like very much to have more *reliable* news of his approach soon, for [the army's rations are reduced again], wich begins to look very suspicious."[115]

Mrs. William Lord had exhausted her patience and she felt only despair as she wrote: "Sunday, June 28th, Still in this dreary cave. Who would have believed that we could have borne such a life for five weeks? The siege has lasted 42 days and yet no relief—every day this week we have waited for the sound of Gen. Johnston's guns, but in vain."[116]

Yet there was no sign of relief; and Grant gave no relief either. Like a bulldog which had its prey by the throat, he tenaciously shook and shook. The cannonade, a Union soldier at Hayne's Bluff wrote his wife, "Is awful It fairly jars the Ground here 14 miles off."[117]

If a soldier at a distance of fourteen miles thought the bombardment was awful, then the comment of Joseph Alison, who was inside the city, may be accepted at face value. He said: "I have read of besieged cities and the sufferings of the inhabitants, but always thought the picture too highly painted. But now I have witnessed one and can believe all that is written on the subject."[118] As Alison looked about him, he saw the sum of trial by fire and privation.

Practically every building bore the sign of the whining fragments which had been flung into the city. Nothing was spared. A Parrott shell struck the Catholic Church during mass and laid figurines and worshipers alike on the rubbled floor. The yellow-flag-marked hospitals were hit (there were almost one hundred of them in the city, so they would have been difficult to miss). One shell landed in a ward of amputees, and men who had had their feet taken off now lost their legs, and men who had lost one arm now had the other cut off. The streets were filled with rubble and a thick coat of dust and powdered mortar covered everything. In the cemetery graves were laid open by the cut of hooves and wheels, allowing corpses to peer out

115. Pepper, Diary, p. 40. 116. Lord, Journal, p. 6.
117. A. M. Gregory to Wife, June 7, 1863, A. M. Gregory Papers, Old Courthouse Museum, Vicksburg.
118. Alison, Diary, p. 16.

through the exposed glass-covered caskets. The reek of death hung over the city.

Dead livestock were "hawled" to the river and thrown in. (When his mare had been missing for several days, James Pepper wryly guessed that "she's at Port Gibson by now.") But the sanitary details could not match the rate of attrition and the work of the June sun. There was a human element also. Green field peas, the main ration staple, were scarcely affected by the soldiers' weakened digestive tracts, and behind the trenches mounds of undigested peas added to the stench. One man said the peas were so thick that if the ground could be plowed they "would have seeded the land for a crop."[119]

The days of privation and pestilence had sapped the bodies of the defenders. Doctor Joseph Alison watched the spread of erysipelas (a highly contagious inflamation of the skin, which with patients' resistance low developed into suppuration and even gangrene). Without drugs, and helpless to treat it, he said: "Where that will end, none can say."[120] An epidemic of measles broke out, first among the children and then among the Negroes. The only treatment consisted of doses of corn whiskey which, thought Anne Harris, who took the treatment, were "frightful in strength and effect."[121] With little opportunity to wash, clothes became vermined, and the people had to accustom themselves to living with lice. Yet some people remained clean and fastidious for, mused James Pepper, "If I had some cooked clothes, what a nice time I could have with the girls."[122]

There was, however, little fastidiousness about diet. "Green" pork was a delicacy at two dollars a pound, and moulding rice sold for one dollar a pound. "An ordinary sized piece of cornbread," noted William Drennan, "sells for $2½."[123] As June came to an end food supplies were almost exhausted. The eating of mule meat became prevalent, and some people who had the choice preferred it to the spoiling remains of beef and pork.[124]

119. Howard, *Illinois Volunteers,* p. 130.
120. Alison, Diary, p. 17.
121. Broidrick, A Recollection, p. 15.
122. Pepper, Diary, p. 19. 123. Drennan, Diary, II, 39.
124. Though there are a few recorded instances in which mule meat was eaten earlier, it appears, according to most sources, that the practice did not become widespread until the latter part of June.

Mary Loughborough's husband sent her a note: "Already I am living on pea meal, and cannot think of your coming to this." His wife thought that she had almost reached that point, for she asked him to send her some mule meat. He refused, saying that he did not want her reduced to that until it was absolutely necessary.[125]

William Kyle, sitting on the Sky Parlor, watched as an officer rode up, dismounted, and tied his horse to a hitching post. A moment later, after a shell fragment wounded the animal, the rider walked into a blacksmith's shop, picked up a sledge hammer, and killed the horse. After the officer had gone Kyle "saw a private soldier stop at the carcas . . . wait a moment and then deliberately commence to cut him off a large chunk."[126]

Other soldiers were promising mutiny unless they were fed, and they sent Pemberton a threatening petition: "We are actually on sufferance . . . . We are . . . not allowed to forage any at all, and, even if permitted, there is nothing to be had among the citizens."[127] But the citizens thought that foraging was permitted, or at least condoned. Anything eatable that could be found was gobbled up—"fruit, vegetables, chickens etc." William Porterfield became so incensed that he picked up his rifle, killed one soldier, and wounded two others, "in protecting his property."[128] Rowland Chambers was also shooting at thieves, and he stripped his unripened peach crop to keep the trees "from being broke to pieces."[129]

Hungry soldiers claiming to be acting in an official capacity began to search homes for food. On June 29, "an officer with a gard came out and serched" Rowland Chambers' property; "but," he said, "took nothing as yet." That night they returned. But now, according to Chambers, they were "a party of armed Ruffians [who] commenced brakeing open the stable . . . . they had an officer [who] said he was acting under authority if so it is

125. Loughborough, *Cave Life,* p. 117.
126. "Memoirs of William D. Kyle," *Vicksburg Daily Herald,* May 4, 1906.
127. *Official Records Navy,* Ser. I, Vol. XXV, 118.
128. *Vicksburg Daily Citizen,* July 2, 1863.
129. Chambers, Diary, June 24, 1863.

a bad state of affairs when Robery is carried on by authority of the government officers."[130]

Robbery was a matter of definition. When Chambers sold five pigs for $430, or when a barrel of flour brought $400, or when a turkey sold for $50, it was not robbery, just honest profit. The *Citizen,* to its last issue, railed at the profitmakers: "If aught would appeal to the heart of stone of the extortioner . . . the present necessities of our citizens would do so . . . . We assert our belief that there is plenty within our lines . . . . We are satisfied there are numerous persons within the city who have breadstuffs secreted, and are dolling it out, at the most exorbitant figure."[131] But money, not humanitarian importunings, was the stuff which lured the food from its hiding places.

However, the price paid for food was no indication of value or worth. William Drennan made a fine distinction between "sells for" and "worth." He said: "Money here is worthless when it comes to buying food—and to say that such a thing is worth so much, only implies that some man is willing to part with it for that; for it is worth much more if this siege holds out ten days longer."[132]

Robbery and extortion were merely synonyms for hunger, and its signs were everywhere. Anne Harris' mother caught her arm to whip her, felt its thinness, burst into tears, and cried: "Oh, I cannot [punish] my poor little half-starved child; it is not naughtiness, it is hunger."[133] A soldier brought Mary Loughborough's daughter a "jaybird" to keep as a pet, but before the day was past the bird was part of a watery gruel.[134] And in the market beside the mule meat hung freshly skinned rats.[135]

Somewhere there was a breaking point. When a soldier had had enough he could slip over to the Union lines, where, one deserter told Seth Wells, he could die a well-fed coward instead of

130. *Ibid.,* June 30, 1863. There is no record which indicates that the military authorities ordered such search and seizure at this date.

131. *Vicksburg Daily Citizen,* July 2, 1863.

132. Drennan, Diary, II, 39.

133. Broidrick, A Recollection, p. 14.

134. Loughborough, *Cave Life,* p. 137.

135. "A Woman's Diary," *The Century Magazine,* XXX, 774; Tunnard, *A Southern Record,* p. 263. Tunnard, whose accuracy with respect to some points is doubtful, makes the sole first-hand claim which the author has seen concerning the actual eating of rats. He states that he ate fried rat on June 29.

a starved martyr. But there was no escape for the civilians. The lines were closed to them, so was the river. One man and his wife attempted to pass through the lines, but were turned back by a politely worded refusal. They then tried the river, but were forced back by gunfire, and returned to their cellar with the "shells flying as thick as ever."[136] Mary Loughborough admitted that her nerve was cracked. When her cave suffered a near-miss by a mortar shell she was seized with "extreme terror and . . . was many days recovering the equanimity" she had struggled so long to attain. She knew other women who had become "utterly sick through constant fear and apprehension."[137] In her diary another woman gave a personal case study of the nerve-breaking process:

> June 25th—Horrible day. The most horrible yet to me, because I've lost my nerve. We were all in the cellar, when a shell came tearing through the roof, burst upstairs, tore up that room, and the pieces coming through both floors down into the cellar . . . . This was tangible proof the cellar was no place of protection from them. On the heels of this came Mr. J— to tell us that young Mrs. P— had had her thigh-bone crushed. When Martha went for the milk she came back horror-stricken to tell us the black girl there had her arm taken off by a shell. For the first time I quailed. I do not think people who are physically brave deserve much credit for it; it is a matter of nerves. In this way I am constitutionally brave, and seldom think of danger till it is over; and death has not the terrors for me it has for some others . . . . But now I first seemed to realize that something worse than death might come; I might be crippled, and not killed. Life, without all one's powers and limbs, was a thought that broke down my courage. [I] must get . . . out of this horrible place; I cannot stay; I know I shall be crippled.

Then her terror, like Mary Loughborough's, subsided and she said: "I must summon that higher kind of courage—moral bravery—to subdue my fears of possible mutilation."[138]

Most of the people must have reached the breaking-point, slipped over into an abyss of terror, then somehow struggled out of it. Somewhere they found a reservoir of sustenance that enabled them to stand the pounding. For some it was an intel-

136. "A Woman's Diary," *The Century Magazine,* XXX, 774.
137. Loughborough, *Cave Life,* p. 132.
138. "A Woman's Diary," *The Century Magazine,* XXX, 773.

lectual exercise, a summoning of "that higher kind of courage," a final screwing up of moral fiber. For others it was a sheer animal will to survive, a crawling into a hole in the ground and lying there, with frenetic scurryings to find something to fill their bellies. For most it was probably a mixture of blind animal will and conscious moral strengthening. Whatever the sources, the people managed to grub up enough tenacity to lead them reeling and staggering into the month of July—the forty-fourth day of siege.

They looked tougher from the outside. Commodore James Palmer, who was having his troubles at Port Hudson, wrote Porter: "I am sorry to hear the Vicksburgians are living on mule meat . . . if it be true, that diet assimilates them wonderfully to the animal that is said to sustain them, for to my mind they have become more stubborn and obstinate than ever."[139]

Palmer was at least partially correct. The stubborn, tenacious fiber was frayed and shredded, but not snapped. Even the sick and wounded had not quite given up. At one of the hospitals those who could walk wrapped themselves in bed sheets and gowns and paraded through a mock wedding ceremony. Civilians as well as soldiers were there, and they thought the satire "was conducted with great magnificence." A blacking-daubed Prince Imperial of Ethopia, swathed in robes made of sheets and bandages, claimed the hand of "the lovely and accomplished . . . Arch Duchess of Senegambia." The spectators laughed and applauded, though, said J. M. Swords, "as is usual in troublesome times the sabler element was predominate."[140]

This was quite an admission from Swords, who did his best to switch up flagging morale. Maybe the gaiety was a hollow shell, form without substance and meaningless so far as being an indication of mind. Perhaps it was merely a conditioned reflex that must occur until the battering ceased. Maybe. Already there was talk that the city's days were numbered. On June 28, the defenders intercepted a message from Porter to Grant which said deserters reported only six days' quarter rations remained in the city and that the city would be surrendered on

139. *Official Records Navy,* Ser. I, Vol. XX, 254.
140. *Vicksburg Daily Citizen,* July 2, 1863.

July 4, "after the rebels fire a salute."[141] A check with a calendar showed that the food would be exhausted on July 3. Perhaps there was something to the story.

Inexorably the fourth day of July grew nearer. A woman looked at her food supplies, found that she had only a barrel of sugar remaining, and confided to her diary that "a few more days will bring us to starvation indeed."[142] William Drennan scrawled a short entry in his diary: "Everything wears a dull hue, and in my own mind I have given out."[143] J. M. Swords, in the July 2 issue of his newsless, wallpaper *Citizen,* set the type for a corner box: "The Great Ulysses—the Yankee Generalissimo, surnamed Grant—has expressed his intention of dining in Vicksburg on Sunday next, and celebrating the 4th of July by a grand dinner . . . Ulysses must get into the city before he dines in it. The way to cook a rabbit is 'first to catch the rabbit.' "

The rabbit was almost caught. On the night of July 2, Pemberton called his major generals to his headquarters. He reviewed the situation, then asked for opinions. From memory the generals repeated Johnston's dispatches. They thought his last message was cheery, but of no hope. General Bowen said that they might as well get it over. The others agreed. They drew up some terms with which they could begin to bargain with Grant, and selected Bowen to open negotiations. The staff secretary read the minutes he had jotted on a scrap of paper; everyone agreed that they were correct, and the conference was over. The next day while the guns roared, the negotiators maneuvered and backed and filled.

As word of the conference reached the civilians, there were howls throughout the city that Pemberton was a proven traitor. When Mrs. Lord learned that General Bowen was one of the group she wished that she could rip out the embroidered wreaths she had sewn about his collar stars. Even as the last hours trickled away the defiance was not dead.[144]

But a woman's vehement wishes could not shore up a sagged and starved army. Finally, after stickling over form, Grant

141. *Official Records Navy,* Ser. I, Vol. XXV, 119.
142. "A Woman's Diary," *The Century Magazine,* XXX, 774.
143. Drennan, Diary, II, 48.
144. Lord, Journal, pp. 7-8.

and Pemberton came to terms; or more precisely, Pemberton met Grant's demand: surrender. At five o'clock on the afternoon of July 3 the last shot rang out from the river batteries.[145] That night rockets arched and exploded over the city in a myriad of holiday colors, and just before daybreak there were a few rattling shots along the lines.[146] Then, after the sun came up, Lewis Guion opened his diary and wrote: "Not a gun [can] be heard . . . this morning."[147]

Now there was only silence. And, a thousand miles away, over the green fields and orchards at Gettysburg there was silence too. High noon had struck and passed for the Confederacy, and the shadows began to lengthen.

For over two years the sounds of the struggle for life had roared over Vicksburg, ringing in the people's ears and hearts. So long as there were the sounds of violence—the inadequate bark of the little field pieces dragged up to Port Hill to halt the *Silver Wave,* the high-velocity crack of Farragut's naval guns, the tortured scream of Whistling Dick, the apologetic cough of Porter's mortars, and the conglomerate roar of Grant's massed artillery—there was defiant life and invincibleness. Now there was only silence.

In one of the battered houses a man leaned back in his rocking chair. He rocked a bit, savoring the silence, then said to his wife: "It seems to me I can hear the silence, and feel it, too. It wraps me like a soft garment; how else can I express this peace?"[148]

145. *Official Records Navy,* Ser. I, Vol. XXV, 123.

146. *Ibid.,* p. 103; Rockwood Manuscript, Old Courthouse Museum, Vicksburg, pp. 1-2.

147. Guion, Diary, July 4, 1863.

148. "A Woman's Diary," *The Century Magazine,* XXX, 774.

CHAPTER IX

"AN ANGRY WAVE HAD PASSED"

THE general was hot, very hot. His shirt was stuck to his body, and when he shifted his weight his blue trousers slid easily over the soaked saddle. His horse's hooves kicked up little spurts of dust which rose and added their bit to the cloud hovering over the snaking column of troops. The afternoon sun blazed down and the dust was choking, but it did not matter. The band was playing "Hail Columbia," "Yankee Doodle," "Home Sweet Home," and when the head of the column reached the courthouse square the soldiers broke into cheers. A division commander climbed to the courthouse's east portico to urge the cheers from the troops. Someone ran up the stairs to the battered cupola and set the stars and stripes flying above it; down in the street the band struck up "The Star-Spangled Banner." The general pulled at the reins and moved off to find a cool spot. He was not an army commander, nor a corps commander, nor even a division commander, and he did not have to be ceremonious. His eye caught a pleasant sight—a lush yard and a fine house over which a British flag floated—and he decided to camp there. He reined in his horse and slid out of the saddle. He was very tired, but very happy.[1]

To the civilians there was nothing tired or worn about the sweaty, dusty, blue columns. One woman, as she watched them march by, thought, "What a contrast [they are] to the suffering creatures we [have] seen so long . . . . Sleek horses, polished

1. "Civil War Letters of Brigadier General William Ward Orme—1862-1866," ed. Harry E. Pratt, *Journal of the Illinois State Historical Society,* XXIII (July, 1930), 289; Rockwood Manuscript, Old Courthouse Museum, Vicksburg, p. 2; Gregory, *Annals,* p. 129.

The rabbit is caught. A Union division marches past the courthouse, which already flies the United States flag, as the people of Vicksburg "celebrate" the Fourth of July, 1863. (From Frank Leslie, *The Soldier in Our Civil War*)

arms, bright plumes . . . the pride and panoply of war." Though she was a Unionist, her heart groaned as she thought of "the worn men in gray, who [are] being blindly dashed against this embodiment of modern power."[2]

If he had known he was being characterized as an embodiment of modern power Seth Wells would have snorted. At the moment he was only hot and tired, and besides that he thought the Confederates were "a good looking set of Rebel troops as we have seen." After cheering at the courthouse he stacked his rifle and sprawled out on the ground until the sun dipped westward and lost some of its heat; then he got up and, like thousands of other Union soldiers, wandered through the city.[3] They had hammered for months and had left comrades buried all the way from the Tennessee border trying to get inside Vicksburg. Now that they were there they wanted to see the formidable city and savor the taste of triumph.

For some triumph was not enough; they wanted obliteration. A newspaper correspondent filed an account of his first impressions of the city: "We expected to see awful havoc from shells and the mortar-bombs. The first sight is a disappointment.

2. "A Woman's Diary," *The Century Magazine,* XXX, 775.
3. Wells, *Siege of Vicksburg,* p. 88.

The place is not damaged so much as might have been expected." He said practically every house had a hole in it ("but a hole made by a cannon-ball is . . . a small matter"), that the streets were cratered, and there was not an unbroken pane of glass in the city; yet to the correspondent this seemed an easy escape from the thousands of shells which had been hurled into the place.[4]

As they picked their way through the rubbly streets other Union men looked about and decided the city had suffered enough. Seth Wells thought the buildings "were torn to pieces," and Charles B. Tompkins, a surgeon, wrote his wife, "Vicksburg has been a very nice city one day but the houses are either injured by our cannon or delapidated & everything looks as if the city had been deserted years ago."[5]

The long sought prize was a different thing to different men. For some it was a blasted shambles, for others it was a disappointment; for Nathan Dye it was a wonder. Vicksburg, he wrote his parents, is "the roughest place that I ever saw . . . . Some places it is bridged 30 or 40 feet high . . . to make the road some houses are up on the top of bluffs so that it takes 40 or 50 steps to go up to the house and some houses you can walk right into the 3rd story from the road. I should call it a den for wolves and other wild beasts."[6]

Throughout the afternoon and into the night the soldiers inspected the city. Seth Wells made his way to the river battery in which Whistling Dick was emplaced; he thought it was a "beautiful" gun, and he sat and listened while the Confederate

4. "A National Account," *Rebellion Record,* VII, 162. The navy fired over 22,000 shells at the city, *Official Records Navy,* Ser. I, Vol. XXV, 104-5. The author has been unable to locate a report which would indicate the number of shells fired by the army, but it is reasonable to assume that it would be several times the navy's total. Material damage was excessive, but the number of civilian casualties, as in the attack of 1862, was surprisingly small. Contemporary accounts differ with respect to the number of people killed, but it appears that not more than five to ten persons died as a result of the bombardment. The number of wounded civilians would be considerably greater. Cf. "National Account," *Rebellion Record,* VIII, 164; "Diary of a Citizen," *ibid.,* p. 170; Gregory, *Annals,* p. 119; Abrams, *Full and Detailed History,* p. 48.

5. Wells, *Siege of Vicksburg,* p. 88; Charles B. Tompkins to Mary G. Tompkins, July 10, 1863, Charles B. Tompkins Papers, Duke University.

6. Nathan G. Dye to Parents, August 1, 1863, Nathan G. Dye Papers, Duke University.

gunners told him its history. Some drunk staff officers climbed the iron stairway of the courthouse, singing the "Star-Spangled Banner" and waving a captured signal flag. One of them saw the name of a Cincinnati foundry cast into the metal and "damned the impudence of the people who thought they could whip the United States when they couldn't even make their own staircases."[7] Max Kuner returned to his house, found a general setting up his quarters there, and asked, "By what authority, sir, do you take possession of another man's house?"

"That's none of your damned business. Who are you?"

"I'm the owner of the house."

"Are you a loyal citizen?"

"That is none of *your* damned business."

The general started to kick at him so Kuner backed out and went to Grant for redress. Grant gave the order for the general to leave, but Kuner had to find him another place to stay.[8]

Charles Wilcox, a Union captain, saw "Rebel officers and Union officers . . . riding together through the streets, and in some instances both parties were so drunk they could hardly sit on their horses." To Wilcox, the women seemed to be most affected by the occupation. They passed by him, heads held high, but with tears in their eyes.[9]

Mrs. William Lord, heartsick from the surrender, climbed out of her cave and went home to find some soldiers rummaging through a basket of clean clothes on her back porch.

"What do you mean," she asked, "by such a liberty? I should think soldiers would have too much feeling in this hour of distress to intrude even to the privacy of a lady's home." The rummagers pointed to her shell-struck house. "Do you call this a lady's home? You ought to keep it in better order."

This exchange evidently put her in an even worse humor,

7. Gregory, *Annals,* p. 130. This was one of the two "offenses" which Gregory thought were committed by the Union soldiers. The other was the selling of copies of *Harper's Weekly,* which carried a cover illustration depicting the execution of two Confederate spies.

8. [Kuner], "Vicksburg and After," *Sewanee Review,* XV, 493.

9. "With Grant at Vicksburg: From the Civil War Diary of Captain Charles E. Wilcox," ed. Edgar L. Erickson, *Journal of the Illinois State Historical Society,* XXX (January, 1938), 496.

for she wrote in her journal: "All . . . day they were streaming through town and in and out of my yard and *so* drunk."[10]

Lewis Guion saw some looting along Washington Street, but there were as many Confederates involved in it as there were Northerners. Hogsheads of sugar were rolled out in the street, the barrels were knocked open, and soldiers from both armies helped themselves to it. Seth Wells was with a group that broke into a store and took "a large quantity of tobacco and other things," and there were Confederates with him. Ephraim Anderson, a Confederate officer, said the homes were left almost undisturbed except for those which were unoccupied, and practically the only things stolen from these houses were mirrors, which the Yankees took to their camps "to survey themselves . . . with evident complacency and [a] most nonchalant air."[11]

They were pleased with themselves, and they wanted to look at their reflections and say to themselves that they were the ones who had cracked the toughest nut the Confederacy had to offer. A good many of them were drunk and they raised the ire of some of the people by "passing rough jokes" with the Negro women. They stole a little, and they trampled through yards and even rummaged through a woman's laundry basket; but there was little wanton destruction of the sort for which General Peter J. Osterhaus' division was noted as it had slashed up through Port Gibson and Raymond. Instead it was as though all the heat and passion were gone. For the most part the soldiers merely wanted to look—to see the mule meat hanging in the markets, to visit the gun emplacements and the caves, to look at the battered homes and earth and know that at last the city was theirs.

They had won—they liked the flavor of victory and they took mirrors to look at themselves in, but they did not rub the victory to the marrow. They had fought the defenders to a frazzle in

10. Lord, Journal, Library of Congress, p. 10.

11. Guion, Diary, July 4, 1863, Department of Archives and Manuscripts, Louisiana State University; Wells, *Siege of Vicksburg,* p. 88; Anderson, *Memoirs,* pp. 358-59. A Provost Marshal's guard was posted as quickly as possible, and such looting as had occurred was soon brought to a minimum. The general impression which the civilians received of the Yankees, considering that after all they were conquerers, was expressed by Gregory, *Annals,* p. 129: "The Federal army . . . conducted itself in an exemplary manner."

a fair fight—Richard Howard, a volunteer from Illinois, could not find "a rugged looking person in the city"—but they respected the losers and they liked their spirit—Howard said the people "stoutly maintained that we had done them very little if any damage"—and they were willing to call it quits.[12] They shared their rations with the soldiers and the civilians, and their doctors treated both the docile and the vengeful. After he had bandaged a girl's gunshot wound, Charles Tompkins wrote his wife, "She has a brother here who is Sergt. in the 22 Miss. He is a fine young man & I like him but his sister is as revengeful towards the Yankees as she can be. I plague her by telling her . . . that her foot will be well in time for the Yankee balls we will have here. But she declares she will never dance with a Yankee."[13]

The summation for the Northerners appeared on a piece of wallpaper. Someone who could set type and operate a press went in the *Citizen* office, found the forms still set for the July 2 issue, changed only the box set in the corner, and printed the famous Fourth of July edition: "Two days bring about great changes. The banner of the Union floats over Vicksburg. Gen. Grant has 'caught the rabbit'; he has dined in Vicksburg, and he did bring his dinner with him. The 'Citizen' lives to see it. For the last time it appears on 'Wall Paper' . . . . This is the last wallpaper edition, and is, excepting this note, from the types as we found them. It will be valuable hereafter as a curiosity."[14] For the victors, Vicksburg and everything for which it stood—pounding artillery, mule meat, wallpaper newspapers, and even rebellion and death—was now only a memory and a curiosity.

The fleet put into the wharves, holiday flags flying, and that night still more fireworks arched and burst over the city. Confederates as well as Federals set them off, and when they ran out of rockets they made roman candles by taking hollowed canestalks and filling them with alternate charges of wet and dry powder. One Confederate soldier said there were thousands of

12. Howard, *124th Regiment,* p. 130.

13. Charles B. Tompkins to Mary G. Tompkins, July 10, 1863, Charles B. Tompkins Papers.

14. *Vicksburg Daily Citizen,* July 4, 1863.

Admiral Porter's fleet, holiday flags flying, puts in to the Vicksburg wharves, as former slaves wait to greet the sailors. (From *Harper's Weekly*)

the improvised roman candles and that he, after forty years, "never saw a display . . . to equal it."[15]

In her home a woman sat at a table and wrote up her diary: "It is evening. All is still. Silence and night are once more united. I can sit at the table in the parlor and write. Two candles are lighted. I would like a dozen. We have had . . . wheat bread once more."[16]

Another woman listened to the band and watched the fireworks. She later made this simple statement: "We cried."[17]

So far as the Union soldiers were concerned Vicksburg was done and past and remained only as a memory to compare with other battles and other campaigns in the reminiscing of years to come. Already they were thinking of moving on—dreaming, wrote a general to his wife, of "that sweet time when we shall meet again to part no more on earth."[18]

But to those they were leaving—"a terribly reduced" people

15. S. R. Martin, Recollections of the War Between the States, 1861-65, p. 81. Owned by John S. Hoggatt, Vicksburg.

16. "A Woman's Diary," *The Century Magazine,* XXX, 774.

17. Rockwood MS, p. 2.

18. Orme, "Civil War Letters," *Journal of the Illinois State Historical Society,* XXIII, 290.

—Vicksburg and everything it meant—stark, shattered defeat—was not finished; in some respects it had only begun. The Northerners did not seem to understand that a light hand and doles of food could not put everything right again. General William Orme wrote his wife of a woman he had met. He had given her and her family some food and wondered why, though "she is evidently a woman of wealth & fine education, [she] wears a small dagger at her side . . . carries a pistol in her trunk [and] talks fierce . . . . What do you think of that." Later he sought out Winchester Hall, whom he had known before the war. He found Hall, his wife and four children in "destitute circumstances"; but when he asked if he might help, all he received was a polite refusal. He shrugged his shoulders, and when he wrote his wife of the incident he said, "They are proud people though, I guess; and do not like to appear asking for anything."[19]

Pride was almost all that remained to them. The moment the last shot from the Confederate batteries fell spent to the ground a way of life crumbled and toppled. Late on the afternoon of July 3 Vicksburg had died. The hills and the houses still stood, and people still ate and slept in them; the river still flowed, and for the first time in almost three years the wharves were crowded with ships; somewhere there was even a laugh and a song—but despite these things the city was a gutted shell. The heart and core of the city—its political, economic, and social structure—which was built and supported within the cradling framework of hills, homes, and river had ceased to exist. Though terribly worn and eroded in spots, this system had functioned to the moment Pemberton bowed his head and nodded acceptance of Grant's demand to surrender; in that split second the system was obliterated and there remained only a void.

19. *Ibid.*, p. 291. There were others who were not too proud to take anything they could get. On the afternoon of the Fourth there was a stampede to the wharves to obtain food brought in by the steamboats. One woman who had a requisition for a dozen hens asked General John McPherson if she might be given at least one rooster. McPherson asked her why she wanted the rooster, and she replied it was because "I [have] not heard a rooster crow in such a long time." The general gave her a rooster. Rockwood MS, p. 4.

Four days after the surrender Jefferson Davis was still trying to learn what was happening at Vicksburg. He telegraphed Governor John Pettus, "What is the State of affairs at Vicksburg . . . ."[20] Pettus, hiding in central Mississippi, had no more idea than did Davis, but someone in Vicksburg might have answered for him: We are a defeated people. We live in a conquered land, yet at the same time it is a limbo-land, for the fighting continues, and thus we are between war and peace. We are subject to the orders of a military governor. Our property is subject to confiscation. Our slaves are freed. Our way of life as we created it is demolished. We live amidst shambles, and on the foundation of shambles we will build again. We do this not willingly, but of necessity, for necessity bears heavily upon us.

Physical wounds scar over quickly. As soon as the shooting stopped workers began shoveling plaster and broken lumber from the houses, caves were closed, shell holes were filled, and grass began to cover the raw earth thrown up before the trenches.[21] A few weeks after the surrender a woman sat in an easy chair, her diary in her lap, looking out at the green slopes. She wrote: "I have looked over this journal as if in a dream . . . . I feel as if an angry wave had passed over me . . . . This book is exhausted, and I wonder whether there will be more adventures . . . to cause me to begin another."[22] She closed the cover and put down her pen, but around her a new struggle was underway, one which would measure the temper of a people as much and as well as did the trial by fire and starvation.

The end product of this new struggle—survival—was the same as the old, but there was a great difference between the contexts in which the two took place. The first was accompanied with all the romantic and glorified trappings of the Confederacy. However shabby and tawdry these overtones and nuances, they

20. Jefferson Davis to John J. Pettus, July 8, 1863, Governor's Military Telegrams, Ser. E, Vol. LXII, Miss. Arch.

21. Jones, *Wisconsin History Commission Original Papers Number 8,* p. 79. This does not imply that the city was repaired overnight. In September a visitor described the interior of one of the churches. There were no pews, no altar, no floor. Negroes were living in the church, and they cooked on the remains of the floor. Dishes and bodies were washed in the marble font. Unsigned letter, September, 1863, quoted in Moore, *Anecdotes,* p. 218.

22. "War Diary," *The Century Magazine,* XXXVIII, 956.

were nevertheless a vital and compelling part of the minds of the people, for they were the things which were cherished and refurbished until ultimately they became the sum and substance of the entire conflict.

The second struggle for survival was more primeval and cruel than the first, for it was stripped of the veneer of honor and idealistic romanticism which surrounded the battle years. It was a rough, brutal shouldering and grubbing to gain or regain those things which had been swept away in defeat. There was little in it which found a pleasant resting place in the memories of the participants. In the distant years the memories of muted drums would call back a flood of wartime reminiscences, but that segment of the mind which harbored the thoughts of the first years of defeat was almost a locked book, and the people who lived through the period scarcely tampered with the lock. Perhaps, if they had a sense of dramatic tragedy, they believed that during the cruel months their story had reached its climax, that they were all somehow touched with a bit of glory, and that the denouement, without glory, should be brief. Perhaps they did not realize that the years of defeat were a time of transition between war and reconstruction, and were as important as the periods they connected. Or perhaps they did not care. Whatever the reasons, when the time came to summon memories of the war years the mind remained curiously reticent when it reached the period immediately following the surrender. But the shards of contemporary evidence remain, and perhaps within them lie the reasons.

The new way of life was rapidly outlined the day the Federals occupied the city. As the troops marched into Vicksburg a new social and economic order was rising from the shambles. An old Negro man, his face split with a grin, provided the keynote for the new social order: "De long-looked-fer done came at lass." Negroes, dressed in the brightest colors they could find, lined the streets to welcome their liberators. Black men lounged at street corners, laughing and jeering in their new-found freedom —some of the people complained they could not speak to the Negroes "for fear of being called a rebel, or some other abusive epithet"—and black women walked arm-in-arm with Federal soldiers. Alexander Abrams said their behavior would have been ludicrous if it had not been so galling.[23]

Now a free man and a free agent, the Negro lost no time asserting his liberty. A cook who asked her mistress for wages and was turned out of the house for her pains, quickly found employment with another woman, though, said the woman, "I am thoroughly pulled to pieces in Vicksburg circles."[24] Most of Marmaduke Shannon's servants left, not to loaf and subsist on government rations, but to work. Two of them joined the Federal army; one became a hack driver, and one worked on a riverboat.[25]

Alexander Abrams, who took special interest in the Negro's behavior, thought the reaction of the Vicksburg Negro ran counter to the stereotype set in the white man's mind. It was generally believed that the city slave or house servant was more attached to his master than the country slave or field hand, probably because he was in closer contact with his master and received better treatment. Yet in Vicksburg, the city slaves more readily deserted their masters and were "abusive," while the Negroes brought in by planters were more loyal and more docile.[26]

Though the people sustained a tremendous property loss in the freeing of the slaves, there was little recrimination. Explaining the slave situation, Alexander Arthur said: "I have some family servants but more have left me, and I have no anxiety on that subject, for . . . it would be more their loss than mine."[27] In some instances there was actual relief that at last the burden and responsibility of maintaining slaves was past. Marmaduke Shannon, who had already lost his more ambitious Negroes, drove away two servants "because they would do

23. Bell, "A Girl's Experience," *Harper's Weekly,* LVI, 13; Abrams, *Full and Detailed History,* p. 64.

24. "A Woman's Diary," *The Century Magazine,* XXX, 775.

25. Marmaduke Shannon to Emma Crutcher, May 18, 1864, Crutcher Collection, Miss. Arch.

26. Abrams, *Full and Detailed History,* p. 65.

27. Alexander H. Arthur to Joseph Holt, July 12, 1863, Joseph Holt Papers, Library of Congress.

nothing but eat"; and a woman positively breathed satisfaction as she wrote: "I have been rid of the negroes . . . & it is a great comfort to be once more alone."[28]

During the months following the surrender, the Negro, poorly equipped to assume his new role of freedman, moved in an ill-defined world of freedom. Some slaves clung to their masters, content with the established paternalistic role; others merely shifted their allegiance and source of support from their masters to the Union army. Still others struck out boldly to seek to make a place for themselves in the new order, while some, whatever their inclinations, were simply shoved into the moil of a free society by masters glad to be quit of their responsibility. In time the Federal government, first through the machinery of tactical army units, then through the Freedmen's Bureau and private philanthropic organizations, would seek to rehabilitate the black man and shepherd him to a secure place in society; but initially the Negro had to shift for himself, and he was in many respects no freer than when he was a slave.

By the end of August the first halting steps were taken to grapple with the mountainous problem of the Negro. Lumped with cotton, drugs, salt, and gold, the Negro was categorized as contraband goods, and a makeshift arrangement was established within the army to care for him. Grant selected John Eaton, a Messianic soldier who was long on fanciful dreams (though he protested he was not) and short on a sense of reality, to organize the Negroes in Vicksburg. After he had looked at the Negroes, Eaton sent letter after letter to his friends in the North begging aid: "The work is to immense for description. It is run, drive, consult, think, write to the end of my strength . . . . Impractical romancing ideas have little place here [he found time to court and wed a Vicksburg girl], good strength sound common sense a thorough Christian spirit of self sacrifice are essentials . . . . [If people would] apply patriotic common sense to the new questions, arising prejudices will give way, Social

28. Marmaduke Shannon to Emma Crutcher, May 18, 1864, Crutcher Collection; Mary L. Blake to Marshall McDonald, August 3, [1863], Marshall McDonald Papers, Duke University.

problems will settle themselves and the country will arise from the bloody ordeal of war to a higher and more glorious career."[29]

Night after night Eaton sat at his letter book, spinning his dreams; yet upon the advent of winter he had somehow found clothes for his contrabands, had organized them into squads under the leadership of "men like all Sgts," and had established a school in which 250 adults and children were learning to read and write. During the autumn of 1863 he held high hopes for his black people, and for the settlement of problems and prejudices through "patriotic common sense." Little did he realize that in his well-intentioned way he was helping to reinforce a legacy of suspicion and hate, for when young Alice Shannon learned of the Negro school she wrote her sister: "Oh the impudence of these Yankees. I hate them worse every day."[30]

Eaton and his glittering, gossamer fancies were long departed from Vicksburg when his faithful lieutenant, now charged with the responsibility for the welfare of the Negroes, wrote up his reports. Samuel Thomas did not hurriedly scrawl messages of "run, consult, think"; his reports were slow recitations of stark reality, written as though the pen was reluctant to record the admission of crumpled dreams:

> The reasons why I think the negro has so little chance for justice at the hands of Mississippians is, that into whatever place I go—the street, the shop, the house, the hotel, or the steamboat—I . . . hear the people talk in a way that indicates that public sentiment has not come to the attitude in which it can conceive of the negro having any rights at all. Men . . . cheat a negro without feeling a single twinge of their honor; to kill a negro they do not deem murder; to debauch a negro woman they do not think fornication; to take property away from a negro they do not consider robbery.
>
> The reason for this is simple and manifest: they esteem the negro the property of the white man by natural right . . . . Other states may, in this matter, be in advance of Mississippi. I suspect they are. If justice is possible, I feel sure they are.
>
> The people . . . boast that when they get . . . affairs in their own

29. Letters Sent by General Superintendent Contrabands, from Memphis, Tenn., and Vicksburg, Miss., 67, 70, 88. NA (RG) 105; John Eaton, *Grant, Lincoln and the Freedmen* (New York, 1907), p. 85.

30. Alice Shannon to Emma Crutcher, November 19, 1863, Crutcher Collection.

hands, the negroes, to use their own classic expression, "will catch hell."[31]

Thomas was an aggrieved and disillusioned man. He had expected what would have amounted to a miracle, and when it failed to materialize he withdrew into a shell of pessimism concerning the fate of his Negroes. What he failed to see, though he lived and worked in the midst of it, was a society uprooted and turned topsy-turvy; and while his charges bore the brunt of the violent change and adjustment, they were not the sole sufferers.

Paralleling the formation of a new social structure, and bearing the same bitter fruit, was the creation of a brawling economic system, which defied every effort to regulate and control it. Had not Vicksburg been the entrepôt for a vast, rich cotton area, the backwaters of war, with all of the flotsam they carried, would have quickly washed past and the people would have been left more or less to their own devices. But as it was, the city became the base for swarms of men who smelled the lush scent of gigantic profits. Regardless of who they were—Yankee speculator, Union soldier, Vicksburg merchant, or private citizen—scarcely anyone was left untouched in the no-holds-barred scramble for wealth.

If the men charged with the responsibility of controlling the commerce had been as sensitive and idealistic as those responsible for the Negro, they too might have retreated into somber disillusionment; but they were not, and if they had ever pinned

31. Samuel Thomas to O. O. Howard, September 28, 1865, Letters Sent, Office of the Assistant Commissioner, Vicksburg, Mississippi, January 22-November 4, 1865, NA (RG) 105. The problem of the Negro was further complicated by the fact that immediately following the close of the Vicksburg campaign, Negroes from the entire region flocked into the city. In April 1865, it was estimated that there were between 20,000 and 25,000 Negroes in Vicksburg. (Marmaduke Shannon to Emma Crutcher, May 2, 1865, Crutcher Collection.) This estimate seems somewhat excessive in the light of census returns compiled eighteen months later (November 1866), which reported 3,793 Negroes living in Vicksburg. (Warren County Census, 1866, Ser. F, Vol. CX, 101, Miss. Arch.) It must be remembered, however, that by November 1866 much of the farm land had been restored to production, and this would tend to drain away a large number of the unemployed Negroes who had come to the city during 1863-65. At any event, even accepting the relatively low figures of 1866, the number of Negroes living in Vicksburg after they were freed was more than triple the number who lived there as slaves. The implications of this increase are obvious.

any hopes on "patriotic common sense," the hopes had long since evaporated into thin air, and in their place was a knowing cynicism. Ten months after the surrender one Treasury agent who had given up the struggle of trying to regulate commerce reported: "We are having gay times here, the town is full of Sechesh Spies, and I think corruption has become corrupted."[32]

While the bases of the economy still rested upon the cotton trade and the businesses clustered about it, the economic life of Vicksburg following the surrender bore as much resemblance to that which had existed before the capitulation as a vicious, flooding river bears to a stagnant millpond. It had taken two years of strangling warfare and months of direct attack to choke off the business life of the city, but when the fighting ceased the flow of trade was revived in less than a month's time. Even as the occupation troops marched into the city, merchants were unbarring doors. Almost like magic, signs appeared advertising fruit and candy, and, not missing a trick, metallic coffins, which were guaranteed to preserve bodies.[33] By the first of August most of the stores were open; and, said Mary Blake, who had been without such things as coffee and tea for over a year, "you can buy anything you want."[34]

During the months immediately following the surrender business sprang back to life; yet it was a haphazard type of operation, depending upon the ability and scruples of the individual and the rulings of the army commanders. (Even Grant was pressed into service as an arbiter and a recorder of deeds, and he probably asked himself if there was no end to the tasks a major general was called upon to perform.)[35] But it was a thriving, opportunity-laden situation and no avenue of profit was left unexplored. Even the scrap from destroyed mills, gins, and factories attracted the profit-seekers; and like vultures descending on a carcass they swarmed into Vicksburg, eager to

32. C. A. Montross to William Burnett, April 14, 1864, quoted in Robert F. Futrell, "Federal Trade With the Confederate States, 1861-1865: A Study of Governmental Policy," unpublished Ph.D. dissertation, Department of History, Vanderbilt University, 1950, p. 306.

33. Abrams, *Full and Detailed History,* p. 46.

34. Mary L. Blake to Marshall McDonald, August 3, [1863], Marshall McDonald Papers.

35. Warren County Deed Book CC, entry for August 29, 1863.

pick the bones.[36] If a man was lucky, and able, and not too scrupulous, fortunes waited for the taking.

Max Kuner was one of these men. As soon as the lines were opened he returned to the city to find his jewelry store in ruins, his safe blasted open and looted. All that remained of his once prosperous business was a single watch. But Kuner had a nose for profit. From a friend with whom he had once shared some precious coffee, Kuner got the option on a cotton crop. Though he had no money, within an hour he raised $32,000 by stepping into the street and borrowing it from a young man who "had plenty of money at his call." He managed to convert Confederate currency (even after the surrender it was worth fifteen cents on the dollar) into Union greenbacks, somehow got the cotton to New Orleans, and cleared $20,000 in the transaction.[37]

But this was merely the bare outline of the business, for Kuner scarcely hinted at the amoral jungle in which the profit hunters operated. William Crutcher, traveling south of Natchez seeking cotton, set the search for profit within its proper moral context as he wrote his daughter, "I expect to close out my cotton matters here in a few days . . . . Our contract will be . . . 2,500 Bales . . . . I hope to make some $15,000 to $20,000 in Sterling or Gold . . . . What a State of morals we find in the land now. Every man is for himself and what watching we have to do to hold our own."[38]

Colonel Charles Gilchrist would have agreed with him. The colonel had marched his Negro regiment from Vicksburg to Grand Gulf and back again hunting recruits and abandoned cotton, and when he sat down to write his report he was still boiling: "The General and the Treasury agents and cotton speculators, by the general's consent or order, took possession of all the cotton I brought in . . . . To sum up, we marched 250 miles, injured our transportation . . . and as far as ending the war is concerned, we did just nothing at all; but, if anything, served to prolong it by assisting a lot of rebels and thieves to sell and get

36. John H. Smith to C. A. Montross, August 7, 1863, Letters Received, Special Agent, Treasury Department, Vicksburg, Mississippi, unboxed, NA (RG) 56.

37. [Kuner], "Vicksburg and After," *Sewanee Review*, XV, 494-95.

38. William Crutcher to Emma Crutcher, August 9, 1864, Crutcher Collection.

Washington Street, Vicksburg's main street, shortly following the war. Ladies complained that the sidewalks were so crowded that they were endangered by flying tobacco juice. (From *Harper's Weekly*)

to market about 1,515 bales of . . . cotton, and a lot of speculators, whose loyalty I very much suspect, in making fortunes."[39]

Complaint also arose from the Confederates. The country beyond the Big Black, rich in cotton, was a shadowy land—neither the Northerners nor the Southerners effectively controlled it—and both sides tried to get the cotton. Dispatches marked "Private" were sent to Jefferson Davis informing him of a "very active trade, carried on between the people of the area and the Federals." When the Confederate cavalry withdrew from Jackson, Davis' informant counted twenty-three wagon loads of cotton passing through the city, bound for Vicksburg; and, he lamented, they added insult to injury by moving "on the Sabbath . . . in view of the whole community." He also reported that women of "good reputation" rode horseback from plantation to

39. *Official Records Army,* Ser. I, Vol. XXXII, Pt. 1, 395-96. Melvin Grigsby, a cavalry trooper, was in a regiment supposed to be hunting Confederate guerillas; but the regiment spent most of its time convoying cotton from plantations into Vicksburg, and, said Grigsby, every officer and man in the unit was "coining money in the cotton business." Melvin Grigsby, *The Smoked Yank* (n.p., 1888), pp. 47-49.

plantation buying cotton to sell to the Yankees.[40] Cotton brought money, and money bought clothes, shoes, and coffee. If the question of disloyalty was raised in the minds of those people engaged in the trade, it was quickly shunted aside. After two years of scarcity the tenuous bonds of a faltering cause were fast falling loose.

Cotton brought other things as well as wealth. It brought to light cases of informers, and traitors, and brothers attempting to cheat sisters of their share of the lucrative trade.[41] Vicksburg was the hub of an entire region in which spiny fingers grasping for greenbacks and gold reached out in every direction, and the city did not remain unsullied.

In September 1863, Grant relinquished the whole perplexing jumble of commercial regulation to the Treasury Department. On paper the Treasury agents appeared to have a sound plan for the regulation of business. Everyone connected with trade was required to take the oath of allegiance, licenses certifying loyalty were to be awarded before anyone could engage in any business operation, and the number of licensed businesses was to be strictly limited. (The plan called for the establishment of only two drugstores, for medicines were highly prized by the Confederates, and unless their distribution were carefully controlled the drugs would find their devious way through the lines.[42])

The plan was doomed from the beginning. Six months after he had arrived in Vicksburg, one agent complained, "I have no blanks and no instructions . . . have ever come to this office. Nor have any of the laws of the U. S. relating to the collection of customs . . . . This place is so far off that it is difficult to know how to do anything right or ascertain if done whether it is done rightly or not."[43]

40. T. J. Wharton to Jefferson Davis, April 16, 1864, Jefferson Davis Papers, Duke University.

41. J. H. Stephenson to T. C. Callicot, October 1, 1864; Maria Buck to T. C. Callicot, November 18, 1864; both in Letters Received, Special Agent, Treasury Department, Vicksburg, Mississippi, unboxed, NA (RG) 56.

42. Futrell, "Federal Trade With the Confederate States," pp. 306-7.

43. John A. McDowell to David G. Barnitz, March 5, 1864, Correspondence Sent, Assistant Special Agent, Vicksburg, Mississippi, NA (RG) 56, Book 123. The agent must not have taxed his brain too severely deciding whether his business was conducted "rightly or not." Approved for shipment into

The trading licenses, reserved for loyal citizens and disabled Union veterans, were juicy prizes, worth any deceit or treachery. The permits for disabled soldiers were issued in many northern cities. Thomas Callicot, who was trying to bring some order to the mess at Vicksburg, said: "The only persons who have [had] authority issued at Cincinnati . . . have been three strong and healthy German Jews not one of whom was ever in the U. S. Army in his life, and at least one of whom is not even a naturalized citizen."[44]

The struggle for trade permits by Vicksburg citizens was equally marked by deception. Max Kuner, who swore he had been awarded a license by Grant for helping map the Vicksburg defenses, was accused of disloyalty by his apprentice. Kuner retaliated by accusing the apprentice of dishonesty and ingratitude (and incidentally throwing in the charge that he was the son of an uxoricide), and both parties brought up witness after witness to rebut the other's claims. The prize was, of course, Kuner's trading license. Before the case was settled even the Treasury agent was charged with corruption, and the military governor who heard the conflicting tales threw up his hands in despair. He refused to render a decision, only an opinion: ". . . present loyalty is influenced entirely by . . . personal interests . . . ."[45]

As time passed the situation was unrelieved; if anything it was worsened. Arthur Burwell, a broadsword-tongued Unionist, said, "I dare not go to any place in the interior, (would be shot, hung or imprisoned if I did). Yet I find men and women going and coming, buying and carrying goods to points over which the United States have about as much control as they have over Japan. This might be allright, but my opinion is, that in time

---

Vicksburg, between December 23 and 29, 1863, as a "military necessity" were: "1 barrell of Scotch whiskey, 30 cases of champagne, 20,000 cigars, 50 dozen white gloves, 420 dozen women's shoes, 15 yards of green velvet, 15 yards of red velvet, 1 pound of silver spangles, 100 barrels of whiskey, 5 barrels of Brandy, 1 case of gin, 50 baskets of champagne, and 100 cases of 'assorted liquor.'" Special Permits to Bring Goods to Vicksburg, unboxed, NA (RG) 56.

44. T. C. Callicot to William P. Mellen, October 4, 1864, *ibid.*

45. Depositions of Valentine F. Vogh, September 6, 1864; Max Kuner, September 8, 1864; B. F. Reamer, September 9, 1864; and others, including letters of T. C. Callicot, and General N. J. T. Dana; all in Letters Received, Special Treasury Agent, Vicksburg, Mississippi, unboxed, NA (RG) 56.

of war trade is more likely to betray than defend the flag . . . . [The army is] encumbered with women and plunder, with pianos, glassware, silverplate, costly silks . . . [and] I hear well authenticated tales of wrong and fraud."[46] Almost a year after she had returned to the city, Lavinia Shannon wrote her daughter in Texas, "Vicksburg is not the place it once was, neither is home."[47]

In the summer of 1864, a new litany of names was stitched into tattered battleflags. Beneath the tarnished silver threads that spelled out names with a victory ring—Bull Run, Front Royal, Cross Keys, Fredericksburg, Chancellorsville—were new names, harsh names—the Wilderness, Spottsylvania, Dalton, Atlanta—names of brutal poundings and sidling flankings which cut bloody trails deeper into the faltering South.

During the Indian summer of the Confederacy the people of Vicksburg waited for the casualty lists to be printed in Swords's revived newspaper. After each battle they picked up the paper, glanced at the reports, then painfully counted down the roster of dead and wounded, hoping against hope. Even those who read through the lists unscathed were touched by what they had seen—"Vicksburg has lost heavily in the battles around Richmond and in Georgia."[48] There seemed to be something futile about the deaths and maimings now; each battle report was a report of defeat, and each defeat was a strengthening proof of the proposition that Vicksburg was back in the Union to stay.

There were still those who refused to take the oath of allegiance, but their defiance carried a note of despair, as if they must continue to be hostile, though they were without hope.[49]

46. A[rthur] Burwell to Joseph Holt, December 20, 1863, Joseph Holt Papers.

47. Lavinia Shannon to Emma Crutcher, July 1, 1864, Crutcher Collection.

48. *Ibid.*

49. Federal treatment and punishment of overt Confederate sympathizers appears to have been moderate. The chief punishment was banishment from Vicksburg, and this was evidently severe enough to control the people effectively. (Marmaduke Shannon to Emma Crutcher, May 18, 1864, Crutcher Collection.) On November 23, 1864, five women were banished from the city. Elizabeth Eggleston was one of them. Her offenses were: "general busy-body with rebel interests, philanthropist, mail receiver, carrier of smuggled goods to prisoners in jail, etc. etc." General Orders No. 82 of Major General N. J. T. Dana, November 23, 1864, Eggleston-Roach Papers, Department of Archives and Manuscripts, Louisiana State University.

Many other people had long since recognized the futility of defiance and rancor, and they made the best of their situation. Alice Shannon, who her father said was difficult to keep "within bounds of propriety," caught both positions in a letter to her sister:

Of course you have heard that we are back in the old place again. I never thought that I would feel so bad at having to come back as I did. I had enough of the Yankees at Raymond . . . . You do not know what a blessing it is to live in the Confederacy where you see nothing but grey. I dont think I shall wear blue any more I hate the very sight of it. It would surprise you to see how mean some of the Vicksburgers are. A great many of them seem to be turning blue . . . . Mrs. West has had several large dancing parties in her house and she invited all the young ladies and yankee officers in town. Lizzie West goes to all the parties given by the Yankee women. I cant call them Ladies . . . . You remember how Miss Lucy Rawlings wore the secesion cockade now she tells the yankees that she always was for the union . . . [She] was . . . shot in the ankle by a ball. I wish it had shot her foot off . . . . Mrs. Cook has had a good deal of trouble, but she says she is ready to take the oath so I dont feel much for her . . . . When we first came in Mrs. Hansford was trying to get up a sunday school—The first sunday the Cooks went but Miss Lucy said it was a secesh school and she would not go again. But she did go [only] because there was a yankee who taught the boys whom she wanted to captivate. The yankees have taken the sunday school in their own hands so we have given it up . . . . This is a dull rainy day I am sitting by the window and evry time [I] raise my eyes I see that hateful flag flying from the courthouse . . . . A little while ago two officers came here to invite Babe and I to a ball . . . . Ma [told] them that we never went out socially [but] they told her that we might as well commense . . . .[50]

Many people were dancing now. A theater was open, a showboat was tied up at the wharf, the gas lights were on once again, and public notice was posted cancelling contracts for all secret Union agents.[51] As the Fourth of July drew near, J. M. Swords, who a year before had taunted Grant to try to take the city, printed in his *Herald*: "No city in the Union has so good a reason to celebrate the fourth of July as Vicksburg, and we

50. Alice Shannon to Emma Crutcher, November 19, 1863, Crutcher Collection.

51. *Vicksburg Daily Herald,* June 7, 8, 1864.

trust it will be an occasion of a cordial greeting among the citizens and soldiers of a common country."[52]

The holiday was met with stony silence.[53] Like the day more than three years past when the people learned they were out of the Union, they marked the day, knew what it meant for them, but refused to celebrate it. There was, even for those who were "turning blue," a thin line which separated dancing and doing business with the Yankees from celebrating a holiday which was really a mockery of their surrender and of their men still in the field. Regardless of what Swords said, there was no holiday less suited to be commemorated in Vicksburg, and four generations would have to pass before the time was ready for "an occasion of a cordial greeting among the citizens and soldiers of a common country."

Perhaps, as the people refused to celebrate the Fourth, they looked deeper into their city, past the Northern gold and the fraternizing soldiers, and saw things which restored commerce and dancing parties could not mask. Women and children were begging in the streets, hundreds of homeless were living in tents and in caves, some persons were selling silver spoons to buy food, miscegenation was openly laughed at, an unrelieved succession of robberies and attempted rapes took place, and from the south end of Washington Street came the rattling sound of firing squads.[54] These were the swirling backwaters of war. Only time would end it, but the time was drawing close.

52. *Ibid.* 53. *Ibid.*, July 6, 1864.

54. *Ibid.*, June-October, 1864, *passim.* With respect to the incidence of lawlessness, the author's conclusion is that the occupation army was fairly free of physical crimes against the civilians. Other than complaints of petty thievery, the only record (seen by the author) of a major crime committed by soldiers appears in a letter written by Marmaduke Shannon, the editor: "I just learned that John H. Babb was . . . killed today. [He] drove some negro soldiers out of his garden and struck one of them with a brickbat for his impudence—they went to their camp, got their guns and . . . shot him dead." Marmaduke Shannon to Emma Crutcher, May 18, 1864, Crutcher Collection.

EPILOGUE

ON the ninth of April 1865, Marmaduke Shannon wrote his daughter in Texas the latest news: "Selma . . . has lately been captured and burned—and I suppose every other place held by the rebels will soon follow."[1] He had moved full circle. Four years previously he had called the secessionists rebels; then while Vicksburg was in the Confederacy he had done his best to make the Confederacy work; now, on this ninth of April, the Confederates were rebels again. As Shannon wrote, Lee was surrendering the Army of Northern Virginia.

Northern travelers began to come down the river, eager to inspect the city. When they looked for Grant's canal, they had difficulty finding it. "It's a little small concern," said one visitor. The "hiding-holes" were filled, the streets were busy with burdened carts and wagons, the wharves were crowded with steamboats, returning soldiers were claiming their welcome, and beyond the city the cotton fields opened in every direction. The fortifications were difficult to identify—cotton plants bloomed in "every little valley"; and, with a gentle irony, the blooms were red and white. One man looked over the fields, then turned away with the thought that "even cotton wore the Rebel colors."[2]

Mahala Roach was living in her house again. After she had settled her family she had some unoccupied hours, and she took out her stack of diaries and began to leaf through them. Yet she did not much care to do it, for, she thought: "The task will

1. Marmaduke Shannon to Emma Crutcher, April 9, 1865, Crutcher Collection.

2. John T. Trowbridge, *A Picture of the Desolated States, and the Work of Restoration* (Hartford, Connecticut, 1868), p. 356; Whitelaw Reid, *After the War: A Southern Tour. May 1, 1865 to May 1, 1866* (Cincinnati, 1866), pp. 281-89.

be a sad one to me, for I will have to turn back my glances to a happy life, now alas! passed away forever."[3]

Though she dwelled on the instability of life and society, she would have done better to have turned her thoughts to the river, flowing broad and ceaselessly, a river which rises in a sudden start in northern Minnesota, then rolls south, swollen by countless other rivers and streams that draw off the rain-glut of half a continent. Beneath her home, the loamy soils of Iowa, Kansas, Illinois, and Ohio washed in the great river. There they mixed and tumbled with earth swept from Tennessee, Alabama, Arkansas, and Mississippi. As the river surged past, there was no telling one particle from the other. It had always been that way. It always would.

3. "Christmas Days," Roach-Eggleston Papers, V, 1.

BIBLIOGRAPHY

Primary Materials

Manuscript Sources

Duke University Library:

Jefferson Davis Papers.
Nathan G. Dye Papers.
Noah L. Gebhart Papers.
Gertrude Jenkins Papers.
Electus W. Jones Papers.
Marshall McDonald Papers.
William H. E. Merritt Papers.
Charles B. Tompkins Papers.
Thomas N. Waul Papers.

Emory University Library:

William H. Brotherton Papers.

Division of Manuscripts, Library of Congress:

Joseph Holt Papers.
Robert E. Jameson Papers.
Journal Kept by Mrs. W. W. Lord During the Siege of Vicksburg.
Earl Van Dorn Papers.

Louisiana State University, Department of Archives and Manuscripts:

Butler Family Papers (E).
Rowland Chambers, Diary.
Eggleston-Roach Papers.
Lewis Guion, Diary.
J. P. Knox Papers.
Jared Y. Sanders Papers.

Mississippi Department of Archives and History:

Charles B. Allen, Plantation Book.
[Emma] Balfour, Diary.

Phillip Crutcher Collection.
William A. Drennan Papers.
Governors' Correspondence, Series E.
J. H. Pepper, Diary of Vicksburg.
Returns for Presidential Electors, 1860, Series F, Volume LXXXV.
Ida B. Trotter, The Seige of Vicksburg, and Some Personal Experiences connected therewith.
Warren County Census, 1860, Schedules 1 and 2.
Warren County Census, 1866, Series F, Volume CX.

National Archives:

Record Group 56. General Records of the Treasury Department.
Record Group 105. Records of the Bureau of Refugees, Freedmen, and Abandoned Lands.
Record Group 109. War Department Collection of Confederate Records.

Southern Historical Collection, University of North Carolina:

Joseph D. Alison, Diary.
Anne Harris Broidrick, A Recollection of Thirty Years Ago.
Samuel H. Lockett, The Defense of Vicksburg—Notes and Sketches from an Engineering Point of View.
Mahala P. H. Roach, Diary.
Roach-Eggleston Papers.

Tennessee State Library and Archives:

John J. Blair, Diary.
G. R. Elliott, Diary.

Vicksburg, Mississippi:

City Council Minute Book, 1860-69. City Hall.
Goodrum Collection. Old Courthouse Museum.
Gregory Papers. Old Courthouse Museum.
John Hughes, Diary. Old Courthouse Museum.
S. R. Martin, Recollections of the War Between the States, 1861-65. Owned by Mr. John S. Hoggatt.
Register. Convent of the Sisters of Mercy.
Rockwood Manuscript. Old Courthouse Museum.
Supervisors' Minute Book, 1853-67. Courthouse.
Warren County Deed Book CC. Courthouse.

Printed Sources

Anecdotes, Poetry and Incidents of the War; North and South, 1860-1865. Edited by Frank Moore. Boston: Boston Stereotype Foundry, 1866.

Brokenburn: The Journal of Kate Stone, 1861-1867. Edited by John Q. Anderson. Baton Rouge: Louisiana State University Press, 1955.

Chambers, William P. "My Journal," Edited by Ruth Polk. *Publications of the Mississippi Historical Society,* Centenary Series, V (1925), 227-386.

"Civil War Diary of Captain James Litton Cooper, September 30, 1861 to January, 1865." Edited by William T. Alderson. *Tennessee Historical Quarterly,* XV (June, 1956), 141-173.

"The Civil War Letters of Brigadier General William Ward Orme—1862-1866." Edited by Harry E. Pratt. *Journal of the Illinois State Historical Society,* XXIII (July, 1930), 246-315.

The Confederate States Almanac for . . . 1862. Nashville, Tennessee: Southern Methodist Publishing House, 1862.

Clarke's Confederate Household Almanac, for the Year 1863. Vicksburg, H. C. Clarke, Publisher, 1863.

The Diary of A. Hugh Moss. [No publisher, no place of publication], 1948.

General Directory for the City of Vicksburg. Vicksburg: H. C. Clarke Publisher, 1860.

Jones, Jenkins L. "An Artilleryman's Diary." *Wisconsin History Commission Original Papers, Number 8.* Democrat Printing Company [no place], 1914.

Journal of the State Convention and Ordinances and Resolutions—Adopted in January, 1861—With an Appendix. Jackson, Mississippi: E. Barksdale, State Printer, 1861.

Newsome, Edmund. *Experience in the War of the Great Rebellion.* Carbondale, Illinois: Printed by the Author, 1879.

Official Records of the Union and Confederate Navies in the War of the Rebellion. 30 vols. and index. Washington: Government Printing Office, 1894-1922.

Proceedings of the Mississippi State Convention Held January 7th to 26th, A.D. 1861. Including the Ordinances, as finally Adopted. Important Speeches, and a List of Members. Jackson, Mississippi: Power and Cadwallader, Book and Job Printers, 1861.

Rebellion Record: A Diary of American Events. Edited by Frank Moore. 11 vols. New York: D. Van Nostrand Publisher, 1867.

Reid, Whitelaw. *After the War: A Southern Tour. May 1, 1865 to May 1, 1866.* Cincinnati: Moore, Wilstach and Baldwin, Publishers, 1866.

Russell, William H. *My Diary North and South.* Boston: T.O.H.P. Burnham, 1863.

The Siege of Vicksburg from the Diary of Seth J. Wells. Detroit: William H. Rowe Publisher, 1915.

Trowbridge, John T. *A Picture of the Desolated States, and the Work of Reconstruction.* Hartford, Connecticut: L. Stebbins, 1868.

"The War Diary of a Union Woman in the South." Edited by George W. Cable. *The Century Magazine,* XXXVIII (October, 1889), 931-46.

The War of the Rebellion: A Compilation of the Official Records of the Union and Confederate Armies. 69 vols. and index. Washington: Government Printing Office, 1880-1901.

"With Grant at Vicksburg: From the Diary of Captain Charles E. Wilcox." Edited by Edgar L. Ericksen. *Journal of the Illinois State Historical Society,* XXX (January, 1938), 441-503.

"A Woman's Diary of the Siege of Vicksburg." Edited by George W. Cable. *The Century Magazine,* XXX (September, 1885), 767-75.

Newspapers and Periodicals

De Bow's Review.
Grand Gulf Advertiser.
Harper's Weekly.
Natchez Daily Courier.
Vicksburg Daily Courier.
Vicksburg Daily Evening Citizen.
Vicksburg Daily Herald.
Vicksburg Daily Times.
Vicksburg Daily Whig.
Vicksburg Weekly Whig.

Memoirs and Reminiscences

Abrams, Alexander S. *A Full and Detailed History of the Siege of Vicksburg.* Atlanta: Intelligencer Steam Power Press, 1863.

Anderson, Ephraim McD. *Memoirs.* Saint Louis: Times Printing Company, 1868.

Battles and Leaders in the Civil War. Edited by Robert U. Johnson and Clarence C. Buel. 4 vols. New York: The Century Company, 1884.

Bell, L. McRae. "A Girl's Experience in the Siege of Vicksburg," *Harper's Weekly,* LVI (June 8, 1912), 12-13.

Bevier, Robert S. *History of the First and Second Missouri Confederate Brigades 1861-1865.* Saint Louis: Bryan, Brand and Company, 1879.

Browne, Junius H. *Four Years in Secessia.* Hartford, Ohio: D. Case and Company, 1865.

Clare, Josephine. *Narrative of the Adventures and Experience of Mrs. Josephine Clare.* Lancaster, Pennsylvania: Pearsol and Geist, Printers, 1865.

DeFontaine, Felix G. *Marginalia; or Gleanings From an Army Note-Book.* Columbia, South Carolina: F. G. DeFontaine and Company, 1864.

DeLeon, Thomas C. *Belles, Beaux and Brains of the 60's.* New York: G. W. Dillingham and Company, 1907.

Dorsey, Sara A. *Recollections of Henry Watkins Allen, Brigadier General Confederate States Army, Ex-Governor of Louisiana.* New York: M. Doolady, 1866.

Fulkerson, Horace S. *A Civilian's Recollection of the War Between the States.* Edited by Percy L. Rainwater. Baton Rouge: Otto Claitor, 1939.

Gregory, Edward S. "Vicksburg During the Siege," *The Annals of the War Written by the Leading Participants North and South.* Philadelphia: The Times Printing Company, 1879.

Grigsby, Melvin. *The Smoked Yank.* 2nd edition. [No publisher, no place], 1888.

Hall, Winchester. *The Story of the 26th Louisiana Infantry, in the Service of the Confederate States.* [No publisher, no place], 1890.

Hart, William O. "A Boy's Recollection of the War," *Publications of the Mississippi Historical Society,* XII (1912), 148-54.

Hogane, J. T. "Reminiscences of the Siege of Vicksburg," *Southern Historical Society Papers,* XI (July, 1883), 291-97.

Howard, Richard L. *History of the 124th Regiment Illinois Infantry Volunteers.* Springfield: H. W. Rokker, 1880.

[Kuner, Max]. *"Vicksburg and After: Being the Experience of a Southern Merchant."* Arranged by Edwin L. Sabin. *The Sewanee Review,* XV (October, 1907), 485-96.

Lee, Stephen D. "The Siege of Vicksburg," *Publications of the Mississippi Historical Society,* III (1900), 55-71.

———. "Details of Important Work by Two Confederate Telegraph Operators," *Publications of the Mississippi Historical Society,* VIII (1904), 54.

Livermore, Mary A. *My Story of the War: A Woman's Narrative of Four Years of Personal Experience.* Hartford, Connecticut: A. D. Worthington and Company, 1892.

Lord, William W., Jr. "A Child at the Siege of Vicksburg," *Harper's Monthly Magazine,* CXVIII (December, 1908), 44-53.

[Loughborough, Mary A.]. *My Cave Life in Vicksburg.* New York: D. Appleton and Company, 1864.

Newcomb, Mary A. *Four Years Personal Reminiscences of the War.* Chicago: H. S. Mills and Company, 1893.

Oldroyd, Osborn H. *A Soldier's Story of the Siege of Vicksburg.* Springfield, Illinois: Printed for the Author, 1885.

Reed, Lida L. "A Woman's Experiences During the Siege of Vicksburg," *The Century Magazine,* LXI (April, 1901), 922-28.

Stevenson, Thomas M. *History of the 78th Regiment O.V.V.I.* Zanesville, Ohio: Hugh Dunn, 1865.

Tunnard, William H. *A Southern Record: The History of the Third Regiment Louisiana Infantry.* Baton Rouge: [No publisher], 1866.

Wilkie, Franc B. *Pen and Powder.* Boston: Ticknor and Company, 1888.

Woods, Thomas H. "Sketch of the Mississippi Secession Convention—Its Membership and Work," *Publications of the Mississippi Historical Society,* VI (1902), 91-104.

Secondary Materials

Barber, Bette E. Vicksburg: Home Town Gibraltar. MS. Mississippi Department of Archives and History.

Bettersworth, John K. *Confederate Mississippi.* Baton Rouge: Louisiana State University Press, 1943.

Black, Robert C. *Railroads of the Confederacy.* Chapel Hill: University of North Carolina Press, 1952.

Dickey, Dallas C. *Seargent S. Prentiss: Whig Orator of the Old South.* Baton Rouge: Louisiana State University Press, 1945.

Encyclopedia of Mississippi History. Edited by Dunbar Rowland. 2 vols. Madison, Wisconsin: Selwyn A. Brant Publishers, 1904.

Futrell, Robert F. "Federal Trade With the Confederate States, 1861-1865: A Study of Governmental Policy." Unpublished Ph.D. dissertation, Department of History, Vanderbilt University, 1950.

Halsell, Willie D. "A Vicksburg Speculator and Planter in the Yazoo Delta," *Journal of Mississippi History,* XI (October, 1942), 231-42.

Lonn, Ella. *Salt as a Factor in the Confederacy.* New York: Walter Neale Publisher, 1933.

McNeily, J. S. "War and Reconstruction in Mississippi: 1863-1890," *Publications of the Mississippi Historical Society,* Centenary Series, II (1918), 165-535.

Matthies, Virginia P. "Natchez-Under-The-Hill," *Journal of Mississippi History,* VII (October, 1945), 201-21.

Rainwater, Percy L. *Mississippi: Storm Center of Secession 1856-1861.* Baton Rouge: Otto Claitor, 1938.

INDEX